Presidential Polls
and the News Media

Presidential Polls
and the News Media

EDITED BY
Paul J. Lavrakas,
Michael W. Traugott,
and Peter V. Miller

Westview Press
BOULDER•SAN FRANCISCO•OXFORD

Copyright © 1995 by Westview Press, Inc., A Division of HarperCollins Publishers, Inc.

Published in 1995 in the United States of America by Westview Press, Inc., 5500 Central Avenue, Boulder, Colorado 80301-2877, and in the United Kingdom by Westview Press, 12 Hid's Copse Road, Cumnor Hill, Oxford OX2 9JJ

A CIP catalog record for this book is available from the Library of Congress. ISBN 0-8133-8943-7 (hc). ISBN 0-8133-8989-5(pbk).

The paper used in this publication meets the requirements of the American National Standard for Permanence of Paper for Printed Library Materials Z39.48-1984.

10   9   8   7   6   5   4   3   2   1

To Barbara, Santa, and Dianne
for their love, friendship, and support

Contents

ΓΑRT ONE
Introduction

PART TWO
Developments in Media Polling

PART THREE
The Methodology of Media Polls

Tables and Figures

ix

Figures

Preface

This volume is a direct outgrowth of an initiative we began in 1988 to study and improve the way that election polls are used by the news media. This effort has involved a collaboration of faculty and resources from Northwestern University and the University of Michigan. Participating units in Evanston have included the Northwestern University Survey Laboratory, the Institute for Modern Communications, the Medill School of Journalism, and the Department of Communication Studies. In Ann Arbor, the Center for Political Studies at the Institute for Social Research and the Department of Communication have been the collaborating organizations.

As part of our effort, we organized a national conference of media polling experts in 1989, published an edited volume in 1991 that focused on the media's use of polling in the coverage of the 1988 Bush/Dukakis election, gave papers and participated in panel discussions at several professional association meetings, published other articles, and modified our curricular offerings to inform our students in journalism, communication studies, and political science about this important topic area.

The present volume contains chapters from many of the same experts who contributed to the previous edited volume (Lavrakas and Holley, 1991). As explained in Chapter 1, this set of chapters presents more original research than the previous volume, with more of an "academic" bent to several of the chapters. Also, it addresses more applied aspects of using information gathered via election surveys and other related methods, such as focus groups, in the production of election coverage by describing several case studies of actual and potential "stories" in the 1992 Bush/Clinton/Perot election.

We thank the many experts who contributed the chapters in the book. We also extend a special thanks to Jenna Powell of the Northwestern University Survey Lab for her editing and layout skills in bringing this volume to production quality. Unlike its predecessor, this volume is unfortunately missing the insightful participation of I.A. "Bud" Lewis, senior journalist and pollster for the *Los Angeles Times*, who died in 1990.

Bud held very high expectations of the news media regarding the manner in which election polls should be used in political campaign coverage. We share his expectations and hope that this volume will encourage journalists and news executives to make a greater commitment to realizing the tremendous potential that exists for news organizations to contribute positively to democratic political processes through enhanced election coverage.

Paul J. Lavrakas
Michael W. Traugott
Peter V. Miller

About the Contributors

Sandra L. Bauman is currently a project director for Roper Starch Worldwide and a Ph.D. candidate in the department of communication studies at Northwestern University. She was the assistant manager of the Northwestern University Survey Laboratory and then exit poll manager for Voter News Service during the 1994 general election.

Robert P. Daves is assistant managing editor for news research at the *Star Tribune* (Minneapolis/St. Paul), and director of The Minnesota Poll, the newspaper's statewide public opinion poll.

Murray Edelman is currently editorial director of Voter News Service. He had been a director of Voter Research & Surveys and deputy director of the CBS News Election and Survey Unit. He recently published on the subject of lesbian and gay voting and has conducted research on exit poll methodology, race of interviewer effects, crowd estimation, tracking polls and mystical experiences.

Susan Herbst, associate professor of communication studies and political science at Northwestern University, is the author of *Numbered Voices: How Opinion Polling Has Shaped American Politics* (1993, University of Chicago), and *Politics at the Margin: Historical Perspectives on Public Expression Outside the Mainstream* (1994, Cambridge).

Larry Hugick is Director of Political and Media Surveys at Princeton Survey Research Associates.

Michael R. Kagay, editor of news surveys at *The New York Times*, heads the newspaper's polling department. Prior to joining *The Times* in 1987 he directed large-scale surveys on public policy and social issues as vice-president of Louis Harris and Associates for five years, and was on the faculty at Princeton University for 10 years where he taught public opinion.

Andrew Kohut is Director of the Times Mirror Center for The People and The Press.

Paul J. Lavrakas, professor of communication studies, journalism, statistics, and urban affairs at Northwestern University, founded the Northwestern University Survey Laboratory in 1982 and continues to serve as its director.

Jennifer Means is a graduate student in the Department of Political Science at the University of Michigan.

Peter V. Miller is associate professor of communication studies and journalism at Northwestern University. He is editor of the Poll Review Section of *Public Opinion Quarterly*, and has written on issues of survey standards and the public opinion industry.

Warren J. Mitofsky is president of Mitofsky International. He had been executive director of Voter Research & Surveys for its first four years and the CBS News Election Survey Unit. He was a founder of those groups and the CBS/*New York Times* Poll, which he directed for CBS for its first 15 years. He originated CBS's election projection and exit poll analysis systems, and a widely used random-digit telephone sampling procedure (with Joseph Waksberg).

Richard Morin is director of polling and a staff writer for *The Washington Post*.

Diana C. Mutz, associate professor of political science and of journalism and mass communication at the University of Wisconsin-Madison, is the author of numerous articles involving mass media and public opinion, and most recently co-edited a book entitled *Political Persuasion and Attitude Change*.

Michael W. Traugott is a professor of communication and the director of the Program in Media and Politics in the Center for Political Studies at the University of Michigan.

Sharon P. Warden is senior polling analyst for *The Washington Post*.

PART ONE

Introduction

1

News Media's Use of Presidential Polling in the 1990s: An Introduction and Overview

Paul J. Lavrakas
Michael W. Traugott

As testimony to the importance of the issue, the past five years have witnessed the publication of several scholarly texts that describe and critique the American news media's use of information gathered via election surveys (polls), in particular in presidential elections. Asher (1992), Cantril (1991), Lavrakas and Holley (1991), Mann and Orren (1992), and Moore (1992), for example, all have striven to demystify either the processes by which election polls are conducted, the manner in which the media do, *and should*, use poll findings in their news stories, or the possible effects this type of news may have on democratic political processes in the United States.

Complementing this increased attention paid directly to election polling and the media is the recent work of Daniel Yankelovich (1991). Yankelovich, in his book *Coming to Public Judgment: Making Democracy Work in a Complex World*, articulates a view highly critical of the news media, focusing on four important issues. First, he believes the media far too often misunderstand the nature and origins of public opinion. Second, they fail to understand or acknowledge how they often negatively affect public opinion. Third, he is concerned that they are not working hard enough to affect the citizenry's opinions and "judgments" in a useful and positive manner. Finally, he believes the media generally ignore the ways in which the present state of affairs hinders, rather than serves, the workings of democracy in the United States.

However, unlike some academic endeavors that aim merely, or even primarily, towards negative criticism, the editors and chapter authors of this volume share a proactive and positive perspective: *That the news media's usage of information gathered via sample surveys, and in particular via election polls, can be extremely interesting and informative to a society, and can produce a more informed electorate, thereby improving the democratic process. Currently, however, the manner in which this type of information is used and disseminated as news too often falls far short of its potential for good; in some instances, it may even hinder the political processes themselves.*

These issues do not just affect the American political process. The Canadian government, for example, recently issued a report on the role of election polls and the news media in Canada (Lachapelle, 1991) as part of an on-going series of policy papers on "reforming electoral democracy." The report noted that "because they are 'scientific,' published opinion polls raise the issues of public confidence in the integrity of the electoral process . . . [Furthermore,] opinion polls are subject to many forms of error and misinterpretation."

Three main arguments, based upon a review of current literature as well as testimony, were presented against the unrestricted release of election poll findings at the hearings held by the Canadian commission that issued the report: (1) due to their "authoritative presentation," polls have "undue influence" on elections; (2) polls can be "erroneous and misleading" and subject to "deliberate manipulation;" and (3) polls often are "presented without proper qualification." The commission concluded that "there are good reasons to oblige news organizations that publish [poll results] during election campaigns to meet certain requirements in order to ensure high standards in the preparation and reporting *of such a powerful source of information*" (italics added). Several recommendations were made by the Commission, including a prohibition of the release of any poll findings "from midnight the day preceding election day until the close of all polls on election day." (Our neighbors to the north already ban the reporting of exit polls on election day.)

Canada is by no means alone in considering formal guidelines and restrictions covering the dissemination of election poll findings by the news media. Many other democratic nations in Europe and elsewhere (e.g., Australia, Brazil, France, Germany, Great Britain, and South Korea) have placed legal restrictions on their news media to prohibit the release of "horse-race" survey findings — i.e., those that report which candidate will be the "likely winner" — within certain time periods prior to and including the country's voting day. There have been legislative attempts during the past two decades in the United States to limit the release of this type of news, but all have failed the test of constitutionality. A crucial difference in the United States is the First Amendment to the constitution and associated case law that has established that no prior restraint can be applied to news.

To us it seems likely that this global trend to restrict the freedom of the news media to use and report election poll findings will grow until critics better understand the positive potential of this type of news and the media demonstrate a greater actualization of this potential. For those who believe that restrictions are a likely mistake, we offer this set of chapters as a guide toward thinking about how the news media can better utilize the information that elections polls can generate.

At another extreme, some well-known "poll bashers" (e.g., Mike Royko) apparently believe that election surveys are an anathema that all good citizens should try at any cost to foil (e.g., refuse and/or fabricate answers to survey interviewers). In contrast, we are optimistic that careful investigation, detailed constructive examples, and level discourse will help the news media to actualize more of the potential benefits that can come from disseminating information gathered via quality election polls. In this way, they can make a significant positive contribution to the workings of our socio-political processes.

Our Mission

This volume is aimed first and foremost at journalists and other news media decision-makers, including reporters, editors, and producers who are dissatisfied with the way their news organizations cover political campaigns. In particular, the information presented in the chapters challenges the news media to evaluate themselves and make a serious and sincere effort to rethink their approaches.

A cynical view of the information presented here would be to discount it as irrelevant for the typical journalist because s/he is employed by a news organization that lacks the resources available at the likes of the ABC News, CBS News, CNN, *The Minneapolis Star Tribune*, NBC News, *The New York Times*, or *The Washington Post*. Instead, we encourage those readers who work in the news business to think about the implications of the chapters for their own news organization, no matter its size, and how the resources they presently commit to election campaign coverage might be better spent. Here the focus should be on uses that are more likely to stimulate the public to engage positively in the political process. Of course, we are not discouraging journalists from also thinking about how and why more resources and time could be devoted to political campaign coverage at their news organizations and still maintain "the bottom line."

A secondary audience for this volume is all other persons who observe, study, or participate in election campaigns. With the omnipresent role of the news media in today's elections, we believe that politicians and their staffs, electoral campaign reformers, media scholars and critics, political scientists and other social science researchers, and the concerned public will better understand what is, and could be, done with election survey data by reading and thinking about the original research and critical analyses in the following chapters. We hope that an enhanced understanding might reinforce some of our readers' willingness to contribute to an improvement of the media's current usage of election polls.

An Overview of the Chapters

In formulating this volume, we sought chapters that would explain how the news media employ election polls, what effects this type of news has on various segments of society, and what might be done differently and better in future election coverage. The volume begins with three chapters that review developments in the manner in which the news media incorporate information gathered via election polls and other research techniques into their news stories. The next three chapters address various aspects of the methodologies of the election polls and the procedures the media use to analyze and interpret their meaning. Following these are three chapters that review and critique how polling information was used in the 1992 election coverage that appeared in some of the major news media. The next two chapters deal with reactions to election news by the public and by campaign contributors. The final chapter provides a synthesis of four themes that we believe unite the issues addressed in the individual chapters and provides a rationale and recommendations for much needed change.

The volume begins with a historical analysis of election polling by communication studies professor Susan Herbst. In Chapter 2, Herbst looks back at the 19th century describing and critiquing the manner in which the American media incorporated public opinion "sampling" into their coverage of presidential election campaigns. Pre-election polling and the use of "quantitative" information in election coverage is nothing new for the media in the United States. Early use of findings from "straw polls" came from a direct effort to get potential voters involved in the election and interested in the news organization's coverage. This type of news was seen as contributing positively to "public discourse" and gave reporters substantial time to interact directly with the voting public. Herbst identifies three sources of these early straw polls: the reporters themselves, the political campaigns, and "peoples' polls," i.e., those conducted by local citizens themselves and passed onto the media.

In the first half of the 20th century, prior to the advent of modern-day scientific sampling techniques, Herbst reports that the large majority of elite journalists were not convinced that the "opinion poll" was either reliable or useful. Using findings from her own in-depth interviews with 44 prominent American journalists who were working in period between the 1920s and the late 1940s, Herbst explains that "some correspondents worried that the widespread use of opinion polling would lead to bandwagon voting, while others were afraid that statesmen could use polling to manipulate the public more effectively." Instead of embracing election polls, reporters in those years were more likely to rely on "public opinion surrogates" — train conductors, cab drivers, bar keepers, even priests — to help them keep "a finger of the pulse of the people." However, since WWII, Herbst notes that there has been a fundamental change in the way journalists approach public opinion due to the diffusion and growing legitimacy of the sample survey.

Clearly Herbst is not as sanguine as are the other chapter authors that this change has been for the better. She concludes with a critical analysis of why, as survey methodology continued to become more scientific, there appears to have been an increasing reliance by journalists to represent "public opinion" merely as numbers that are measured in surveys. This greatly concerns Herbst and she challenges journalists and students of public opinion to "use the history *of their own field* to ask fundamental questions about the appropriateness, format, and reporting of survey data" in election coverage and other issues, "lest we become slaves to the very methodological tools we've created."

Chapter 3 reports findings from the largest content analysis to date of the front page usage of pre-election poll findings by prominent American daily newspapers. Here, media and survey researchers Paul J. Lavrakas and Sandra L. Bauman review the impetus for the news media to increase their use of election survey findings in their coverage of presidential election campaigns. Viewing the past two decades' apparent "proliferation" of poll findings in the news as highly consistent with Phil Meyer's (1973) call for more "precision journalism" by using social science methods to gather and to make "news," Chapter 3 begins with a discussion of *why* such an increased usage of polling news would be expected. Discussing the "norm of objectivity," the media's "role as watchdog," technological advantages in gathering and processing election survey data, the decline in the importance of political parties, and competitive pressures, Lavrakas and Bauman chronicle the rationale supporting the apparent increased use of poll findings in election stories. Lamentably, this appears to have coincided with a decrease in so-called "shoe-leather" journalism.

However, as Chapter 3 notes, although there is a widespread belief that there has been a tremendous increase in poll-related election news, there has neither been a large-scale documentation of its actual existence nor its magnitude. Although many media critics and "poll-bashers" alike have articulated the view that this proliferation has been taking place during the past two decades, this view has remained only their *impression* until systematic research could document it.

To close this knowledge gap, the authors started in 1988 to develop a content analysis database of the Page One news stories of 11 prominent daily newspapers. The database included all stories in these dailies from July 1 through election day for each of the last four presidential election years; in the end it totaled more than 5,500 front pages.

Comparing the 1980, 1984 and 1988 years, there was not that much difference in the number or the rate of Page One news stories that reported poll findings. However, in 1992 the flood-gates opened with between a two- and three-fold increase over the previous three election years in the absolute number of Page One presidential election stories with poll findings. Furthermore the *rate* of the increased reporting of poll findings in 1992 was more than seven times greater than the rate of the increase in the election news stories themselves. That is, although the Bush/Clinton/Perot election generated many more Page One news stories than the previous three presidential elections, this by no means explained the amount of polling news that was reported in the 1992 front pages. Lavrakas and Bauman observe that, unfortunately, this increase in poll-based news "does not mean that this news necessarily informed the electorate in any meaningful fashion" and suggest that if journalists have, in fact, "become lazy in covering elections by relying too heavily on information gathered by polls, then we all have lost."

In Chapter 4, political scientist, communication studies professor, and survey researcher, Michael W. Traugott, explains the research support services he and the Center for Political Studies at the University of Michigan provided to *The Detroit News* in 1992 to help the newspaper incorporate the results of several *focus groups* into their presidential election campaign coverage. (These small groups involved moderated and structured discussion sessions lasting 90-120 minutes that were typically made up of fairly homogeneous participants, e.g., conservative Democrats.) The newspaper used the focus group findings: (1) in combination with news reports of standard election poll findings; (2) as part of "event-centered" coverage of the campaign (e.g., President Bush's 1992 State of the Union address; Clinton's performance at the Democratic convention); and (3) as material for the paper's columnists.

Traugott begins his chapter with an in-depth analysis of the ways that journalists have come to incorporate social science techniques into election campaign coverage. (This section both supplements and complements the related reviews in the previous two chapters.) This leads to his explanation of how the of use of focus groups to enhance the study of public opinion vis-a-vis the campaign is a logical extension of the recently heightened efforts of many news organizations to "personalize coverage and provide local pegs for stories that frequently have a major national theme." Traugott also notes the competitive advantage this strategy can provide a news organization by generating feedback from its audience — whose members typically comprise the focus group participants — "often with the goal of modifying [the coverage] to maintain reader interest and satisfaction."

For any media organization that has yet to incorporate focus group techniques to supplement issue-specific news coverage, Chapter 4 provides a detailed game plan for how to devise, implement, and utilize this type of information as "news." For those media already using focus groups for news purposes, the chapter affords each organization an opportunity to compare its own approach with that devised by Traugott and *The Detroit News* for the 1992 presidential campaign.

Focus groups are especially relevant to presidential election campaign coverage because of the many predictable aspects of such a news story that occur every four years. Traugott explains how focus groups can allow a local newspaper, television or radio station to "'humanize' political coverage," thereby making for both "good news and good business as it can provide a vehicle for satisfying the newsworthiness criteria of reflecting the impact of news events on the local audience while at the same time establishing more direct links between a news organization and its audience."

Traugott suggests that focus groups can have a very cost-effective news value, especially for small- to medium-sized news organizations. He estimates that a focus group could cost about one-fourth of the price of a small local survey. The potential problem of inference from focus groups notwithstanding — Traugott correctly warns about over-generalizing from a small, highly selective group of citizens — the technique, when supplemented with photos and direct quotes, can undeniably provide reporters, editors and producers "a way to personify the impact of politics and an on-going campaign that aggregate statistical data from a survey does not."

Far from advocating the replacement of election surveys with focus groups, Chapter 4 convincingly shows how the technique is best used to complement the information that polls can generate. In this, Traugott reinforces Herbst's theme in Chapter 2 that journalists must think more flexibly and more creatively about how to gather reliable "news" about public opinion.

The next section of the book includes three chapters by prominent media pollsters who address various methodological and statistical aspects about what news media have been doing, and should be doing, with election poll data. In Chapter 5, former CBS News and VRS executive pollster Warren J. Mitofsky, the dean of exit poll practitioner-scholars, takes a controversial stance by calling for a completely different approach than that commonly used by the journalists to report the "methodological details" of election polls, e.g., sample size and sampling error, questionnaire item wording, and survey dates and sponsorship.

There may be no one else living who has had more occasion to think about how election polls should be conducted and used by journalists, who has explained election poll findings to more journalists, or who has had more occasion to observe and evaluate the effects of poll-related election news on the public, politicians, and the media than Warren Mitofsky. As such, one should take his call for an entirely "new way" to go about reporting election poll findings in 1996 very seriously.

Mitofsky's senior perspective has led him to believe that it is generally illogical and wasteful of a news organization's talent and resources to try to train its journalists to become polling experts. It is dysfunctional to ask reporters both to write about the strengths and limitations of the research methods that an election survey has deployed and also about the "meaning" of election poll findings. Certainly there are individual exceptions where some persons have demonstrated both polling and journalistic expertise, including several chapter authors in this volume, but Mitofsky does not believe this is a prudent use of resources for most news organizations.

Instead, Mitofsky strongly advises that written interpretation of election poll findings is better left to the research experts. In reaching this conclusion he is not advocating that the researcher's "news story" would be the one that is published or broadcast, but that it would provide the typical political reporter "with a much better starting point." As with former senior Los Angeles Times pollster, Bud Lewis (1991), Mitofsky believes that it is not numbers that make poll findings newsworthy, rather it is their *meaning* — the implications of these numbers for the election campaign. For Mitofsky, the researcher is much better equipped to explain the meaning of quantitative poll findings than the typical political reporter.

His ideas are not merely general comments. Rather in Chapter 5, he provides specific examples of how he would write a "researcher's news story." Possibly the most provocative section is the one in which he calls for researchers who are writing the first version of these polling stories to "discuss the level of generalizations that can and cannot be made from the data." Here he provides a fascinating hypothetical example of a first pass on a news story that might be written about the limits of an election survey's methodology and the implications of these limitations for the final news story. Mitofsky argues that the expert researcher should be able to speculate about the limitations of the survey design and devise a summary statement such as the following: "[In this survey,] 15 percent of the population had no chance of selection in the sample, . . . they likely comprise nine percent of the voters, and could be expected to change the margin between the Democratic and Republican candidates by two percentage points at most."

In addition to this, Chapter 5 is filled with specific ideas for improving the way that pollsters, reporters, and the discerning public should use election polls in 1996 and beyond.

With the explicit intent of "publishing a systematic evaluation of [the 1992] VRS exit polling," former long-time colleagues Warren Mitofsky and Murray Edelman provide in Chapter 6 a description and critique of the exit polling that was done for the 1992 elections by the now-defunct Voter Research and Surveys — the organization created in 1989 from a pooling of resources by ABC, CBS, CNN, and NBC to collect exit poll data that each network would analyze separately.

Having first learned about the tradition of post hoc self-disclosure and the evaluation of survey methods under the tutelage of Morris Hansen at the U.S. Bureau of the Census prior to joining CBS News, Mitofsky and Edelman detail how the sampling, questionnaire design, interviewing, tabulating, and dissemination of the exit polling data was done for the 1992 general election.

Approximately 177,000 voters were interviewed for the national and state exits polls conducted on Election Day, November 3, 1992. The authors' self-critique notes that it is their opinion that "the questionnaires put together by the VRS survey committee were consistently better than those from earlier exit polls conducted separately by each of the networks before VRS was formed." However, despite the efforts that went into questionnaire development and sampling methods, they report that a bias leading to an overestimate of the success of Democratic congressional candidates was observed, although at a lower level than in some previous election years.

Coupled with Mitofsky's chapter in our previous edited volume (Mitofsky, 1991), Chapter 6 provides the most detailed publicly available explanation of exit polling methods. Although reading their explanation will not make anyone an expert in gathering or analyzing exit poll data, the elaboration of the methodologies Mitofsky and Edelman have pioneered for exit polls is nonetheless impressive. For the first time, too, the authors present analyses of questionnaire order effects and questionnaire response category biases. They also explicitly address the issue of nonresponse in exit polls due either to sampled voters refusing to participate or to the interviewer being otherwise occupied and unable to query a sampled respondent. In 1992, the level of nonresponse averaged 42%;

thus, about two out of every five voters who were sampled did not provide any data. However, the "good news" was that the *rate of nonresponse* was not associated with the extent to which the exit poll findings conformed with the actual voting.

Mitofsky and Edelman also provide an insiders' view and critique of how their data were used by the network journalists on election night. As noted earlier, each news organization conducted its own analyses of the data provided by VRS in 1992. However, all the networks had "agreed not to present any state analysis on the air prior to poll closing that would suggest anything about the outcome of a contest." The authors comment that the networks "almost all were pretty good about observing this restriction." This is not to say that Mitofsky and Edelman observed no problems with the ways their data were disseminated by the networks the night of November 3, 1992; they did, and provide a telling example of how one network got "burned" by failing to heed VRS's warning not to use "preliminary" data prematurely.

In Chapter 7, Rob Daves, assistant managing editor and pollster for the *Minneapolis Star Tribune*, and Sharon Warden, senior polling analyst at *The Washington Post*, provide a detailed technical explanation of how data, gathered in pre-primary and pre-election polls to predict the possible outcome of a contest, must be very carefully analyzed in order to increase the likelihood that the predictive findings about the outcome will be correct. The specific issue they address is the process, which heretofore has remained mysterious to many, of how undecided voters should be treated in the calculations that derive the prediction of the outcome of a primary or general election.

Unlike the surveying of almost any other topic, pre-primary and pre-election polls that are used to predict a winner have an objective criterion against which their accuracy is judged — the actual outcome. As such, there are tremendous competitive pressures on news organizations not to make mistakes in their polls' predictions. One of the thorniest issues that has challenged pollsters is how to "allocate" sampled persons who, at the time the poll is conducted, respond that they are undecided about how they will vote or choose not to express an opinion.

It may come as a surprise to some that there is no widely agreed upon method for doing this. As there also is no one "standard" for how polls should screen for "likely voters" in the introductory scripts that are used to begin an interview, various pollsters have devised their own "secret" methods for handling undecideds. Daves and Warden begin by explaining how polls can incorporate techniques that are likely to reduce the proportion of persons who are truly undecided. They then explain four different approaches for doing this and put each to the test using data from five polls gathered (separately) by their respective organizations.

Chapter 7 will be of special interest to practitioners (both pollsters and journalists) and political junkies who want to learn the details about how news-related methodological and statistical decisions are made by those who gather poll data and analyze them for their news organizations. As the authors suggest, "assigning undecided respondents in pre-election polls is a chancy business, no matter which method is used." However the findings they present show that "assigning all undecided respondents to a challenger [i.e., the "Incumbency Rule"] resulted in the most error."

As an admonition to reporters, editors and producers, Daves and Warden recommend that it would be best to allow for both the time and resources to calculate pre-election predictions using several methods of assigning undecideds, and then disseminating a "best estimate" where possible. The issue is a clear example of the complexities of election polling, the implications of which too often are ignored by the news media.

The following three chapters report on various aspects of what was done by a few of the nation's prominent news organizations, and in some cases on what else might have been done, with election polls in news coverage of the 1992 presidential election campaign.

Chapter 8 comes from Sharon Warden's colleague at *The Washington Post*, Richard Morin, *The Post's* director of polling. As a seasoned pollster and journalist — someone who often writes public opinion and survey-related news stories in *The Post* — Morin is eminently qualified to advance an expert assessment of how the national media's polls fared in 1992. In short, he concludes that "1992 saw a maturing of the major media polls — in terms of technique and content, the polls were more sophisticated. Journalists in the major news organizations used polls more wisely and more cautiously than in the past."

In describing and critiquing the major "polling events" of the Bush/Clinton/Perot election campaign — including some in which he would have preferred that his own organization had done otherwise — Morin presents several conclusions about the '92 experience and considerations for election campaign coverage in 1996 and beyond:

- More polls were better than fewer polls — "America has more to fear from too few polls, rather than too many."
- Most news organizations remained "overly fond" of reporting horse-race findings and "remained too dependent on them to shape their coverage"; however, the blame lies with reporters and editors, not the polls or pollsters.
- Simultaneous with reporting the horse race too much, there was too little attention paid to other, non-horse race, types of survey

results — "prescient findings that challenged conventional wisdom."
*   "Tracking polls and focus groups were more widely used than ever [in 1992, but] with mixed results."

Morin's most compelling lament is his observation that "the media remained *data-rich but analysis poor*." Reading Morin's explanation of what *The Post* tried to do with its 1992 election polling, shows how journalists' use and dissemination of poll findings might more often serve "as a window into the concerns of voters." Along this line, he lauds the efforts of *The Charlotte Observer* for the way in which it used polls along with qualitative research techniques to determine a "voter's agenda" and then used that agenda to shape their campaign coverage.

Included in Chapter 8 is Morin's analysis of what was wrong with *The Post's* own reporting of a 21-point lead for Clinton in late September, 1992. This faux pas led their executive editor to pledge that a poll number for a horse-race lead would never again appear in a *Post* headline. Also of interest is Morin's explanation of the difference of opinions over the value of tracking polls between his organization and its polling partner, ABC News, *The Post* being far less sanguine about the method. In Morin's view, "tracking poll numbers are about as perishable as fresh fish."

Of special interest to all politicos is Morin's section on the effects that polling news had on the course of the 1992 campaign. He argues that, "it was the polls that legitimized Perot as a presidential candidate, forcing the political establishment to treat Perot and his message seriously." By the establishment, Morin surely includes political reporters and editors who ultimately make the decisions about which candidacies are viable and worthy of news coverage.

From all indications, it appears that *The New York Times* commits more resources over a broader period of time to using surveys to frame their presidential election campaign coverage than any other news organization. As he did in our previous volume on the Bush/Dukakis election coverage, Michael R. Kagay — political scientist, pollster, and news survey editor of *The Times* — again has provided a welcome treatise, filled with state-of-the art journalistic details, statistical tables, and figures from his organization's coverage of the Bush/Clinton/Perot election campaign. He does this in a way that illustrates how *The Times* used election polls throughout the 1992 campaign coverage. At the same time, Kagay weaves a compelling tale of why Bill Clinton was elected President.

Even more explicit than Morin's message in the previous chapter regarding the way that a news organization can be impacted by its own poll findings, Kagay states that "*The Times* used public opinion polling to aid its *reporters, editors,* and readers in understanding how the American electorate was reacting to the personalities, issues, and events of the Presidential election campaign" (italics added). There were six major types of polls that *The Times* used in 1992: (1) frequent national telephone polls to measure voter preferences and attitudes throughout the year; (2) a regional pre-primary poll in the South during the early, "trend identifying" stages of the campaign; (3) statewide exit polls on primary election days from February through June; (4) polls of delegates to the two major political party conventions; (5) statewide pre-election polls in five major states in the fall to study how the national contest was playing out at the state level; and (6) a national exit poll and additional key state exit polls on Election Day.

Without question, journalists and media scholars who read Chapter 9 can gain tremendous applied insight into the value of the long-term planning of election campaign coverage that utilizes surveys as a central element. That is, Kagay's presentation is not theory with abstract value; rather, it is packed with operational details that demonstrate exactly how poll findings were reported and helped to structure the entire election campaign coverage. Furthermore, with Kagay's useful notations of many of the *Times* articles that were generated and/or enhanced by the various poll findings, an enterprising reader could retrieve the original articles and systematically review them while referring to Kagay's explanation of their origins and the import of the news they presented.

Overall the varied polling *The Times* conducted and sponsored for the 1992 election was used in 50 news articles that relied heavily on polling data, 150 other articles in which the poll data were used to a lesser extent, and in many "free-standing graphics" which conveyed statistical snapshots of campaign-related topics. Furthermore, these polls "helped inform reporting and editing [throughout the year] by permitting reporters and editors to check hunches, to test the claims of candidates and pundits, and to avoid [being] manipulated." Here, certainly, is the current definitive role model for a news organization that is considering how to incorporate polling information into its election campaign coverage.

As with some of the previous chapters, Kagay includes many specific ideas for others to consider in planning the use of polls in their future campaign coverage. For example: why is one type of survey design preferred for a certain news purpose over another? Why do certain questionnaire items serve information gathering needs better than others? A most creative and informative use of the *Times's* poll data was a graphic that displayed the "ideological center of gravity" of various subgroupings of the American population along the liberal-conservative continuum.

Consistent with the goal of this volume, and as is the case for some
other major news organizations, Kagay notes that "measurement of the
'horse race' has always been a secondary consideration in polls sponsored by *The Times*. Our first priority has always been to measure the
public's reactions to issues, personalities, and events, and to try to understand the public's political attitudes." To do this, Kagay and his colleagues tried to design a "program of survey research" that was "responsive, flexible, and adequate to the task its faces." Few would question
that they succeeded.

Complementing the many examples in Chapter 9 of how a news organization can proactively plan to gather election survey data and use it as
news for specific purposes during an election campaign, Chapter 10 presents a detailed case study of a specific issue that had considerable consequences during the 1992 election season — the Gennifer Flowers story
and Bill Clinton's "problems of character."

In Chapter 10, Michael W. Traugott and Jennifer Means, political communications researchers at the University of Michigan, discuss their secondary analysis of data gathered in a 1992 ABC News/*Washington Post*
poll. Their case study illustrates how such data could be plumbed in
more depth, thereby leading to markedly different conclusions about the
campaign events and issues measured by the poll. A different analysis,
in turn, could have changed substantially the nature of the news coverage the "story" received, thereby altering significantly the campaign
itself. The authors do this not to criticize the specific story that was written from the data, but rather to demonstrate the behind-the-scenes effort
that *can and, more often, should* go into the interpretation and dissemination of newsworthy poll findings, as also noted by Mitofsky in Chapter 5.
Unfortunately, it is quite likely that there was a plethora of instances
across various news media in 1992, and in earlier years, that could have
served as case studies for Traugott and Means. As noted by Rich Morin
in Chapter 8, election poll data are too often vastly underutilized by the
very news organizations that pay for the poll to be conducted, but rarely
commit the time and resources needed to actualize the data's news
potential.

This concern is not a mere "academic" nitpicking matter. Rather, it is
one with serious consequences for the nation's political processes, as
Traugott and Means demonstrate: Too often news organizations must
quickly turn around poll findings as part of the coverage of breaking
news; "Their presentation of survey results is typically limited to marginal frequencies for single questions . . . Poll-based coverage makes significant sacrifices for the sake of journalistic brevity and simplicity: infrequent discussion of complicated relationships that reflect the nuances of
public opinion on an issue . . . This dilemma becomes more acute as news
organizations increase their use of public opinion polls in news stories."

Traugott and Means' mission was to determine if "a different story, equally newsworthy, could have been prepared from the same data." Through their re-analysis of poll data that ABC News and *The Washington Post* gathered on the public's reactions to Bill Clinton and the Gennifer Flowers story, they demonstrate that "there was a more interesting and telling news story than the obvious one that was presented through marginal frequencies for selected variables." In Chapter 10, they show that the citizens most concerned about Clinton's alleged "infidelity" and "credibility" were potential voters who were not at all likely to support Clinton anyway. Rather than playing the original poll findings and their implications as a story which highlighted Bill Clinton's problems with voters, thereby severely threatening his campaign's momentum and viability, the media should have played it more for what it was: partisan politics as usual.

The next two chapters address some of the effects this type of news coverage has on the public and the campaigns themselves. Chapter 11 describes the public's reaction to news coverage of the 1992 election campaign using findings from the polls that were commissioned to study this issue by the Times Mirror Center. Here, pollsters Andrew Kohut, Director of The Times Mirror Center for the People and the Press, and Larry Hugick of Princeton Survey Research Associates, base their assessment on the results of 13 surveys conducted in 1992 for these purposes and similar surveys that were conducted in earlier years. Kohut and Hugick conclude that "in reviewing the survey results from 1988, 1990, and 1992, it becomes apparent that these public attitudes [towards the media] have impacted on the evolution of presidential campaigns and how they are covered by the news media."

Kohut and Hugick report that, overall, the American public was slightly more positive in its assessment of the news coverage of the 1992 election than the coverage of the 1988 election. However, in an absolute sense rather than a relative one, the citizenry was clearly far from satisfied, giving the media's performance an average overall grade of "C+". "People's general feelings about the media's role in society were as much responsible for these low ratings as their beliefs about actual press performance during the campaign."

Telling of the public's reactions to the kind of news that has come to dominate election coverage, the authors note that Americans have "become extremely wary of the intrusiveness of the media." The news media are neither respected nor viewed by the public as impartial observers of the political process. Supplementing the findings reported by Traugott and Means (Chapter 10), Chapter 11 explains how the Times Mirror poll findings showed that the news peg that *60 Minutes* put on the Clinton infidelity issue was out of touch with majority opinion about how it should have been covered.

The Times Mirror surveys showed that the majority of the public would prefer to see the news organizations less involved in the election process. This most certainly extends to the public's attitudes towards use of election polls by the news media, attitudes that likely reflect a profound misunderstanding of the potential value of quality election polls. Undoubtably linked to concerns about the ways in which most news organizations are covering elections is Kohut and Hugick's documentation of the increased importance in 1992 to many citizens and journalists of radio and television talk shows vis-a-vis public opinion and its impact on the campaign process.

Kohut and Hugick finish their chapter with an especially interesting observation that "in 1992, there was little controversy about the polls driving the election or dampening voter interest." As evidence for this conclusion, they reason that, "the polls made it clear that Ross Perot had little or no chance to win, but did not seem to keep his supporters from participating."

Many of the earlier chapters in the book address sincere concerns about the effects that election polling news might have on the workings of various political processes in democratic societies. As noted earlier, the trend in many other democracies has been to place legal restrictions on the news media's release of horse-race results as election day approaches. In Chapter 12, Diana C. Mutz, political science and communication studies professor at the University of Wisconsin-Madison, presents the findings of an original research study in which she investigated "the impact of horse race media coverage on candidates' abilities to obtain campaign donations." She concludes that it is most likely that horse-race polling news has its largest impact on the course of the election campaign *during the primary season.* Ironically, it is at this very time in an election campaign that it is most difficult to accurately measure voters' preferences, which are often used as a critical gauge of "candidate viability," *and yet the news media typically commit the fewest resources to polling during this phase.*

Chapter 12 begins with a scholarly review of the news media's role in the primary process and of "strategic motivations" among political campaigners and contributors. Mutz notes that, "despite widespread agreement as to the importance of horse race coverage in influencing fund raising, there is little empirical evidence bearing on its validity and widespread confusion as to its role."

Using an impressive and robust database that she created for the period from the fall of 1987 through the spring 1988 Republican presidential primaries, Mutz reports her findings about the linkages between the media's poll-based "spin" on the successes and failures of George Bush, Bob Dole, Jack Kemp, and Pat Robertson and the weekly donations to their respective campaigns. Her conclusions are provocative, including finding that there is a minimum elapsed time of about two weeks before changes in horse-race news spin can be expected to impact a candidate's contributions. Surprisingly, the specific effects she documents were not all direct and positive. For example, coverage of George Bush's viability vis-a-vis the polls had no effect on contributions to the Bush campaign; however as Kemp's poll numbers deteriorated, Bush's contributions increased significantly.

Chapter 12 concludes with Mutz's discussion, bolstered by her findings, of how horse-race coverage by the media appears to influence the early stages of a political campaign. Here she notes that the news released by the media regarding the level of support the candidates, or potential candidates, have among the electorate plays "an important role in determining which candidates enter the primary season well funded, and which candidates continue to find supporters with checkbooks in hand." Just as importantly, Mutz explains that even if horse-race poll findings were eliminated (e.g. legally restricted) from public dissemination by the new media, they would likely have strong effects — albeit, behind the scenes — through their influence on the journalists covering a candidates' viability.

If, as we stated earlier, our central mission with this volume is to influence the manner in which the information gathered in election polls is used by the news media so as to enhance democratic political processes, then the chapters identify several themes for further thought and action.

Chapter 13 concludes the book with a discussion of four themes that we (Lavrakas and Traugott) see as pervading the other 11 chapters. We believe that these themes are highly consistent with most of what has recently been written by other scholars about this topic area, especially since 1990. First, we believe that the "power of the polls" has been adequately documented — in this volume and elsewhere — and that there is no longer any reason to question that the news media's use of election polls influences democratic political processes both directly and indirectly. We also heartily agree with Rich Morin's observation that the news media are "data-rich but analysis poor" when it comes to taking advantage of the potential benefits that could be derived from the information that election polls can generate. Related to this, and in line with several of the chapters, we believe that traditional approaches to formulating and "packaging" election news coverage must be extensively modified for significant improvements to result. Finally, we challenge media executives and journalists to accept more responsibility for the effects of their work on the values they profess to serve, and to recommit themselves and their organizations to actively strive to enhance democratic political processes.

PART TWO

Developments in Media Polling

2

Election Polling in Historical Perspective

Susan Herbst

Many textbooks and edited volumes about public opinion trace the roots of polling to 1936, the year when George Gallup demonstrated that the sample survey was a far more reliable predictive tool than the crude *Literary Digest* poll. Focusing on this year as the birth date of modern polling is not without merit, since 1936 was a turning point in the history of survey research: After that year social scientists and pollsters began to refine the sample survey and improve their accuracy in predicting elections even further. Yet if we think of the 1930s as the start of serious or "important" opinion measurement, we ignore the fascinating (and rather extensive) history of opinion measurement in America. The goal of this chapter is to remind students of public opinion about the lengthy chronicle of opinion assessment and to underscore some particularly interesting lessons from the pre-1936 past.

In the 1992 presidential race, polls were omnipresent: On a typical day that autumn, any attentive citizen could locate a variety of election or issue polls in newspapers, newsmagazines, or on the evening local and national news broadcasts. Although there has been an uneven but steady increase in the number of polls reported (Ladd & Benson, 1992; See also Lavrakas & Bauman, Chapter 3), Americans are already quite accustomed to the presence of polls in the public sphere. In the mid-nineteenth century, for example, major newspapers like the *Chicago Tribune* reported the results of numerous straw polls in the months before a national election. One could say, in fact, that quantification has been a discernable part of American political culture ever since the diffusion of the general election. In his mid-nineteenth century travels across America Alexis de Tocqueville (1850) argued that

[Americans] carry a trader's habits over into the business of politics. They like order, without which affairs do not prosper, and they set an especial value on regularity of mores, which are the foundation of a good business; they prefer the good sense which creates fortunes to the genius which often dissipates them; their minds, accustomed to definite calculations, are frightened by general ideas; and they hold practice in greater honor than theory.

As Patricia Cline Cohen puts it, we are and always have been a "calculating people" (Cohen, 1982). Placing the 1992 polls in historical perspective demands attention to larger issues like quantification and power differentials among citizens. Such a contextualized look at polling can help us better understand changes in survey practices as well as great transformations in political culture. In this short chapter I cannot hope to cover the large, complex history of public opinion in America, but I can point to some suggestive phenomena and trends which illuminate parts of that history. I begin by exploring the nature of early straw polls in the mid-nineteenth century, then move to the 1930s and 1940s, when "scientific" polling was in its youth. Finally, I'll discuss some of the implications and lessons of this history for contemporary pollsters, journalists and public opinion scholars.

A note of qualification: This chapter concerns the sorts of election polls that Americans see in their newspapers and media broadcasts, not academic survey research. Although many academic survey labs and individual scholars have begun to work with journalists at major newspaper to conduct polls, it is still fairly easy to differentiate between horse-race polls or quickly conducted issue polls and the much longer surveys academic labs produce. So, "surveys" and "polls" are used interchangeably here to refer to polls conducted by journalists, commercial pollsters, citizens, or parties — not by scholars.

Straw Polling in the Nineteenth Century

Beginning in the early nineteenth century, political party activists, journalists and interested citizens engaged in the practice of straw polling. Straw polls, which are still commonly used today, are simple oral or paper and pencil polls conducted without sampling. Although the most famous straw polls were those conducted by the *Literary Digest* in the early decades of the twentieth century, political activists and reporters have long been aware of the usefulness and rhetorical power of such surveys.[1]

In a study of straw polling, I systematically analyzed newspaper coverage of American presidential races at twenty year intervals, from 1856 to 1976. I've also evaluated the 1860, 1988 and 1992 campaigns, since the first contest was particularly interesting from a historical standpoint, and the latter two races are the most recent ones we've witnessed.[2] In my analysis, I studied three newspapers: the *Chicago Sun-Times*, the *Chicago Tribune*, and the *New York Times*.[3] In general, there were three types of straw poll articles: reports from journalists in the field (either a paper's own correspondent, or a journalist from a like-minded paper), polls by party workers sent to the newspapers, and citizens' polls or what I call "peoples' polls."

Journalists who covered the typical nineteenth or early twentieth century presidential campaign spent an enormous amount of time on the road, as they do today. Yet poor roads, the absence of air travel, and the lack of electronic communication technology (fax machines, laptop computers with modems, etc.) gave reporters substantial time to interact with voters, whether they sought this interaction or not. Many journalists spent long hours travelling to rallies, parades and speaking events, and formally polled citizens on trains, steamers and at public events. Results of such polls were considered "news" by all three papers in this sample, yet the partisan nature of such reports should be kept in mind. Although newspapers of the late nineteenth and early twentieth century were far less partisan than their predecessors (see Baldasty, 1992), there was no real separation between news and editorial content in the text of a paper. As a result, straw polls were reported with the strongest of partisan bias, and it is doubtful that journalists even bothered sending unfavorable poll results back to their editors: A newspaper's chosen candidate was almost universally favored in the straw polls that newspaper published.

Polls by journalists were a vital and interesting genre of partisan rhetoric for many reasons. Straw polls had an air of science because they were quantitative, and in that way echoed the legitimacy of the already-thriving hard sciences (see Porter, 1986). Also, "straws," as they were often called, were democratically conducted: All those in a train car or steamer sitting area were included in a poll. Finally, straw polls were authentic journalistic reports from the field that demonstrated just how wide support was for a paper's chosen candidate. A poll taken during the 1860 contest between Lincoln and Douglas exemplifies the "traveling" polls conducted by journalists:

> They had an excursion from Hillsdale to Goshen, Indiana on Thursday. A vote for President was taken, with the following result: For Lincoln, gentlemen 368, ladies 433 — total 796 [sic]; for Douglas, gentlemen 156, ladies 60 — total 216; for Breckinridge, gentlemen 5, lady 1. Lincoln over all 574 (*Chicago Tribune*, 10/7/60, p. 2).

In a similar sort of poll during the 1876 race, a reporter queried voters as they walked from a train to their hotels:

> An excursion train containing some 200 people from Dayton, O., and neighboring towns, arrived last evening via the Pan Handle Road. They are stopping at the Commercial, Gardner's St. James, and Ruhn's Hotel. Coming up, a vote was taken, resulting as follows: Hayes 65, Tilden 13, neutral 3, Cooper 2 (*Chicago Tribune* 8/25/76, p. 2).

The *Chicago Tribune* editors were particularly interested in straw polling, and these two reports are indicative of their rhetorical style. Both accounts are straightforward, and without obvious editorializing, yet from the perspective of the 1990s we know just how problematic these reports actually are. Did the journalists interview all who would participate, or did they pick and choose among potential respondents? How did they phrase their questions? Were the polls taken before or after a political discussion? Were they anonymous? And finally, were these the only polls journalists conducted on those two fall days, in 1860 and 1896, or were others taken and then discarded?

Beyond conducting their own polls, journalists accepted polls handed to them by factory managers or political operatives. An example from the 1896 race:

> Estimates received at Republican National headquarters indicate that 90 per cent of the railway employees favor the St. Louis platform and nominees. The activity shown by them in organizing sound money clubs throughout the country is given as evidence in proof of these estimates. . . . A visitor from Nebraska said he knew of thirty sound money Populists in one neighborhood out there who would cast their ballots this year for the Republican candidate (*Chicago Tribune*, 8/27/96, p. 12.)

Again, we know very little about how the poll was conducted, and the source seems dubious, given that the *Tribune* was itself a Republican paper. Yet these problems did not plague the editors of the typical nineteenth century newspaper, who were intent on *reinforcing* the existing beliefs of their partisan readers.

Newspapers also published a large number of polls conducted by readers themselves. Some of these readers were travelling on business, such as the gentleman who polled 2,886 voters during the summer of 1856. He wrote to the *New York Times* that

> Of literary men, collegiate professors, teachers [etc.], seven-eighths were Republicans. . . Of forty-two ministers of the Gospel, thirty-nine affirmed they should vote for Fremont; one for Buchanan, and two for Fillmore (*New York Times*, 9/13/56, p. 4.)

During that same year, the *Tribune* published this poll, which they received from another paper:

> The New Haven *Journal of Commerce* has seen a letter from a workman in Samuel Cole's pistol factory, at Hartford, stating the politics of the workmen in one department to be as follows: for Fremont, 109; Buchanan, 37; Fillmore, 3. That, he says, is an immense change of opinion, as Buchanan used to have about 100 majority in these shops (8/15/56, p.2).

And in yet another poll, a voter contributed his own editorial comments along with his statistics:

> CAR VOTING. - Editors Tribune: Gents — The following is the result of a canvass I made on the Saturday evening train to Milwaukee. Among the gentlemen, Fillmore 5, Buchanan 13, Fremont 41.— Among the ladies, of whom about one half only voted, the vote was, Fremont 9, Fillmore 2, Buchanan ("purely out of sympathy for his lonesome condition,") one (*Chicago Tribune*, 8/26/56, p. 3).

Some citizen contributors sent in humorous polls, which both expressed their hopes for the upcoming election and probably made readers laugh:

> To the Editor of the New York Times:
> On a south-bound train on the Delaware and Hudson Railroad last Thursday, in one car an enthusiastic drummer took the now popular straw vote to determine the political affiliations of the passengers. The poll showed the 23 occupants divided — 18 for McKinley, 5 for Bryan. This was satisfactory, but more was to come. When the train halted at Ballston, among those who got off were the five Bryan sympathizers, and then it was seen that they were handcuffed together, and were a gang of prisoners on their way to the county jail at that place.
> Sound Money.
> Ballston, N.Y., Oct. 5 (10/7/96, p.4).

Although citizen polls were commonly found in newspapers before the 1930s, they largely disappeared after that point, replaced by the more reliable surveys of Gallup, Roper, Crossley, and others (see Herbst, 1993). While one does on occasion see unscientific polls published in newspapers (e.g., the "roving photographer" who takes one's picture and asks his or her opinion on a single issue), major dailies primarily use sample survey techniques. Yet despite the improvements in election prediction we have witnessed, the early straw polls served many useful social and political functions. For one, straw polling was a way to get voters involved in the election, since any citizen could poll his or her colleagues or neighbors about the upcoming election, tally those results and possi-

bly get them published. Straw polls were a concrete avenue for participation in the pre-election excitement that we no longer enjoy: These days
pollsters have taken over the "chore" of surveying the electorate, depriv-
ing citizens of this task. Additionally, straw polling probably served as a
basis for interpersonal dialogue about the campaign: In many reports on
straws, we can see that such tallies were made before or after a political
discussion. When voters were themselves conducting polls, those surveys served to enhance engagement in, and excitement about, the presidential contest. In the 1990s, it is difficult to understand the enthusiasm
(and indeed joy), that surrounded the typical election campaign of the
previous century. Yet we have enormous amounts of archival evidence
attesting to this enthusiasm, of which straw polling was a vital part (on
nature of nineteenth century political participation, see Baker, 1985;
Dinkin, 1989; or McGerr, 1986).

This is not to say that the straw polling of the nineteenth and early
twentieth century is somehow "better" than today's surveys. But it is
clear to the historian of polls that progress in some respects (predictive
power) can also lead to regression in others: Peoples' polls were a means
of citizen public expression during campaigns, and a starting point for
discourse among voters.

Journalists and Polls, 1930-1950

Even though George Gallup did accurately predict the outcome of the
1936 presidential race, embarrassing the *Literary Digest*, the large majority of elite journalists during that period were not convinced that the opinion poll was reliable or useful.[4] Some correspondents worried that the
widespread use of opinion polling would lead to bandwagon voting,
while others were afraid that statesmen could use polling to manipulate
the public more effectively. On the whole, however, journalists working
in the decades just before and after the introduction of the sample survey
were more skeptical than fearful: How could polling help them to assess
public opinion, during and between elections, when the method could
only tally categorical data? These were journalists accustomed to talking
with citizens and leaders at great length, probing them on the subtleties
of their beliefs. To them, polling seemed a superficial means for understanding the complex nature of public sentiments.

A few years ago, I conducted a study of 44 prominent journalists who
worked during the period when survey research was new, and its real
value was yet undetermined.[5] Using a combination of oral history techniques and open-ended survey questions, I was able to learn quite a lot
about their views of the new opinion poll, and about the alternative

methods they used for assessing public attitudes.[6] Not surprisingly, some journalists began by telling me that newspapers were more interested in persuading public opinion than in evaluating it during the 1930s and 1940s. This put serious journalists in something of a bind, since their paper's biases constrained their public opinion reporting to a great extent. One correspondent explained that

> It should be borne in mind that during the 1930s and 1940s, most American newspapers regarded themselves as political *leaders* as well as political chronicles. Therefore, most of them looked for signs that public opinion was in step with the publisher's biases. For example, in 1936 the *Chicago Tribune* featured stories on the heavy run on Alf Landon campaign buttons in Chicago (they consisted of felt cut in the shape of a sunflower with a Landon picture on a button in the middle). The *Chicago Daily Times*, on the other hand, featured stories about the number of school children who were looking for the buttons because the felt made an ideal pen wiper — an article that sold for one or two pennies. . . . Newspapers did not really become interested in articles on public opinion until World War II loomed on the horizon (of course there were some exceptions).

He concluded that, "You really aren't interested in public opinion when you are trying to lead it."

Journalists working during this period were largely ignorant of advances in survey methodology despite the growing number of professional and academic researchers working in the field (see Converse, 1987). Of the journalists I spoke with, or corresponded with, some indicated a familiarity with polling operations like Gallup's, and their newspapers subscribed to these services. About one-third of the reporters went "door-to-door" at some point in the period before 1950, in an attempt to better understand voter behavior in their area. One journalist, working in the far west, used the door-to-door technique to help establish a new magazine: "Never west of the Hudson, I didn't know one end of an abalone from another. But a door-to-door canvass from Eureka to Encenita convinced me that [the publication's] only hope was to stay and grow as a [specialty] magazine."

Given that journalists were unfamiliar with survey methodology (see also Price, 1953), and only used non-random door-to-door techniques sporadically, how did they measure public opinion? Several journalists said that they tried to assess popular attitudes by querying large numbers of citizens and by sharing that information with other journalists. As one former correspondent noted

> In our time we were in *personal* (not "electronic") touch with each other. Journalists lived nearby and had their communal "watering holes." In New York, for example, we had Bleeck's now-vanished, once-famous

"Artists and Writers" bar in the old *Herald Tribune* building. . . the Round
Table at the Algonquin Hotel. . . plus clubs: Dutch Treat ("The Literary
Kiwanis"), the Coffee House, and for all its stuffiness, the Century. In
Boston, the *Globe, Post, Transcript,* and the Hearst papers were side-by-side
on "Newspaper Row."

These days, press clubs have almost disappeared. But in previous
decades, over drinks or coffee, journalists would trade knowledge about
public opinion, gleaned from their contacts. From my interviews, I got
the sense that journalists, while interested in measuring public opinion,
had a certain confidence about that process that reporters lack today.
Contemporary journalists depend upon polls, in many cases, and find it
difficult to assess the climate of opinion without such tools. Compare
journalistic attitudes of today with this quote, from an informant in my
study:

> In the 1930s on [a large newspaper's] staff in New York I tried to envision
> my average reader and then spoke to him. As [a foreign] bureau chief. . .
> starting in 1946 I tried to think of the average New York subway goer —
> why should he care? I tried to understand the mind of the average reader
> and then set out to tell him what I could about Europe and North Africa.
> "Public opinion" merely identified the reader and his interests and preju-
> dices; it was a starting point for converse. My source on what readers
> thought? Just my memory of folks I have known all my life.

Beyond trusting their own instincts and sharing these thoughts with
other journalists, reporters working in the 1930s and 1940s depended
upon what I call "public opinion surrogates" — unofficial experts who
kept a finger on the public pulse. Journalists in my study mentioned all
sorts of surrogates — Pullman operators, cab drivers and others who
interacted with the public for a living. Reporters used these surrogates,
in addition to their own interviews with citizens, as evidence of public
attitudes. One reporter noted that he "had [his] own favorite device on
gauging elections. I approached Catholic clergy to ask how the vote
would go in their area because I knew most priests love politics. I had a
favorite bishop who never missed an election."

Now this is not to say that journalists today don't socialize with each
other,[7] use their intuition about public opinion, or converse with surrogates. And there is a tendency on the part of veteran journalists to believe
that the "old ways" of reporting are somehow better than contemporary
practices. Without initiating a debate about which practices are superior,
however, we can recognize that there has been a fundamental change in
the way journalists and their editors approach public opinion with the
diffusion and growing legitimacy of the sample survey.[8]

Lessons from the Past

Although the history of public opinion is full of lessons to contemporary pollsters and journalists who use polls, I'll concentrate on only a few
here, all of which should be useful in thinking about how surveys are
used in the public sphere. This section is not intended as a guide for editors and journalists, suggesting how they might better use and report on
polls. Plenty of academics have already listed such suggestions (e.g.,
Meyer, 1973; or more recently, Holley, 1991; McBride, 1991; or Miller,
Merkle & Wang, 1991). Instead, I try to make links between history and
current practices, in order to show the usefulness of looking back.

First, the resistance to polls that was so pervasive in journalistic circles
before the 1950s was not simply due to ignorance about the advantages
of sampling. This resistance was a thoughtful sort, based upon some
intelligent insights about the limitations of polling. For example, while
open-ended survey questions are often used in academic polling, commercial pollsters and those who sell political polling services most often
use closed-ended questions. The textured opinions that earlier journalists gathered, by talking to citizens at length, often get crushed today as
reporters, editors, and producers use surveys to squeeze such opinions
into categories. Journalists were right to be concerned about the loss of
in-depth interviewing, because it *has* become less common during political campaigns, and between campaigns. Recent interest in focus groups
(see Traugott, Chapter 4) among journalists is probably a reaction to the
diffusion of polling: We need to find ways to supplement poll data, and
to help us to gain perspective on mixed or complex survey results. Many
of the complaints and fears about polling, expressed by journalists who
witnessed the rise of the sample survey, are still valid, and still worth
thinking about. If they had looked to the history of public opinion twenty years ago, journalists and other newspaper professionals would be
much more sophisticated in how they use focus groups and in-depth
interviews in conjunction with polling.

During every contemporary election, there are pleas to take polls
"with a grain of salt." Many of these appeals are voiced by candidates
and managers, upset with their performance in pre-election polls (see
Bauman & Herbst, 1994). But many other complaints are from citizens
and journalists themselves. Despite these longstanding objections, journalists still have much to learn about the reporting of polls, and how to
critically analyze poll results. Beyond a few elite papers which make
some effort to analyze survey data critically (e.g., *The New York Times*),
many news organizations still leave out crucial statistics when reporting

data (see Mitofsky, chapter 5). Even when journalists do report basic statistics such as sampling error, it is doubtful that they understand what that error is, or why it matters. Journalists of the nineteenth and early twentieth centuries seemed to have a more ironic and sensible stance to polls than contemporary correspondents and editors. It is most certainly true that polling has improved, but that does not mean that healthy, informed skepticism should disappear.

Even though today's polls are rarely reported in a partisan manner, journalistic writing about surveys is still confused and unsatisfying to academics and probably to readers as well. Instead of the partisan commentary which framed reports of nineteenth century straw polls, journalists and pollsters use technical language to avoid just such editorializing. Unfortunately, since most journalists lack a technical sensibility when it comes to polls, citizens are sometimes subjected to nonsensical poll reports, as in this example by the *Chicago Tribune*'s Jon Margolis during the 1992 campaign:

> That trend [showing Bush closing the gap] was what statisticians call "regression to the mean," with the top going down, the bottom going up, and the middle staying where it was, raising the possibility that each of the three candidates would soon have the support of about one-third of the electorate (10/26/92, p. 1).

"Regression to the mean" is an important statistical concept, but it is unclear how even a well-educated citizen would make sense of this poll report. Voters shouldn't need a course in linear modeling in order to read their daily newspaper during an election campaign.

My argument in this essay is not that pollsters should conduct fewer polls, or that journalists should report fewer of them. And I am not making a simple plea for better poll reporting, although that is clearly a necessity. I am asking that students of public opinion use the history *of their own field* to ask fundamental questions about the appropriateness, format, and reporting of survey data. If we think long and hard about the problematics of nineteenth century poll reporting, for example, we realize that we have replaced partisan discourse with technical discourse, and that the technical discourse is often used just as irresponsibly as the partisan one was used. Do we need a new language, to help us communicate polling results to voters? What might a language, that is intelligent, skeptical, and contextualizes data, actually look like? I believe that we are a long way from finding the answer to this question, but we need to ask it before much longer, lest we become slaves to the very methodological tools we've created.

Notes

1. On straw polls also see Smith (1990).
2. The 1860 campaign was a particularly exciting one, since the slavery debate raged, and war was near. Also, Stephen Douglas made extraordinary efforts to win the campaign, even though his chances were slim.
3. Although one could conceivably study any of a number of major metropolitan dailies from the mid-nineteenth century, these three papers are especially good candidates for analysis. The *Tribune* and *Sun-Times* are strong, competing papers with different political ideologies, while the *New York Times* has long been a national opinion leader among the press. For each newspaper, 15 sample days were randomly selected between July 1 and election day.

The *Sun-Times* has not been a continuously published periodical: For elections beginning with 1856, I studied the *Chicago Times*, for 1896, I used the Chicago Times-Herald, and in 1936 I evaluated the *Chicago Daily Times*. For 1860, certain editions of the *Chicago Times* could not be located, so those in the Illinois State Historical Library were included in the sample. Only a few issues of the 1856 *Tribune* were located, and 1856 issues of the *Chicago Times* were missing.

4. The same was true for congressmen, who debated the merits of the sample survey on the House floor. See Herbst, 1993.
5. See Herbst (1993) pp. 192-3, for methodological details on this study.
6. There are limitations associated with the "data" collected in any oral historical study, since informants are asked to remember events and activities which occurred long ago. Although one can find a variety of sophisticated discussions of these problems in history journals — particularly the *Journal of American History* and the *Oral History Review* — see Herbst (1993; pp. 94-5) for my perspective on memory problems in this study.
7. Perhaps the most vivid and entertaining portrait of socialization and cameraderie among campaign journalists can be found in Crouse (1974), who describes press activity during the 1972 presidential campaign.
8. For a broad discussion of varying conceptualizations of public opinion in history, and some documentation of alternative routes for public opinion expression, see Herbst (1994).

3

Page One Use of Presidential Pre-Election Polls: 1980-1992

Paul J. Lavrakas
Sandra L. Bauman

The media long have been interested in evaluating and presenting public opinion as a part of their news coverage (cf. Cantril, 1991; Crespi, 1989; Gollin, 1980; and Herbst, 1993). Recognizing the public's need for such information, newspapers in particular have increasingly become involved in the business of polling — by conducting their own polls, by commissioning private polls, and/or by using results from syndicated polls (cf. Demers, 1987; Holley, 1991; Traugott, 1992). The use of media-sponsored polls, especially in presidential election campaign coverage, has become a staple.

Prior to the mid-1970s, the press usually contracted with outside firms to conduct surveys of public opinion, such as pre-election polls (Holley, 1991). Large-scale, routinely conducted media polls — ones that generally employ sound methodologies — came into being when CBS and the *New York Times* joined forces in 1975 (cf. Kagay, 1991). Consistent with Meyer's (1973) call for the deployment of "precision journalism" techniques in news reporting, these two news organizations recognized the value of conducting their own polls to inform their own news coverage of major issues, such as presidential elections; (however, each always has done its own analysis of the data). When the news media began to design, conduct, and analyze their own polls and used this information to inform both their news staffs and the public, "it could be seen as part of the movement toward more investigative reporting, rather than merely reporting and/or reacting to polls done by others" (Lavrakas, 1991, p. 11). That is, it was a form of "enterprise journalism" in which the media themselves created information which had news value (cf. Von Hoffman, 1980). Today, it is estimated that about half of all U.S. daily newspapers report on their own pre-election polls, as do almost all of the nation's largest print and broadcast news organizations (cf. Holley, 1991; Ladd & Benson, 1992). Not only has the number of news organizations conducting polls increased, but so has the sheer number of polls sponsored by the media. And, in each election year since the early 1970s, the number of media polls appears to have increased. According to a Roper Center study, there were two major news organizations in 1972 that conducted a total of three polls; seven news organizations conducted 122 polls in 1980, whereas in 1988, eight organizations conducted 259 polls (Ladd & Benson, 1992). The *Los Angeles Times*, for example, conducted twice as many polls during the 1988 election as it did in the 1984 election, with about a 90% increase in the sheer number of respondents interviewed (Lewis, 1991). Miller (1993) reported that the findings from 130 polls were published in print media between June, 1992 and Election Day.

Several factors have contributed to this "proliferation" of media pre-election polling (Dionne, 1992; Mann & Orren, 1992; Traugott, 1992). First, two of the basic tenets of American journalism have spurred journalists' use of scientific polling: (1) the Norm of Objectivity; and (2) the Role of Watchdog.

In terms of objectivity, the news media are expected to present information in a balanced, unbiased manner. Polls, with their scientific methodology, allow the media to present information in a seemingly objective fashion (cf. Dionne, 1992; Gitlin, 1990; Miller, Merkle & Wang, 1991; and Traugott, 1992). Instead of having to rely on "the riveting anecdote and dramatic personal experience" (Mann & Orren, 1992, p. 5) that long have been the staple of so-called "shoeleather" journalism, poll results put the issues of the election into a more holistic perspective. Hickman (1991) goes further by arguing that in election coverage reporters can address the likely outcome of an election contest from "behind a veil of objectivity" by citing poll data, and at the same time, poll data offer these same reporters a scapegoat when the election outcome differs from the polls' prediction.

The media's role as watchdog is ostensibly enhanced with the sponsorship and presentation of pre-election polls. Journalists no longer need to "blindly accept the claims of politicians who try to peddle their own information" (Mann & Orren, 1992, p. 4). Media-sponsored polls allow news organizations to put candidate claims into perspective and challenge conventional wisdom (Kagay, 1991). Journalists recognize they cannot be everywhere at once, and public opinion surveys can help them catch faulty facts while evaluating candidate messages and pinpointing the public's concerns.

Another contributing factor to the proliferation of election surveys is the technological advances in the practice of polling (Frankovic, 1994). For example, relatively small probability samples make it possible to generalize to enormous populations, and the advent of statistical software makes analysis relatively quick and simple (Altschuler, 1982; Herbst, 1993; Moore, 1992). New telecommunications technologies now provide news organizations with nearly "instant" poll results (Frankovic, 1994).

A final explanation for the proliferation of election polls is the hypothesis that the decline in the importance of political parties has contributed to news organizations becoming more involved in polling (Altschuler, 1982; Mann & Orren, 1992; Moore, 1992). This decline has left the media with the "responsibility for vetting presidential candidates and deciding who among them should be considered seriously" (Mann & Orren, 1992, p. 13). Especially in the election primary season, journalists appear to rely heavily on poll results to determine which candidates, among a field of several, are "viable" and therefore "worthy of coverage" (cf. Hickman, 1991; Meyrowitz, 1992).

Each recent presidential election campaign has seen its share of media critics (e.g., Crotty, 1991; Dionne, 1991; Greiter, 1992; Jamieson, 1992) and "poll-bashers" (e.g., Looney, 1991; Greenberg, 1992; Royko, 1992) questioning, and, in some cases, lamenting the escalating use of polls in election news coverage. However, no one has robustly documented the extent to which this assumed increase has actually occurred.

To partially address this knowledge gap, we began in 1988 to conduct a content analysis of the front pages of 11 major U.S. daily newspapers focusing on their coverage of presidential elections. We have completed this data collection for 1980, 1984, 1988, and 1992 — a database totaling more than 5,500 front pages.

Content Analysis Methodology

The front pages of 11 large circulation U.S. newspapers were analyzed to determine the frequency and the percentage of Page One presidential election stories that reported findings of a pre-election poll. The newspapers were the:

Atlanta Constitution,
Boston Globe,
Chicago Tribune,
Cleveland Plain Dealer,
Denver Post,

Houston Post,
Los Angeles Times,
New York Times,
St. Louis Post-Dispatch,
Wall Street Journal, and
Washington Post.

These newspapers were chosen because of their geographic distribution, their varied editorial objectives, and their ready availability on microfilm.

The front page of each of the newspapers from July 1 of the given presidential election year through the November election day of that year was coded for 1980, 1984, 1988 and 1992. For each front page, two trained coders *independently* read each story to determine whether or not it was about the presidential election campaign.[1] If it was a presidential election story the coder determined whether or not the story — at least the Page One portion — reported findings of a pre-election poll.[2] These two variables served as the primary data for this chapter: (1) the number of presidential election stories on a front page of a given day; and (2) the number of these stories that reported pre-election poll findings.

As noted above, each front page was coded independently by two coders and their counts were compared. In cases where the data for the same front page did not match, a third coder returned to the microfilm to resolve the inconsistency. (Despite this level of coding some measurement error is likely to remain, given that some discretion was exercised by the human coders. However, we do not believe that this imprecision has biased the findings; i.e., whatever errors remain, they are likely to be random in nature.)

These data provided three types of information about the newspapers. First, they provided a count of the absolute number of Page One stories which focused on the presidential election a newspaper ran between July 1 and the election day in a given year. Second, they provided a count of the absolute number of Page One presidential stories with pre-election poll news the newspaper ran in the time frame. Third, they provided the percentage (relative frequency) of the Page One presidential pre-election news stories which reported poll findings as part of the Page One copy.[3]

In addition to this intensive effort, we conducted a follow-up content analysis of 400 front pages randomly selected across the 11 newspapers and the four years. In this follow-up study, additional information about the poll stories was coded, including: (1) placement of the story on the page; (2) information about the content of the headline and the story lead;

and (3) more details about the "prominence" of the poll information within the story.[4]

Page One Pre-Election Polling News

In all, 5,521 front pages were read for the 11 newspapers during the four presidential election years. These pages had 6,431 Page One news stories about that year's presidential election. This is an average of a little more than one such story per front page (mean = 1.16). Of these stories, 883, or about one in seven (13.7%), reported the findings of at least one pre-election poll on the front page portion of the story. Overall, this translates to an average of about one presidential poll story *per week* in the front pages of these newspapers from the July through Election Day time period during 1980, 1984, 1988 and 1992. On the surface, this does not appear to be a situation in which these major newspapers have bombarded the public with so called "horse race" journalism.

However, it is a year-by-year comparison that better answers the question whether or not the use of pre-election polls has increased since 1980 and, if so, by how much.

Number of Presidential Pre-Election Stories

As shown in Table 3.1, there were 1,446 presidential pre-election front page stories on the 1980 Anderson-Carter-Reagan election campaign in the July-November timeframe in these 11 newspapers. In 1984, for the Mondale-Reagan campaign, there were 1,393 stories, or about 4% fewer than in 1980 — basically the same amount. For the 1988 Bush-Dukakis campaign there were 1,559 stories, or about 8% more than in 1980 — a slight increase the over previous two election years. However, in 1992 there were 2,033 Page One stories about the Bush-Clinton-Perot election, which was *more than a 30% increase over the 1980, 1984 and 1988 years.*

The left-most columns of Table 3.1 present these data grouped by year and by newspaper, respectively. It can be seen that there was a good deal of variation across the 11 newspapers in their own respective year-by-year coverage change: e.g., whereas the *Denver Post, Cleveland Plain Dealer, Houston Post,* and *Chicago Tribune* basically doubled the number of pre-election stories they ran on Page One in 1992 compared to 1980, the *Atlanta Constitution, Boston Globe, St. Louis Post-Dispatch,* and *Washington Post* ran a fairly similar number of Page One stories in each of these presidential election years.

TABLE 3.1 Number of Page One Election Stories, Poll Stories, and Percentage Poll Stories by Year and Paper

Paper	Number of Election Stories				Number of Poll Stories				Percentage Poll Stories/ Election Stories			
	1980	1984	1988	1992	1980	1984	1988	1992	1980	1984	1988	1992
Atlanta Constitution	115	100	94	120	12	2	8	38	13.8	1.9	8.5	31.5
Boston Globe	200	148	179	218	10	7	10	44	6.3	4.3	6.8	18.1
Chicago Tribune	75	107	142	156	7	25	37	48	11.2	25.9	30.5	29.7
Cleveland Plain Dealer	76	73	108	139	16	4	5	44	11.9	7.1	5.0	31.1
Denver Post	54	83	108	102	2	10	14	29	4.8	16.7	14.6	30.1
Houston Post	79	126	170	178	2	8	8	46	2.2	9.1	5.9	22.8
Los Angeles Times	145	106	92	219	9	32	10	42	6.0	29.6	11.0	20.1
New York Times	152	175	144	259	13	38	15	42	8.3	17.0	12.1	17.3
St. Louis Post Dispatch	162	156	163	172	5	8	2	28	4.2	6.9	0.9	14.0
Wall Street Journal	204	147	176	262	13	12	21	67	6.3	8.3	8.7	18.9
Washington Post	184	172	183	208	15	33	20	24	9.9	21.3	12.2	13.4
TOTAL	1446	1393	1559	2033	102	179	150	452	7.1	12.8	9.6	22.2

Number of Presidential Pre-Election Poll Stories

In 1980, there were 102 Page One stories in these newspapers about the Anderson-Carter-Reagan election campaign in the July-November time frame that reported the findings of pre-election polls. In 1984, there were 179 such stories, or about a 75% increase over 1980. In 1988, there were 150 front page stories with poll findings about the Bush-Dukakis election campaign, or about 50% more than in 1980, yet 16% fewer than in 1984. However, during the 1992 campaign there were 452 Page One poll stories. This is *more than a 300% increase over 1980* and *more than a 150% increase over 1984 and 1988.*

The middle columns of Table 3.1 present these data by year and by newspaper, respectively. Here one can observe the considerable variation across the 11 newspapers in the amount of stories with poll news that they ran across the four election years.

Percentage of Page One Presidential Pre-Election Stories with Poll News

Although absolute numbers of stories and stories with polling news tell part of the picture, it is the *percentage* of stories that contain poll findings that speaks more directly to the issue of the prominence of presidential pre-election polling news in these major U.S. dailies.

As shown in the right-most columns of Table 3.1, the proportion of Page One presidential pre-election stories in 1980 with poll findings was 7.1% or about one in 14. In 1984, the proportion was greater: 12.8% or about one in eight. In 1988, it dropped back to 9.6% or about one out of 10. However, in 1992, the proportion of stories with polling news *jumped to 22.2% or more than one in 5.* In fact, four of the newspapers (*Atlanta Constitution, Cleveland Plain Dealer, Chicago Tribune,* and *Denver Post*) had nearly a third of their 1992 presidential campaign front page stories reporting a pre-election poll.

Variation over Time

Figures 3.1, 3.2, and 3.3 plot these data, combined across the 11 newspapers, by each half-month before the election.

As shown in Figure 3.1, there was a fairly similar pattern in the total number of Page One stories per newspaper for 1984, 1988, and 1992 from

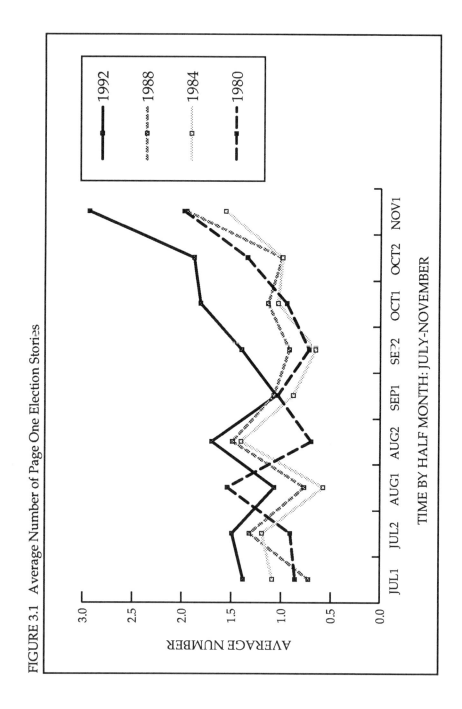

FIGURE 3.1 Average Number of Page One Election Stories

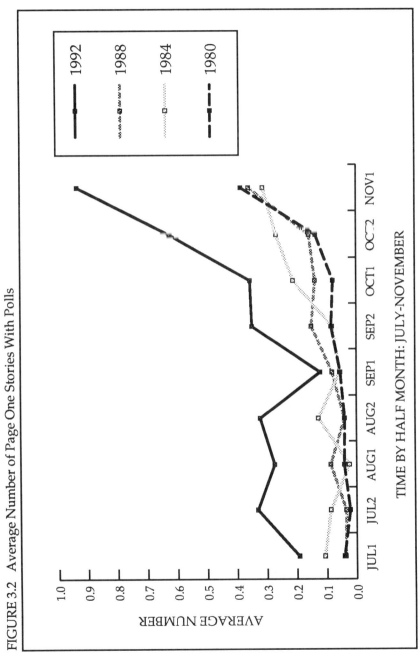

FIGURE 3.2 Average Number of Page One Stories With Polls

FIGURE 3.3   Percentage of Page One Stories With Polls

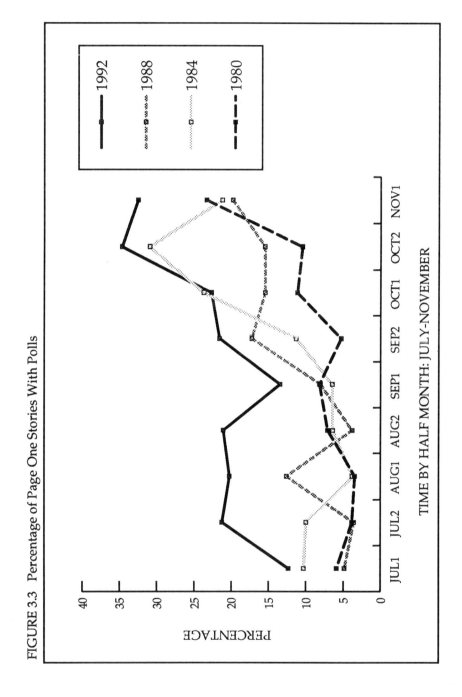

July through the first half of September: a slight increase from early July through late July, followed by a decrease in the first half of August; then a rise in the second half of August; then a decrease in the first half of September. This pattern closely matches the timing of the Democratic Party and Republican Party conventions. In 1980, the Democratic convention was in mid-August, after the Republican convention, which was in mid-July; in the other three years, the timing was reversed. After the first half of September, the 1980, 1984, and 1988 patterns were nearly identical in number and slope: a slow rise in Page One stories through late October; then a greater increase through Election Day. In contrast, 1992 stands out in Figure 3.1 after early September through Election Day, with a greater number of stories and a steeper rise to an early November peak of an average of nearly three Page One stories per day per newspaper.

As shown in Figure 3.2, 1992 clearly stands out above the other three years across the entire July-November time period in terms of the average number of Page One stories per newspaper that reported pre-election poll results, with the exception of the dip in the first half of September. The pattern for the other three years was quite similar: a fairly constant level, with some variation, from early July through early September; then a slight increase though late October, culminating with a greater rise in early November.

Figure 3.3 shows that 1992 also stands out from the three previous presidential election years in terms of the *percentage* of Page One election stories reporting poll findings. In fact, with the exception of the 1984 increase in poll stories in October of that year, the other three years' patterns are fairly similar. In contrast, throughout the July-November period in 1992, these newspapers changed their presidential election news mix by increasing their usage of poll-based news compared with the three previous years. If there has been a proliferation of polling news, Figure 3.3 suggests that the change may not have occurred until 1992.

In-depth Follow-up Study

Placement

From our follow-up content analysis of 400 front pages, which were selected randomly from the 5,500-plus pages, we found that most Page One stories with poll results were placed above the fold (70%), with four in 10 running in the upper-right quadrant (i.e., the most prominent placement on the page). There was considerable variation across newspapers, with the *Wall Street Journal* and *New York Times* running nearly all their poll stories above the fold, whereas the *Los Angles Times* did so only a third of the time. In 1992, four in five stories (83%) ran above the fold, nearly double the percentage in 1980 (42%).

Headline Content

Nearly half of all poll stories (46%) had a headline with an explicit (e.g., "Poll Shows Carter Running 3rd") or implicit (e.g., "Bush's Lead Slipping") reference to the poll.

Again there was considerable variation across papers and over time. At the high end, four-fifths of the headlines in the *Denver Post* referred explicitly or implicitly to the poll findings. On the low end, only a third of those in the *Wall Street Journal* and *New York Times* did so. In 1980 and 1992, about one in three poll-based stories used a headline that explicitly or implicitly referenced poll findings; in contrast, twice that ratio occurred in 1984 and 1988 (i.e., approximately two in three).

Lead Content

A third of the poll stories had a lead that explicitly referred to the poll. Another one in five made implicit reference to poll findings in the lead. The same pattern of variation as found with headline content was observed for lead content: 1980 and 1992 had fewer leads that referred the poll findings (42% and 34%, respectively) than in 1984 (79%) and 1988 (56%).

Story Content

On average, poll results were first mentioned in the third or fourth paragraph of news stories. This, too, varied considerably with newspapers: the *St. Louis Post-Dispatch* generally report the poll findings in their lead paragraph, whereas the *Wall Street Journal* and *Cleveland Plain Dealer* did not do so until the fifth paragraph, on average. In 1988, the poll findings were first reported in the second or third paragraphs, on average. In contrast, in 1980, 1984 and 1992, it was the third or fourth paragraphs.

Discussion and Conclusions

Before addressing the implications of our findings, we want to acknowledge some of the limitations of this type of research: Our content analysis was limited to 11 U.S. daily newspapers. It also was limited to the front page news of these dailies and to simple counts of this news, with the exception of the more detailed information we gathered in the smaller follow-up study. Our research tells nothing about the prevalence of pre-election polling news *inside* these newspapers.

Overall, it seems likely to us that many or most major U.S. newspapers have increased their reporting of presidential pre-election polling news to an *even greater extent* than we have documented by this research. For example, in 1992 the *New York Times* routinely ran inside stories and/or graphics showing the Bush-Clinton-Perot poll standings. This was not done with such frequency in previous election years. This notwithstanding, we believe our findings provide a valid documentation of the change in prevalence of prominent usage of poll news (i.e., running it on Page One) by a broad sample of the nation's most read newspapers.

1992 Page One Poll News Proliferation

Our findings document that the 1992 election — with the addition of a "third-party" candidate who would not go away — generated more election campaign news that these major dailies chose to put on Page One than was the case with the three previous presidential elections.

With a greater front page newshole given to the 1992 presidential campaign, the sheer number of stories reporting polls would be expected to have increased over the previous years, even if the papers did nothing other than use polling news on their front page at the same rate as they had done previously. However, despite an increase in Page One presidential pre-election stories in 1992 of about 40% compared to the 1980, 1984 and 1988 average, there was a more than 300% increase in the use of poll findings in Page One news in 1992 compared to the average of the previous three election years. Thus, the rate of the increase in using pre-election polling news on their front pages was *more than seven times greater* than the rate at which these papers increased the number of pre-election stories they ran on Page One.

Although 1992 stood out from the other three years in the relative frequency of Page One polling news, the results of our follow-up study showed that it did not differ in other measures of "prominence." Headline content and lead content in 1992 was less likely to make explicit or implicit reference to poll findings than in 1984 or 1988. The positioning of the poll findings in 1992 was not further up in the story, on average, than in 1980 or 1984, and was lower into the story than in 1988. The only exception was the finding that poll news was more likely to be run above the fold in 1992 than in any of the other three years.

Differences Across Dailies

The individual variation that was seen for the 11 dailies can be summarized as follows: By 1980, the *Los Angeles Times*, *New York Times*, and

Washington Post had begun to conduct their own presidential pre-election polls and have routinely incorporated this type of news into their coverage ever since. Some of the other papers (*Chicago Tribune* and the *Denver Post*) increased their usage of this type of news as early as 1984, although they did not always sponsor the surveys themselves. Finally, the flood gates appear to have opened in 1992, with the rest of these major dailies using polling news to such an extent that it was almost as though they were trying to make up for lost ground in the three previous elections.

Poll Reporting and Press Responsibility

We believe that the responsible use of pre-election polls is a highly newsworthy and informative component of election campaign coverage (cf. Dionne, 1992; Mann & Orren, 1992; Meyer, 1990). However, the increased use in presidential pre-election polling news documented here does not mean that this news necessarily informed the electorate in any meaningful fashion.

It remains the responsibility of journalists to look critically at their own behind-the-scenes use of these polls and their of use of polls as news. If reporters and editors become lazy in covering elections by relying too heavily on information gathered by polls, then we have all lost. If on the other hand, reporters and editors use pre-election poll findings to investigate and report on issues in greater depth and with greater insight, then we have gained considerably. And, as several of the other chapters in this book point out, there are many ways for the media to use polls creatively, with insight, and responsibly — ways which we believe will enhance the process by which our nation elects its political leaders.

Notes

An earlier version of the research in this chapter was presented at the Midwest Association for Public Opinion Research conference in Chicago in November, 1993.

1. A "story" was defined as a body of copy, at least one paragraph in length, that had its own headline. In the case of the *Wall Street Journal*, each item in the "What's News" section of page 1 was counted as a story under this definition. A story was counted as a presidential election story if the main focus was the upcoming presidential election.

2. A story was counted as a poll story if it reported the results of a presidential pre-election poll as a part of the Page One copy. That is, a poll was specifically mentioned or actual poll results were reported. A story with a visual presentation of poll data was also counted if the graphic accompanied a story on the presidential election campaign.

3. This content analysis was extremely labor intensive. Nearly 6,500 Page One stories about that year's presidential election were read closely by at least two different people, and more than 25,000 other Page One stories were read closely enough by at least two different people to determine that the stories were *not* about that year's presidential election. In all, the coding process required reading more than 60,000 stories.

Although computer routines exist to aid with the straight-forward content analysis of certain newspapers (e.g., those available via Lexis and Nexis) it would not have been possible to conduct this research via computer for two primary reasons. First, most of these front pages are not in a computer-readable database. And second, the decision-making task engaged in by the coders was too sophisticated for existing software.

4. We would like to thank the Northwestern University Survey Laboratory and the Medill School of Journalism for the work-study research assistant support that made this content analysis possible.

4

The Use of Focus Groups to Supplement Campaign Coverage

Michael W. Traugott

The marriage of social science, especially survey research, with the imperatives of political reporting has evolved over a long period of time. In the same way that journalists and political candidates enjoy a symbiotic relationship, so increasingly do political reporters and pollsters. All of the networks and major daily newspapers are actively conducting their own survey research as part of their news operations. There is strong reason to suspect that the generation of polls by the major news organizations in the United States is close to saturation and now constrained primarily by the availability of funds and space in the news hole. But among all news organizations, the reporting of polls from a variety of sources, including data supplied by candidates, may still be increasing (Ladd & Benson, 1992; Traugott, 1992; Lavrakas & Bauman, Chapter 3).

In this environment, many news organizations — especially newspapers — have turned to the use of qualitative research methods like focus groups to supplement their reporting. Focus groups provide a low cost method of data collection that can supply a direct link or "peg" for a story to the paper's readers. When used under conditions that acknowledge the problems of lack of generalizability from small, unrepresentative samples, focus groups can provide a technique for humanizing a political story in terms of a locally affected population.

During the 1992 campaign, the Center for Political Studies conducted focus groups for *The Detroit News* for the purpose of supplementing their coverage in this fashion. By organizing and conducting groups around critical dates or important events in the presidential campaign, the newspaper was able to supplement its coverage packages by incorporating reports of the discussions in these groups with other more traditional forms of reporting, including straight news, reports of surveys conducted at the same time, and political columns. This chapter describes the use of such qualitative information in the form of a case study in contemporary political reporting, illustrating how the process worked and the various forms that the resulting coverage took. This is as much a story about the pressures on newspapers to maintain readership as it is one of new styles of political reporting.

Journalists and Social Science

Political campaigns have always been very newsworthy events because they so easily lend themselves to coverage (Traugott, 1985). Elections have a major impact on the American political system, and they involve a stylized form of conflict between highly visible figures. From an organizational perspective, campaigns make good news because they occur on a schedule. This facilitates the assignment of reporters and permits the allocation of resources to coverage on a relatively predictable basis. The drama of the campaign is resolved on election day in the determination of a clear winner, making possible a neat wrap-up of the story. Media coverage of campaigns and elections has consistently contained a strong analytical — even predictive — element, with the emphasis on expected winners building toward the end of the campaign.

Tankard (1972) dates the earliest use of polls by media organizations to two newspapers in Delaware and North Carolina that employed unsystematic samplings of public opinion as part of their coverage of the election of 1824. This was a campaign that "centered around eliminating the (Congressional) caucus as president-maker and demonstrating the will of the people" (p. 365). In the beginning, then, independent measures of public opinion were reported as a means to interject popular sentiment into a process that had effectively been controlled by political elites.

The main difference in contemporary coverage is the use of polls to support "horse race" journalism (Broh, 1980), a long-time stylistic tendency in political reporting that was formerly satisfied by reporters' reliance upon political leaders like state and county party chairmen who expressed their opinions about what was likely to happen and why (Meyer, 1973; Ismach, 1984). As a means of establishing independence from such biased sources, media organizations were only too happy to turn to public pollsters like Gallup, Harris and Roper for independent assessments of the "pulse of democracy." And other stylistic changes in reporting that emphasized scenarios, benchmarks and standards of candidate performance during a lengthening presidential campaign inevitably began to include polling and the reporting of poll results as an integral part of the coverage (Arterton, 1984).

Given these predispositions and tendencies, polling has become a relatively natural and comfortable complement to contemporary political reporting. The application of systematic survey research means that information can be obtained directly from voters without the intervening application of "spin" by party officials and the candidates' handlers. While polls can be used to assess public attitudes about issues as well as the candidates, most journalistic attention is routinely directed to the relative standing of the candidates (see Lavrakas & Bauman, Chapter 3). This tendency to rely on polls for reporting who is ahead increases across the campaign (Traugott & Rusch, 1989). Even when news organizations are not reporting the results of their own polls, they are frequently giving results from other newsworthy findings compiled by their competitors or the news wires. And there is a suggestion that references to "the polls" to explain a candidate's strategic behavior have become the equivalent of "unnamed sources" in other standard forms of reporting.

The use of polling in journalism has become more frequent over time. Merton and Hatt (1949) conducted a survey among a small sample of newspaper editors after the public polls experienced problems in the 1948 election. They reported that about half their sample (47%) indicated that they had "made use" of polls previously while 49% indicated they had not. Unfavorable opinions of polling that resulted from the 1948 election performance apparently led about half of those who had previously used polling to discontinue the practice.

Contemporary data on a more representative sampling of industry practices are available for newspapers, based upon three surveys. Rippey (1980) was the first to solicit such information from informants representing a probability sample of newspapers in 1978, and his effort was essentially replicated by Demers (1987, 1988) eight years later. Holley (1991) conducted another such survey in 1989, after the 1988 presidential election. Rippey's survey disclosed that 37% of the papers reported they had "conducted an opinion poll on which to gather information to base stories," and Demers found this proportion essentially unchanged in 1986, as did Holley in 1989.

In the 1970s, media organizations began to establish their own polling operations in order to exercise greater editorial control over what elements of public opinion would be reported and when they would be reported. By designing and fielding their own questionnaires, media organizations could frame and measure what they themselves considered to be the important dimensions of opinion in the electorate, including group bases for candidate support, citizens' policy preferences, and the voters' perceptions of who the candidates were and what they stood for. This action also freed them from reliance on the topical coverage and timing of surveys conducted by the public pollsters.

In an interesting and provocative analysis, Herbst (1993) has suggested that the trend toward "precision journalism" is an inevitable outgrowth of a number of social trends that have generally led to a rationalization of public policy formulation and implementation in contemporary society (see also Herbst, Chapter 2). Citing such disparate theoretical underpinnings as Weber and Foucault, she describes the joint interest of politicians and news organizations in focusing on a public opinion that can be expressed through survey research and quantified to support certain forms of social policy. From the perspective of her synthesis, this is the result of increasing bureaucratization of political life (Weber) as well as politicians' interest in invoking public support for policy in the discourse about the role of government in a democracy that favors the established and existing order (Foucault).

Herbst makes only passing reference to focus groups as a detour along what she sees as the inevitable developmental path to the wholesale adoption of survey research (1993, p. 171). However, there is a set of economic forces at work on the business side of newsmaking that is propelling news organizations toward greater use of qualitative research techniques like focus groups. Simply put, it is a fear of losing their audience — both readership and viewership. Newspapers are concerned about lost readers who have become viewers, and network executives are concerned about viewers who are leaving mass media programming for more specialized programming on the myriad channels of cable television.

For newspapers in particular, declining readership has forced editors and publishers to consider ways of (re)establishing contact with members of their communities in ways that emphasize their linkages and common interests while, at the same time, maintain the size of their audience (Bogart, 1991). Many news organizations are using focus groups composed of audience members to personalize coverage and provide local pegs for stories that frequently have a major national theme. They are also using focus groups to obtain feedback on their coverage, often with the goal of modifying it to maintain reader interest and satisfaction.

Focus groups have long been used by campaigns to evaluate the issue preferences and candidate evaluations of selected groups in the electorate, as well as to screen new commercials.[1] On rare but significant occasions, such focus groups have become newsworthy, as was the case with one organized by Republicans in Paramus, New Jersey, in May, 1988.[2] During this session, observed by five senior campaign operatives including Lee Atwater, the Republicans realized the vulnerability of Michael Dukakis because the electorate knew so little about who he was and what he stood for. By 1992, the use of focus groups by candidates had become a newsworthy topic in and of itself (Kolbert, 1992; See also Morin, Chapter 8).

More commonly, news organizations have turned to focus groups as a cost-effective way to report on how citizens are reacting to political events, issues and candidates in a personalized way that provides direct contact with their readers.[3] While the total cost of a focus group may be only about one-quarter of the cost of a small survey, the main appeal is news value. Focus groups can provide a direct link to readers as members are usually identified by name, age, occupation, and place of residence; and many of these stories include photographs of the participants as well. Often using a scheduled event or a national news story or trend as a news peg, a story can be produced on the basis of a focus group discussion that shows how local citizens react to or are affected by politics. In this way, the news is personalized to demonstrate the impact of events on local residents, satisfying many of the criteria of newsworthiness.

The Methodology of Focus Groups

Focus groups have advantages and potential pitfalls for journalists, just as surveys do. First and foremost, there is a potential problem of inference, as focus groups are usually composed of small numbers of carefully selected participants. While their views can be analyzed in detail and with nuance, it is difficult to generalize from a small number of individuals to the electorate as a whole. But the use of photographs, direct quotes, and discussions of the tone of the conversation provide journalists with a way to personify the impact of politics and an ongoing campaign that aggregated statistical data from a survey does not.

The methodology of focus groups differs from that of surveys in several distinct regards (Krueger, 1987; Morgan, 1988; Stewart & Shamdasani, 1992). First and foremost, there is the matter of *representation*. Surveys involve the methodology of scientific sampling, by which the laws of probability are used to select a large number of respondents from a well-described population. Knowing about the sample design allows the researcher to generalize back to the population; given a particular sample size, a level of confidence in the generalization can be calculated as well.

In a focus group, a small number of participants are purposefully selected on the basis of a limited set of criteria. The goal is to construct a relatively homogeneous group on the basis of a limited number of common characteristics such as race or gender, for example, or the criterion that the members are self-described Democrats who voted for Ronald Reagan and George Bush. Typically numbering from 8 to 12 participants, a focus group may be assembled to evaluate a candidate's speech or a debate, or to discuss the relative strengths and weaknesses of various candidates before a primary. The results of the discussion can be used to represent the range of opinions that prevail in the electorate, but they can not be used to generate a statistical estimate of the prevalence of such views.

There are several ways that participants can be recruited, and this can affect the quality of the resulting discussion. For *The Detroit News* contract, all subjects were recruited by the local field staff of the Survey Research Center at least one week in advance of the group meeting, based upon specifications provided by the study director. Advance planning and preparation are clearly preferable to last minute methods like recruitment in malls or other public places.

In the typical survey, a series of questions are consistently administered in a predetermined fashion. The *questionnaire* is designed to minimize context effects and in some sense to constrain responses so that they may be combined for the analysis of respondents with shared characteristics. The vast majority of questions are asked in the "closed" form in which specific response categories are offered as part of the question (Converse & Presser, 1986). The essence of this approach is to search for patterns of responses to individual items and for relationships between responses to multiple items. Based upon scientific sampling and the systematic administration of a questionnaire in this manner, the existence of these relationships can be generalized to the population as well.

Within a focus group, a discussion takes place that is organized around a *script* rather than a questionnaire. The script defines the topics to be covered and the general order in which they will be covered. A discussion can range in length up to two hours and takes the form of a long interview (McCracken, 1988) in which virtually all of the questions are administered in an "open" form designed to eliminate the possibility of short answers such as "agree" or "no." Rather than the researcher completely defining terms and concepts in the framework of a pre-existing theoretical framework, participants are encouraged to respond in their own terms and with their own frame of reference.

Given these essential differences, then, there are correspondingly different roles to be played by the moderator of a focus group and an interviewer. An *interviewer* deals with one respondent at a time and must remain faithful to the questionnaire. Comparability of responses and the ability to group respondents for analysis comes from an assumption that the data were collected in a series of systematic dyadic interactions. The *moderator* must try to adhere to the script, as a means of ensuring coverage of all relevant topics and avoiding any context effects that it has anticipated, but digressions are permitted and sometimes encouraged. And the moderator must of course be sensitive to the dynamics of the group, ensuring that all participants have an opportunity to express their views and that the conversation is not monopolized by a few loquacious or extroverted members. The moderator has the benefit of knowing about the script and the intent of the discussion but cannot impose his or her own view of appropriate topics and tone. He or she acts more like a facilitator than an interviewer does, but too much direction will distort group interaction and discussion.

Integrating Focus Group Results into Campaign Coverage

The contract with *The Detroit News* called for the Center for Political Studies (CPS) to be available to arrange and conduct multiple focus groups during the year leading up to the November presidential election.[4] These focus groups were as event-based as normal campaign coverage is, and a general schedule of groups was established on the basis of a preliminary lineup of expected stories. This schedule corresponded directly with a story budget to be produced on the basis of the content of the discussions. The initial schedule was predicated on beginning one year out from the November election and convening successive groups around such events as the Michigan primaries, each party's nominating convention, the Labor Day start of the campaign, and perhaps one or two during the general election campaign.

For any particular focus group, the schedule was arranged so that the news coverage could appear in the Sunday edition of the paper. These stories combined properties of straight news and feature writing, and many political stories were prepared on this basis because the Sunday paper has the greatest circulation of the week. In addition, a peculiarity of the Detroit market is a joint operating agreement (JOA) between *The Detroit News* and *The Detroit Free Press*. Among the negotiated conditions of the JOA were separately published weekday editions of the two papers, *Free Press* control of the front page and major sections of the Saturday paper, and equivalent *News* control over the Sunday paper. So the focus group articles usually appeared on the front page of the Sunday paper under *The Detroit News* banner.

There was flexibility to change the preliminary schedule, and after an initial success with the first effort on October 29, 1991, the newspaper expressed an interest in assembling a group to view President Bush's State of the Union address on January 28, 1992. During the discussion of this proposal, it was decided to organize two groups. The first involved citizens actually watching the speech and then commenting on it after it was delivered; a second was convened one week later to assess the speech in light of intervening news coverage and commentary as well as political spin.[5] That date was approximately one week before the Iowa caucus and just after the Gennifer Flowers press conference organized by *The Star*.

In general, the standard set of participants were registered voters residing in southeastern Michigan, essentially the region of dominant circulation of *The Detroit News*, consisting of Wayne, Oakland and Macomb Counties. Recruitment was conducted by members of the field staff of the Survey Research Center at the Institute for Social Research. The sessions were held in meeting rooms of public libraries and a community center, as well as in a rented conference room in a motel. Because the participants frequently traveled some distance to get to the site, the discussions usually began at 7 p.m. and lasted between 90 minutes and two hours. Held during the week, this provided participants with an opportunity to get to the site after work and to return home at a reasonable hour. The participants were compensated with $20 as a token amount to cover their travel expenses.

The first groups were heterogeneous by political party, race and gender. Before the April primaries, separate groups of Democrats and Republicans were convened. Prior to the Democratic convention, a group of residents from Macomb County who could be classified as "Reagan Democrats" were assembled to get their reactions to Bill Clinton, Ross Perot and the Democratic party. At the end of the campaign, this group was reassembled to get their reactions to the general election campaign and how it had affected them.

Each focus group was held with a CPS researcher as moderator, and a reporter from the newspaper sat in on each session. This was typically the Washington bureau chief of *The Detroit News*, Jim Gannon, although other reporters participated as well. Dual audio tape recordings were made of each session, and the reporter kept one copy as an aid in preparing the news stories. No video taping was done of the sessions because the newspaper had no use for such footage. However, as part of the procedure, photographs of the participants were taken at the time of the meeting and often later in a home or work setting.

Because of the unusual nature of these arrangements in relation to the University of Michigan's standard human subjects' review procedures, a special informed consent and release form was developed. Before any of the discussion began, therefore, the participants were required to sign the release to acknowledge these conditions. There were no refusals because the recruitment process explicitly described the purpose of the group session. And, of course, there was eventually some limited, cumulative publicity of the effort because of the newspaper articles that followed each session; in the later sessions, many participants knew when they were being recruited what would be done with the discussions.

The scripts for each session were prepared collaboratively between the CPS researcher and the reporter. A general set of topics was generated independently and exchanged, and a proposed ordering of the flow of the discussion was prepared after a discussion. In most regards, this followed the same procedures used to develop a standard pre-election questionnaire; and the resulting script was very similar to such a questionnaire. For example, respondents were first given the opportunity to discuss the general state of affairs in the country in their own words before the discussion turned to focus on any particular problem. And evaluations of George Bush's performance as president were solicited before discussing specific issues like the economy.

The general news peg for each focus group was determined by judgements of the prevailing state of affairs in the presidential campaign. In most cases, this represented a combination of assessments of recent events, the results from recent national surveys, and political intelligence collected at the newspaper's Washington bureau and in the Detroit newsroom. For each story, the issues were cast in terms of their impact on Michigan citizens or the reactions of Michigan citizens to candidates and events.

The primary purpose of the focus groups was to generate content for news stories. The typical "package" consisted of at least one lengthy story accompanied by a photo montage of the participants. Each person was identified by name, age, occupation and place of residence. In addition, there was usually a quotation from the participants accompanying their photos. The bulk of the photographs were taken just before or after the discussion took place; in some cases, participants were photographed at work or home, sometimes with other family members who were of course not present at the focus group discussion.

Examples of 1992 Campaign Coverage
Based upon Focus Groups

The Detroit News incorporated the focus group results into their campaign coverage in several different ways. These included in combination with standard survey results, as parts of event-centered coverage of the campaign and as material for columns. These three kinds of uses provide a framework for evaluating current practice and anticipating future uses of such content.

Combining Focus Group and Survey Results

The material from the very first group discussion was incorporated into a news package that included results from a statewide survey conducted at approximately the same time. This combination of approaches is rare under most social science circumstances (Morgan, 1988: 35-36), but it has an appeal from a journalistic perspective. Survey analysis involves the grouping of anonymous replies from respondents so that frequencies can be calculated for individual variables and relationships between variables can be evaluated. In general, a guarantee of confidentiality offered at the start of interview means that respondents remain anonymous. This is certainly the case for survey results released by candidates and by the wire services. News organizations that collect their own data have now developed procedures for asking respondents at the end of their interview whether they would be willing to talk further with a reporter about their views.[6]

In the story package prepared by *The Detroit News* one year in advance of the November election, the focus group discussion provided a local, personalized anchor for statewide survey results. The group-based article received somewhat greater prominence than an accompanying survey-based article, presumably because the package incorporated photographs of the focus group participants. Under the heading "Middle class boils about U.S. 'decline'," the article led with concerns expressed by the nine participants about erosion of their middle class standards of living (Gannon, 1991a). The first article of a brief series that was to run across the next few days presented results from a poll of 600 registered voters; it discussed the negative attitudes of the electorate and the fact that the most prominent concerns were about the recession and unemployment (Gannon, 1991b). The focus group story told about the specific economic concerns of the participants and their families, at home and at work.[7]

Just prior to the Michigan primaries, which were "closed" by the two parties for the first time in recent memory, separate groups of Democrats and Republicans were convened. The newspaper also sponsored a brief survey with a very restricted field period to measure candidate preferences among likely primary voters. Because of the JOA arrangement for the weekend papers, the survey was fielded in such a way that Republican respondents were interviewed earlier, and the results reported on Friday, March 13. These data were reported first because the Republican primary was not expected to be very close. The "better" story, involving the greater conflict between the Democrats and the less certain outcome, was reported on Sunday, March 15. The single article based upon the focus group discussion also ran on Sunday.

For logistical reasons, participants were recalled from previous groups. The purpose was not explicitly to employ a panel and ascertain how specific attitudes or candidate preferences had changed. Rather, in order to write about the views of Democrats and Republicans on a timely basis, a decision was made to conduct two focus groups on the same evening. This meant limiting each group's discussion to about one hour in order to fit both in and to give the second set of participants time to get home. The feeling was that the "warm-up" period in the discussion could be substantially reduced by using participants who were already familiar with the nature of the conversations and the moderator and reporter, as well as with how to get to the site. A total of 14 former participants, six self-described Republicans and eight equivalent Democrats, were called back for the two groups.

A single article summarized the results of both groups (Gannon, 1992d). For the Republicans, the discussion focused on evaluations of George Bush and Patrick Buchanan. This included growing concerns about Bush's performance in office and the quality of his campaign effort that were not present in October. A portion of the discussion was devoted to protest votes; in the Michigan context, this included Buchanan and David Duke. There were two distinct groups of disgruntled Republicans present among the participants. One was a set of conservative Republicans who felt that Bush had been a designated successor to Ronald Reagan who had gone astray ideologically. They would vote against Bush with an eye toward having him replaced on the ticket by someone with more conservative views. Another was a group who remained loyal to Bush personally but who felt either the president was drifting in policy terms and/or was running an ineffective campaign. These participants saw a value in having the insurgent Buchanan campaign light a fire under Bush, but they did not see the challenger as the eventual nominee of their party.

This example illustrates an interesting potential link between focus group and survey data, along the lines that focus groups have historically been used as a device to pretest eventual survey measures. Learning from the focus group discussion just cited, these two distinct groups of dissatisfied Republicans could have been identified, distinguished and interrogated in a subsequent survey. Such an analysis of these two groups of "protesters" could have produced an interesting story about the relative size of each group and the intensity of their members' feelings. This story would have been uniquely suited to survey data and appropriately different from the standard reporting of "who's ahead and who's behind."

Among the Democrats, Clinton was the most appealing on the basis of his personality, while Tsongas generated little support among the assembled group. In this discussion there was a palpable sense of the Democrats' strong interest, by almost any means, in winning the White House again and the value of a candidate who would battle the Republicans all the way through the campaign.

Using Focus Group Results in a Political Column

Jim Gannon used material from the focus groups in his own weekly columns. In the first one based upon the focus groups, he presented his reactions to the anger and cynicism expressed by the participants about politicians and the political system (Gannon, 1991c). The use of direct quotations from local citizens made the abstract reporting about these concerns in the national media more concrete. And in prophetic anticipation of the candidates' eventual shift in the summer of 1992 to talk shows, call in programs, and, eventually, new debate formats, one participant was quoted as saying "I would like to see us be the questioners on television."

On occasion, features of the discussion like their tone or tenor became elements of Gannon's regular column in the newspaper. Cynicism about politicians and the political system, concerns about media coverage of the campaign, and questions about Bill Clinton's character were all the focus of Gannon columns in which portions of the focus group discussions were incorporated. And one column focused on a topic he found significant because it was never raised by any of the participants, the role of abortion as an issue in the campaign.

Organizing Focus Groups Around Specific Campaign Events

A common approach to political reporting is to organize coverage around specific campaign events, and focus groups were used by*The Detroit News* in this fashion. One such occasion for which groups were convened was the State of the Union address by George Bush on January 28. Two groups were actually convened, one in a motel conference room to comment on the speech just after it was delivered and another approximately one week later. The first meeting took place from 8:30 to 10 p.m., and reporter Colleen Fitzpatrick wrote about the discussion among seven participants for a late evening deadline for the next day's paper (Fitzpatrick, 1992). The initial reactions to the speech raised as many questions in the minds of those who watched it as points of agreement and satisfaction.

One week later, a second group of participants was convened to get their more considered opinion about the speech and the president's performance in office. In the intervening period, politicians and officials from both parties, as well as the White House communications operation, had an opportunity to put their own "spin" on the speech. This group was coincidentally assembled about one week before the Iowa caucuses and two weeks before the New Hampshire primary.

The main article reporting on this discussion focused on Bush's vulnerability in the Michigan electorate and the relative invisibility of the Democratic challengers (Gannon, 1992c). With the passage of time, reactions to the president's speech were more reserved, as would be expected from the tone of the intervening commentary. Among the 11 participants, Gennifer Flowers was better known for her recent disclosures than any of the Democrats. There was concern about the weakness of the Democratic field, and expressions of hope that other candidates might enter the race. And none of the participants expected that Bush would have serious trouble with re-election in the fall. Gannon pegged his Sunday column (1992b) to questions about Clinton's character and the reaction of the focus group's participants to the issue.

A second occasion involved the Democratic convention. As it neared, the Clinton nomination was assured and the Bush campaign continued to falter. Since the March discussion preceding the Michigan primaries, the candidacy of Ross Perot had taken off; he had become the first independent candidate to lead both of the major party candidates in a national survey. In this three-way contest, an important question was whether Clinton or Perot would attract "Reagan Democrats" or they would stay with Bush. Michigan, and Macomb County in particular, have a special place in reporting about the state of the Democratic party and recent Republican successes in attracting certain of its members. Peter Brown (1991) wrote an analysis of the Democratic party's prospects, including a description of this group based upon Macomb County demographics and interviews.

Eight self-described Reagan Democrats, all white, were recruited for a two-hour discussion of the presidential campaign ten days before the Democratic convention. The meeting was held in the Mt. Clemens Community Center in Macomb County. The resulting article presented the clear message of the group discussion indicating that they were prepared to abandon George Bush; only one participant remained a loyal supporter. But it was not clear in early July whether they would return home to the Democrats and support Clinton or they would go with Perot (Gannon, 1992e). Disillusionment with Bush was based on several factors, including a sense that he lacked conviction, his poor management of the economy, and a sense that the country was adrift and without leadership. As for Clinton, the participants responded positively to his ability to take attacks and endure, as well as a perception that he had "stood up" to Jesse Jackson.

These Reagan Democrats also became panel participants because of the movement of Ross Perot in and out and back in the campaign. Just after their first session and before the Democratic convention, Perot withdrew. When his re-entry was being widely discussed and anticipated in late September, these same participants were reconvened. The results of this group suggested that Perot would have trouble regaining all of his earlier momentum, although anti-Bush sentiment remained high, as did perceived levels of the need for a change from the Bush administration (Gannon, 1992a).[8]

On a third occasion, a focus group composed of formerly undecided voters was recruited to discuss debate reactions after the entire series of four had been completed (Gannon, 1992f). Because of the "debate about the debates," they were eventually scheduled for very late in the campaign. Therefore, a discussion of post-debate reactions with such a group of voters in the next to the last week of the campaign was also an occasion for writing a wrap up piece on how the campaign had gone, how it had affected voters' decision making, and what it portended for election day. This time, the focus group was scheduled two weeks in advance of the election so *The Detroit News* could run one Sunday special story based on this form of voter reaction and then a final pre-election poll a week later, just before Election Day.

Conclusions

The development of social science approaches to the reporting of political news continues with the advent of focus groups to supplement campaign coverage. This technique can be used to "humanize" political coverage by creating local pegs for national news stories during a presidential campaign. This is both good news and good business as it can provide a vehicle for satisfying the newsworthiness criteria of reflecting the impact of news events on the local audience while at the same time establishing more direct links between a news organization and its readership.

The experience with *The Detroit News* suggests that there are three distinct ways that focus groups can be employed as part of campaign coverage: to complement the reporting of survey results by presenting real life examples of patterns of survey response; to focus on significant events during the campaign by presenting readers' reactions to them; and to provide substance and pegs for political columnists who write about the campaign.

The use of focus groups is especially well-suited to newspapers. Even small and mid-sized papers can design news packages around focus groups by combining knowledge of the campaign calendar with the relatively predictable schedule of national surveys conducted around major primaries, the conventions and debates. For example, editors and reporters can schedule focus groups around their state's primaries or just prior to or immediately after the parties' nominating conventions. In either case, it is very likely that statewide or national surveys will be available. Similarly, groups can be assembled to watch and evaluate presidential debates or major policy addresses, other occasions when instant analysis and surveys are likely to appear on television. In these circumstances, newspapers can establish a link to their own readers by providing a local interpretation of the meaning of national events.

This is generally a positive development if it can also make campaign politics more understandable and accessible to average citizens. By showing that other citizens share their views or that national issues have a particular impact on local citizens, readers and viewers may be stimulated to pay more attention to campaign events and eventually to vote in greater numbers when they see that the election has some consequence for them. Reporting what goes on in a focus group discussion can provide important contextual information for readers and viewers. But journalists have to be sensitive to the prospects of over-generalizing or drawing incorrect inferences from small, highly selective groups of citizens. Estimating candidate support from eight to ten citizens in a focus group is even riskier than the use of quota samples was in the pre-election forecasts in 1948.

Notes

An earlier version of this chapter was prepared for presentation at the annual meeting of the American Political Science Association in Chicago in September, 1992.

1. Focus groups are increasingly being used by academic researchers to increase their understanding of citizens' reactions to politics (Delli Carpini & Williams, 1990; Gamson,1992), especially during the campaign (Jamieson, 1992; Kern and Just, 1992a and b).

2. One of the more compelling news stories appeared in *The Washington Post* on October 28, 1988 under the byline of Paul Taylor and David S. Broder. The Paramus focus group was given significant attention by Germond and Witcover (1989) in *Whose Broad Stripes and Bright Stars*.

3. Several experiments in political coverage were conducted among Knight-Ridder papers as part of their 1992 campaign coverage, designed to "connect readership and citizenship" (Hoyt, 1992). This effort took place at the chain's properties in Wichita, Kansas; Charlotte, North Carolina; and Columbus, Georgia. The evaluations of these efforts have just begun to become available (Dykers, 1993; Greer, 1993)

4. The recruitment procedures were developed under the basic agreement, and a separate fee is charged for each focus group held.

5. This plan was proposed on the basis of Steeper's work (1980), among others, showing that the public's immediate evaluation of an event like the 1976 Ford-Carter debate can be quite different from a subsequent evaluation colored

by intervening news coverage. This was clearly the case with regard to public reaction to Ford's comment about Soviet domination over its eastern European satellites.

6. In effect, these respondents are being asked to waive the guarantee of confidentiality that they were offered at the start of the interview. Respondents may be selected for such treatment by interviewers because they have been responsive during the interview or particularly outspoken in their views. A form of such a question wording employed in the past by the author is as follows:

> Some of the information obtained in this survey will be used in the preparation of newspaper articles about the attitudes and opinions of people here in Michigan. Would you mind if a reporter called you back to discuss your views further?

Very few respondents are needed to supply quotes for a newspaper article, especially in relation to the typical survey sample size. Therefore there is no need to pressure any respondents to cooperate on this matter, and interviewers are so instructed.

7. When the two data collection techniques were paired in news coverage, in our experience, there never was a discrepancy between the main findings of a survey and the relevant parts of a discussion among focus group participants. For a variety of reasons, including chance, such a discrepancy could occur on occasion. In this case, a journalist working with a trained social scientist would have to proceed first with results of the scientific sample and might face the prospect of forgoing some of the discussion in the focus group. The alternative would be an explanation of the relative representativeness of the survey sample and the possibilities for bias in the selection of the focus group participants.

8. It is also interesting to note that many had become media "personalities" in their own right by the time of the second focus group. Because of a general media interest in "Reagan Democrats," some had appeared on U.S. and British television, and many had been interviewed by other reporters. Because the participants were publicly acknowledged, self-described members of this group, an enterprising reporter who identified them through searches of recent coverage usually found a willing source for another interview.

PART THREE

The Methodology of Media Polls

5

How Pollsters and Reporters Can Do a Better Job Informing the Public: A Challenge for Campaign '96

Warren J. Mitofsky

Getting meaningful survey reports to a reporter and ultimately to the public is something akin to the childhood game of telephone. Here is how it's played: One child whispers a message to his nearest neighbor, who in turn whispers it to the next child, and so on until the last child repeats the message out loud. The garbled end result is compared to the original, usually to the amusement of all.

That is the paradigm I have in mind for the reporting of survey results to the public. Far too often there is very little resemblance between the researcher's findings and the journalists' and the public's understanding. The reports of Ross Perot's popularity with the voting public during May and June of 1992 are a good case in point. Perot was a creature of voter discontent with the other candidates. It is doubtful that his following at that time was as substantial as news reports would have had you believe. We will come back to this example.

I would like to continue with this child's game of telephone as a model for what I believe has been an almost futile attempt by survey researchers to educate the press, who in turn inform the public. Let me explain.

Disclosure of Methods Is Not Improving Reporting

Survey researchers have tried promoting disclosure of methods, self help courses for journalists, newsroom guides about surveys for editors and reporters, discussions with all who will listen about what is wrong with particular surveys or pseudo-survey approaches. There is no end to the number of efforts. Unfortunately, this education happens over and over again with the converted and not with those most in need of the researchers' message.

Many journalists, on the other hand, hear today's plaintive wail, perhaps write a story about it, but more likely not, and then continue doing what they always do. They write stories about surveys by repeating numbers. Far too often they don't draw conclusions from the numbers. It is easier for them to just cite the numbers and let the reader draw the conclusion. And they don't try to assess the quality of the survey research unless something is glaringly suspicious. It is my experience that reporters of campaign politics will usually take numbers, usually uncritically, and repeat them.

They have regard for disclosure about sample size, source and sponsor of the survey, dates and method of conducting the survey, question wording and the sampling error. However, there is very little evidence that the methods disclosed form a basis for inquiry or skepticism about the meaning of the numbers reported. It is as though disclosing methods by the researcher and the media is the equivalent of the Good Housekeeping Seal of Approval. Somehow, if methods are disclosed by the press the survey is thought to have validity

Of course, nobody should believe that. What is needed are journalists who evaluate the survey, once they hear the facts. But that is not what happens. The journalist, not to be outdone by the researcher, passes these disclosures to the listener of a broadcast or the reader of a newspaper. Now it is up to the public to do the interpretation.

Something is wrong! The researchers and the journalists have all done their jobs of disclosure and still almost no one has made a clear interpretation or evaluation of the research for the public.

Used uncritically, these disclosures are not very useful beyond being an article of good faith between the researcher and the consumers. Disclosure implies that the researcher has nothing to hide. It argues for the credibility of the researcher. It does little for serious evaluation in its present form. Disclosure to a trained survey researcher may be useful, but it is not helping most journalists or the public.

Let me suggest why I think disclosure alone is not adequate to improve the reporting of surveys. First, it requires the journalist or the public to reach a level of expertise that is better left to a researcher. The burden of interpretation might best be carried out by a statistician. Not by a journalist! And not by the public!

There is another equally important reason why disclosure alone is inadequate. The requirements for disclosure, as stated by many professional survey research groups, are a minimal list of disclosures at best.

Items Disclosed

There are problems with the items that are usually disclosed by the survey researcher. What follows is a discussion of the items usually presented.

Sample Design

Researchers usually refer to the sample design by the single word "probability" or some variant such as a "modified probability" selection, whatever that means. But this is not sufficient information. We don't know if there are biases or gross inefficiencies in the selection. For example, the typical national election survey by the media leaves out Alaska and Hawaii, non-telephone households, and most of the population living in quarters other than housing units. Sometimes there is a bias in the weighting related to multiple residential telephone numbers for reaching a person. And all too frequently there is a bias related to the selection and/or weighting of a person *within* a household.

If disclosure did a good job, it might reveal these details. But knowing these details still won't provide useful information to the public. What might better be known, as a minimum, is the size of the population excluded or misrepresented. Does this effect 10 percent of the population, 20 percent, 30 percent? And do they vote differently or have different opinions on issues or any other characteristics measured in the survey?

Sample Size

Knowing the sample size is most useful if one assumes simple random sampling. It tells us little about the size of the subgroups or the effects of clustering for these subgroups. For example, in an election-day poll of voters leaving the polling place, the clustering of sample voters by polling place will produce a much larger sampling error for minorities than for most other subgroups of the same sample size. In a Random-Digit-Dial telephone survey, the size of the cluster within a working block can have order of magnitude effects on the sampling error for minority subgroups.

Who Conducted the Survey

As for disclosing the name of the organization conducting the survey, it is useful for making judgments about the work of well-known companies. But during the 1992 elections, did you know the names:

Political/Media Research, ARG, Potomac Research, Mason-Dixon or KRC? They conducted most of the political surveys people read or heard about in local newspapers and on local television stations. Did you know anything about the state surveys done by the University of Connecticut or the University of North Carolina? If you did, you would likely have regard for their current work, but one of them, a decade or more ago, did highly questionable work, worse than any commercial work you might imagine.

Survey Dates

The dates when the survey was conducted are not useful, except for the most current polls. What one needs to know to make survey dates meaningful is a current events context. If a 1992 political poll was conducted before or after the Democratic or Republican Conventions it had a very different meaning. After the Democratic Convention the Clinton image soared and was only slightly diminished by the events at the Republican Convention.

But how about a political poll before or after November 4, 1979? Two significant events that changed the course of the upcoming presidential election happened that day. One was the taking of hostages at the American embassy in Iran. The other was the Roger Mudd hour-long documentary on CBS about the life of Ted Kennedy. Both events destroyed Kennedy's challenge to President Carter for the Democratic Presidential nomination. Before November 4th, Kennedy was leading by two-to-one in the polls. The positions were reversed soon afterward.

The same problem exists for studying unemployment surveys without knowing a current events context for the dates. Significant economic events like a stock market crash or a change in the income tax laws can influence employment rates. The introduction of a drug or vaccine can influence health surveys. The point of all this is that dates alone, without context, places the burden back on the journalist or the public to find out for themselves whether events could have changed the meaning of survey results.

Question Wording

Disclosure of the question wording has often been suggested. It is generally useful. It is not practical, however. Most news stories do not have the space either in print or on a broadcast to include the question wording. Besides, the question wording is often not meaningful unless you know the questions that preceded it. Context effects may be more important. There is an example later on in this chapter that expands on this point.

Sampling Error

Sampling error seems to be the most controversial of all the disclosure items. It is usually misleading and misunderstood. What you usually hear in political polls is a crude approximation of a sampling error for a 50 percent characteristic based on the whole sample, where the researcher assumed simple random sampling. This is frequently done even when the sample is a non-probability design. This may be a useful approximation, but only to a handful of people.

The sampling error for many surveys is reported as plus or minus three percentage points. While the level of magnitude of the sampling error may be a useful clue for people comparing two numbers in the same survey or numbers in different surveys it also can be misleading. For example, the sampling errors for characteristics measured by an exit poll will vary enormously due to the large clustering effect on some characteristics. The sampling error for a characteristic of black voters may be orders of magnitude larger than a voting characteristic for an age group of the same size. The former is subject to large clustering effects, and the latter to almost none.

A news story would better serve its readers if all comparisons that implied something changed, or said that two variables were different, had been tested for statistical significance. It should not be the responsibility of the reader or listener to conduct their own significance test!

An Alternative to Disclosure as We Know It

Having said why I think disclosure as now recommended by professional groups is not nearly as useful as it might be, I would like to offer an alternative approach for consideration. Survey researchers have struggled with this problem over the years. The suggestions that follow will serve their purpose if they stimulate further discussion by other survey researchers.

My alternative approach has two parts: First, the researcher, and not a journalist, should try writing what he or she wants to see in a newspaper. And second, the researcher should do his or her own evaluation of the limitations of the survey.

The Researcher's News Story

Writing a news story may be a new burden for some researchers. Others have done it before. Its value is to shift the burden to the researcher for correctly presenting the most reasonable interpretation of the newsworthy findings of the survey research.

The researcher's news story should be no longer than two or three pages. It should be aimed at a lay audience. And it should draw whatever conclusions the researcher wants the reader to draw from the work. If anyone wants more details there should be a more complete report.

Notice, disclosure was not included in the prescription for the news story. This was not necessarily meant to exclude relevant details. What was wanted was authoritative interpretation of the relevance of background facts in the researcher's news story. The job is to tell what the research means (cf. Lewis, 1991). If the researcher included informed speculation and it is properly identified as such that would be acceptable. For example: Bill Clinton's lead over George Bush following the Democratic Convention in many polls was over 20 percentage points. It would be acceptable to include a statement from a researcher that said, "Even though challengers usually lead presidential incumbents between party conventions, my experience suggests that the size of Bill Clinton's lead at this time makes him a better than even money bet to win the election in November."

The researcher's opinion is a legitimate part of the press release. It would not be acceptable for a reporter to offer his or her own opinion as part of the news story. A reporter would quote a researcher's opinion if expert interpretation was desired.

A front page story in *The New York Times* compared *The New York Times*/CBS News Poll's 1992 post-convention jump in the public's preference of Bill Clinton for president to that recorded for Dukakis in 1988, Mondale in 1984 and Carter in 1980. The reporter did not offer his opinion or cite an expert's opinion about what the results might portend for November. You, gentle reader, were left to draw your own conclusion.

While that would not have been difficult in this example, I believe the reader will generally be better served in most survey reports with more interpretive assistance. The point of the story was the likely effect in November and not the current level or change in support.

I believe survey researchers can write good news stories. They can probably do it more readily than a journalist can learn enough statistics to interpret a research report.

That does not mean that the researcher's news story will be published in the newspaper or broadcast on television. It likely will not. But it will provide the reporter with a much better starting point. It also will force the researcher to separate the newsworthy portion of the research from the scholarly material that is out of place in most news stories. The press is not a substitute for a more complete exposition in a journal or report.

A New Form of Disclosure

The second change I would like to see calls for a new type of disclosure that would require both professionalism and judgment on the part of survey researchers. Journalists should not have to ask a third party to evaluate survey research. Evaluation should be an integral part of the research report. I am asking the survey researcher to explicitly state the limitations of his or her work. Rather than the familiar disclosure of a few details about the conduct of a survey, *the researcher should discuss the level of the generalizations that can and cannot be made from the data.* This is the most important point I want to make in this essay. If researchers can start with this notion on the road to interpretation, I believe a real improvement can be made in the reporting of surveys.

Let's start by continuing the example about the portion of the potential voting population excluded from election surveys. Earlier it was suggested that the researcher should report the portion of the public excluded from most media telephone surveys. My estimate is that it is approximately 13 percent - 15 percent of the population.

A researcher might know from previous work the likelihood of these people going to the polls and casting a vote, and something about their voting behavior. Are they more Democratic or Republican than the voting population included in the survey? A statement that said, hypothetically, that "15 percent of the population had no chance of selection in the sample, and that they likely would comprise nine percent of the voters, and could be expected to change the margin between the Democratic and Republican candidates by two percentage points at most."

I would submit that this is a much more useful statement than the one usually made. All that would typically be said is, "In a national survey...," etc. Not even a mention of the under-representation of the sample.

Or how about saying: "We limited our results to the 55 percent of the residential population that seemed to be the most likely to vote. We know that all of them will not vote, perhaps 20 percent will not. And, we know from other research that about 15 percent of those thought not likely to vote will go to the polls and vote. These misclassified groups could affect the margin between the candidates by from three to seven percentage points." That's what I call disclosure!

Similar statements can be made about the dates of the survey, sponsorship, sampling error, question wording and question order effects.

Presidential preference, as measured by public surveys in the first half of June of 1992, was affected by question order effects. At different times during the presidential campaign year all three candidates were in first place in the polls. Early June was when Ross Perot was leading, Bush was second, and the eventual winner, Bill Clinton, was third in most polls but not all. Varying news reports must have confused the public about the size of Perot's lead or whether he was leading at all.

Each news organization that conducted its own poll reported its results as though no other poll reported something different. Other journalists, without a poll of their own, reported each new poll as though there was some remarkable shift in public sentiment from day to day. The truth of the matter is that most differences in these polls were probably due to question order effects. Most of the researchers conducting the polls were aware of this problem.

In an op-ed piece on June 27, 1992 in *The New York Times*, my former CBS News colleague, Dr. Kathy Frankovic, explained some of these differences. Questions asked prior to the presidential preference question changed the results. CBS and *The Times* first asked a question about favorable or unfavorable views about all the candidates. Many people did not know enough about Perot to express such a view. As a result, Perot was third in presidential preference in this poll.

Time/CNN first asked: "How well do you think things are going in the country these days...?" Perot got his biggest lead in this poll and Bush was last. Gallup first asked preference between Bush and Clinton, and then asked about presidential preference among all three candidates. Perot does better when the questions were asked in this order.

The underlying reason for the conflict is because the majority of voters knew very little about Perot and only a little more about Clinton. They all knew Bush, and he was dropping in almost every measure of his job performance.

Frankovic concluded her analysis with this statement:

> Pollsters are not asking the wrong questions, but journalists and politicians are focusing on the wrong answers. This is not the time to concentrate on "Who's ahead?" The apparently conflicting poll results on the horserace masks the non-conflicting results of public dismay and confusion about this year's election. Those are the responses journalists and politicians — and pollsters — all need to concentrate on.

I submit that a CBS poll, reported on June 22, 1992, would have been much more useful for journalists and the public if it had included Frankovic's subsequent views expressed in her op-ed piece five days later. That is the type of disclosure that is useful.

As Frankovic illustrates, meaningful disclosure can best come from the people doing the surveys. This is a general conclusion I would like to draw. Its implications are not to be limited to political surveys. The rationale applies to all survey research. The researcher is the one to evaluate the limits of the survey results. Not the journalist! Not the public! They are ill-equipped to do this. The researcher is not.

What Reporters Can Do

I would like to conclude with a few other things that I believe can be done to improve the reporting of surveys.

News organizations can do several things. They can train a reporter or a newspaper editor or a television producer to understand the rudiments of survey research, at least enough so that they can ask researchers insightful questions. Hopefully, these journalist will know enough about when to get additional guidance from an experienced researcher.

Another thing news organizations can do is develop guidelines or news standards before they publish someone else's survey. CBS News did this many years ago at the urging of its then president, Richard Salant. The survey-reporting standards were published in an internal book of standards governing all news reported by CBS. It insisted on minimum disclosure on air, validity of the methods used to conduct the survey and broadcast approval by the head of survey research. These guidelines kept bad survey work off CBS.

Salant asked for an up-to-date evaluation of the methods used by all survey organizations conducting public polls. The guide was strictly for internal use and it characterized surveys as acceptable, questionable or not acceptable for broadcast by CBS News. If a survey organization's work was of questionable quality it was subject to case-by-case review. This approach kept a lot of bad work off the air.

What Professional Associations Can Do

This next suggestion is something professional associations like the American Statistical Association, the American Association for Public Opinion Research, the National Council on Public Polls and others can do. They can create advisory groups that will give *ad hoc* assistance to journalists when they have questions about surveys. What journalists want is someone they trust to answer their questions about surveys. There is no reason, other than concern for lawsuits, why such groups couldn't be set up and made known to journalists.

The advisory group must be prepared to give valuative answers to direct questions and on short notice. This does not mean that the group must do the journalists' work if additional information is required. The journalist can and should be told what he or she must acquire in the way of information to facilitate an evaluation. It is not imperative that an advisor be identified in print or on the air. The comments of an advisor can be for background purposes only and not for attribution. You should know, however, that most journalists would prefer the assistance on background to no assistance. But they also would prefer attribution to no attribution.

Some Other Things Survey Researchers Can Do

These next remarks are for survey researchers. It may be of use if they are asked to advise journalists about other researchers' work.

First, it is more important for an advisor to clarify what *can* be said based on a survey, rather than doting on what cannot be said. News stories are not written about the denial of a survey's findings. Anything negative that comes out of an evaluation is only useful to shape the limits of what can be said positively.

Next, generalizations about the survey process are not nearly as useful as specifics. The researcher's evaluation is not a tutorial on survey methods. It is a pointed appraisal about specific material.

Just a final note about jargon. I once got verbally assaulted by a somewhat eminent statistician for using the term "margin of error." To satisfy this man, I should have said "two times the sampling error" or maybe he would have preferred "two sigma." It doesn't matter! I submit that the man was wedded to jargon — jargon that does not have a common meaning for many journalists and the public. If there is a simple way to say something, try it, even if it is not exactly the politically correct phrase among statisticians.

A "mean" can be an "average." A "median" can be the "halfway-point," or some other notion of the midpoint. How about "related" instead of "correlated"? Or, something is "very likely" instead of "statistically significant." Or, "not different" rather than "the difference is not significant." Statistics has a language of its own, but journalists and the public do not speak it. It should be easier for statisticians to describe poll results more simply than they have in the past.

These next two points are obvious, but I want to say them anyway. Criteria for evaluation should not be absolute. If they were, we would have a good case for performance standards. The evaluation depends on the purpose of the survey. For example, I do not have the same statistical criteria on election night for concluding a candidate has won an election as I do for reporting an estimate of his or her winning percentage.

For announcing a winner on network television, I want a maximum risk of one chance in 200. For announcing the percentage, I will accept a risk of one in 10 that the estimate is within three percentage points. These are not comparable risks. Similarly, a survey to report the approximate level of public opinion does not require the same precision as a determination of change on a key variable. A survey may be adequate for one purpose but not another. Survey evaluation should fit the complexity of the problem.

My last point is to ask you to assess the audience for all this survey enlightenment. Some people can take more enlightenment than others. Others need more, but can't take it.

Conclusion

At the start I said the child's game of telephone was the model of the past, that is, the way survey researchers had been passing their message to journalists and they, in turn, relaying it to the public. It was the intent of this essay to help ungarble the end result of our research.

I believe this can be done if those of us who produce surveys start by shifting the emphasis away from the type of disclosure that has been our practice in recent years. It is too limited to be the sole product we produce for assisting those journalists or members of the public who want to evaluate our surveys.

Second, survey researchers should write their own version of a news story. This role reversal is more practical than making survey experts out of reporters. It will force the researcher to identify the newsworthy findings of his or her work. And, it will present the researcher's interpretation of those findings.

Third, and most importantly, researchers should tell the journalist the limitations of the research and the generality or specificity of the conclusions that can be drawn from the survey research.

It is time for survey researchers to abandon their whisper and speak with a clear voice about their work. I believe this can be done, but only if the process is changed.

Notes

An earlier version of this chapter appeared in the 1992 Proceedings of the Section on Survey Research Methods of the American Statistical Association as "A Challenge for Campaign '92: Training Reporters and Informing the Public."

6

A Review of the
1992 VRS Exit Polls

Warren J. Mitofsky
Murray Edelman

Exit polls have become a staple of election reporting for the news media. In 1992, these polls were used in the reporting of almost all the presidential primaries and all general election contests for President, Senator and Governor. Since their first use as an analytic tool in the 1970 general elections, exit polls have been an increasingly more dominant source of information for news stories about the election.

Exit polls were conducted by Voter Research & Surveys in 1990 and 1992. Before that, starting in 1967, the authors conducted exit polls for CBS News. VRS was a broadcast pool sponsored by the major television networks — ABC, CBS, CNN and NBC. Its purpose was to conduct exit polls and produce election analyses and projections for presidential primaries and for the general election contests for President, Senator, Governor and House of Representatives.[1] VRS distributed its results to its participants on an election night computer system. Correspondents and producers used this material for live broadcasts. Graphics devices presented the material to the broadcast audience.

Other news organizations shared in the cost and also made extensive use of the VRS materials. During 1992, 85 television stations, newspapers and news magazines made use of the VRS exit polls in their news reporting. On election night, news organizations reported VRS material not only in the United States, but in England, Germany, Japan and Italy. It was heard in other countries on CNN and the World Service of the BBC.

Given the wide distribution of VRS material by the news media, it is important to its credibility to have complete disclosure about its methods and the evaluation of its performance. Disclosure about the evaluation of survey methods is a tradition the authors learned first at the Census Bureau. The Bureau published post-Census evaluation reports under the leadership of Morris Hansen. The research in those reports was responsible for improving Census methods. It is not overstating the case to say that these evaluation studies were responsible for improvements in surveys everywhere that used probability-based methods. The work of VRS cannot be compared to the level of the work at the Census Bureau. However, it is the authors' intent to follow in this tradition by publishing a systematic evaluation of VRS exit polling.

How Exit Polls Were Conducted

By way of background, this is what was done in the United States for the 1992 general election:

Sampling

In each state, a stratified sample of precincts was selected proportionate to the number of votes cast in a previous election. This provided the basis for each state's exit poll. A stratified subsample of 300 precincts was selected from the state samples. It was done so that national sample precincts had a probability of selection proportionate to the number of votes cast in the 1988 presidential election.

The voters within each precinct were chosen by the systematic selection of every *nth* voter leaving the polling place. The rate of selection was expected to produce at least 100 sample respondents over the course of the voting day. The high average of 134 was due in part to increased voter turnout for this election.

Interviewing and Tabulating

An exit poll consists of interviews with a probability sample of voters outside the polling place after they have voted. Including the state polls, interviews were conducted with 177,000 voters on election day in 1,310 precincts. Interviewers were hired and trained by Chilton Research Services. They collected the data at their offices in Radnor, Pennsylvania, where it was edited and passed from their computer to the VRS computer. VRS did the weighting, tabulating and other processing.

There was usually only one interviewer working at a polling place. Interviewers arrived before voting began and worked 50 minutes of each hour. During their 10-minute break, they did a hand tally of the number of respondents who said they voted for each candidate. Interviewers telephoned results of the hand tally and the individual responses to each question to a central site three times during the day. Before reading the individual responses, questionnaires were subsampled.

The subsampling was controlled by the operator receiving the call at the central site. The subsampling produced 62,024 questionnaires, of which 15,256 were from national questionnaires. The rest were from state exit polls.

The first call from interviewers was in the late morning. The second call was several hours later and the last call was about an hour before poll closing. New estimates and tabulations were produced after each call. This was done so that journalists could start looking over the vast amount of preliminary data and develop story ideas.

The Questionnaire

VRS conducted surveys in all 50 states and the District of Columbia. Some parts of each questionnaire were unique for each state. There were three different national exit poll questionnaires.

Questions for the exit polls were drafted by a committee made up of representatives of the four networks. VRS had the final responsibility for the questionnaire. It chaired the committee and coordinated the preparation of the questionnaires and computer files.

It is tempting to think that a committee would not do the best job of preparing questionnaires. The early meetings of this committee gave strong evidence that the strongest held opinions in America are those of public opinion researchers about their own ways of asking others their opinions. After an initial struggle, this committee was able to function effectively and gain from each other's strengths. It is the opinion of the authors that the questionnaires put together by the VRS survey committee were consistently better than those from earlier exit polls conducted separately by each of the networks before VRS was formed.

Having a limited amount of space on the questionnaires had been a problem in the past when the networks worked separately. As members of VRS, the networks were required to share the space on the questionnaires and the problem was more acute. The solution was to have three national questionnaires. This gave the networks more common space and also allowed them space to ask their own questions.

The National Questionnaires

The national survey was more complex than the state exit polls. There were three different national questionnaires administered in each voting precinct. States only had one questionnaire, except California, which had two.

National exit poll interviewers were given bound pads of questionnaires. Each pad had the different questionnaires interspersed so voters
and interviewers had no choice about which questionnaire was handed
to a particular voter. Questionnaires were identified by color. The first
questionnaire had two versions. One was on white paper, the other was
gray. The questions on the two versions were the same. The only difference was a *rotation of the order* of the answer categories for two questions.
The first questionnaire, the white and gray versions combined, was given
to twice as many sample voters as the yellow and pink questionnaires.
The 15,256 national questionnaires included 8,503 white plus gray combined, 3,899 yellow and 2,854 pink.

All three national questionnaires asked respondents about their votes
for President and House of Representatives. And, if there were contests
for Senator and/or Governor, it asked for their votes in those races. Also
common to the three questionnaires were seven questions — questions
on sex, race, age, party identification, income, sexual orientation and 1988
presidential vote.

The white/gray questionnaire had 29 questions. These questions
were available to all networks and subscribers. The pink questionnaire
was made up of the seven common questions, the vote for political
offices, plus 22 questions that were available only to the network that
requested the question. The yellow version was mostly shared among all
participants but had some network-specific questions.

There was one other complication that increased the number of versions of each questionnaire. Because the names of the candidates running for Senator and Governor were listed, the preparation varied in each
state. Preparation included not only printing, but also creating computer files for processing and distributing the results.

In prior years, the names of House candidates were put on each questionnaire, actually printing a different questionnaire for each precinct.
This was done to get a more accurate report of the House vote. In 1992,
it was not felt that this could be done. VRS was already committed to
print 204 different questionnaires, four for each state. If names of House
candidates had been added VRS would have had to prepare 1,200 different questionnaires.

The names are important as some people only recognize the name of
the person they voted for; they don't always know their candidate's political party. Research conducted in 1984 when the authors were at CBS
showed this problem was more acute in House races that were won by
wide margins. The interpretation of this phenomenon was that popular
incumbents who won by landslides often avoided party identification in
their campaigning because it encouraged support from voters that were
mistaken about the candidate's party.

In 1992, the names of candidates running for the House of Representatives were not listed. They were just identified as "Democrat" or "Republican," or some other party, where appropriate. The candidates' names were attached to the interviewer's clipboard. It was hoped that the bias found in past years when the names were not on the questionnaire could be minimized.

Table 6.1 shows by how much the estimates were in error in 1984. (Those exit polls were conducted for CBS News.) The easy winners — the ones in safe seats — had larger errors. After that, the names of the candidates were put on each questionnaire and the bias virtually disappeared. The 1990 column, when names were on the ballot, shows no relationship between the safety of the seat and the error.

In 1992, the congressional names were once again missing from the questionnaires. A preliminary evaluation of a compromise approach, based on only 115 of the 300 national exit poll precincts, shows the bias still remained. Obviously, further research is necessary.

Distribution of the Results

The output of these polls was coordinated so that each news organization received tabulations of only those questions it was entitled to. For example, CNN could not see NBC's questions and non-network participants could not see any of the unilateral questions.

One other detail about the output: Some questions were placed on more than one questionnaire, while others were restricted to just one. When someone requested a tabulation, they saw results that were an accumulation of all responses to a question across all versions of the questionnaire that had the question.

TABLE 6.1 Difference Between % Democratic from the Exit Poll Estimate and the Official Vote for House of Representatives

Expected Result in Cong. District	House Candidate Names on Questionnaire?		
	No Names	Names On Qs	Names Nearby
	1984	1990	1992
Safe Democratic	-7.1%	-0.1%	-1.5%
Safe Republican	5.4%	-1.6%	7.4%
All Other CDs	-3.6%	0.7%	4.1%

For example, vote and age were on all versions of the national questionnaires. Therefore, the sample size for a cross tab was the combined number of interviews from all three versions of the questionnaire. On the other hand, political ideology was only on one version, making the resulting sample size for tabulations of this characteristic smaller.

The News Organizations' Reporting of the Results

Each news organization was at liberty to interpret the results and report them as it saw fit. However, there were guidelines for use of the information. Sometimes these guidelines were not observed.

Calls

The networks agreed to let VRS call the winners of the different state contests. They had the capability of doing this themselves, but before 1994, no one had.[2] Non-network participants did not have this capability.

All parties had agreed not to announce winners prior to the time the polls closed in a state. In 1992 everyone kept this agreement, with one exception. There was one lapse during the New York presidential primary when NBC thought a few minutes before poll closing was acceptable. It wasn't! The other networks strongly objected to breaking the embargo, even by a few minutes.

All participants were notified ahead of time about the calls VRS planned to make at the next poll-closing hour. This was necessary to prepare graphics for on-air display and to prepare the networks' anchors for what they would say. What the participants were told shortly before poll closing was the name of the winning candidate in each contest where the exit poll indicated there was a winner. At that time, the candidates' percentages were not available for on-air use. They came later when VRS had better estimates — that is, estimates based on the actual vote returns in the same sample precincts.

For the primaries, VRS also provided a verbal characterization of the size of the win and something about the showing of the other candidates in the contest. For the general election, there were so many states closing at each hour, a verbal characterization was not given.

Analysis

News organizations did their own analysis. VRS provided formatted crosstabs available on computer screens. The networks' analysts could create additional crosstabs, controlling on any number of variables. Other participants could not generate extra crosstabs themselves, but they were able to request them from VRS by telephone. The networks agreed not to present any state analysis on air prior to poll closing that would suggest anything about the outcome of the contest. Almost all were pretty good about observing this restriction.

The problem was less amenable to a solution when it came to the national exit poll. The networks tried to make a responsible rule that would fit all electoral situations, but it just was not possible. There was no such thing as an appropriate logical time for reporting the national exit poll.

At first, the networks planned to wait until one candidate had a majority of the electoral votes before reporting based on the national exit poll and say nothing before then. That would have been a good rule in a landslide situation, but it was not acceptable for reporting a close contest. For reporters to say nothing about why a contest was close until after it was decided would leave a gaping hole for most of the night in the news reporting.

If reporters were prohibited from using the exit poll results for this purpose, they would do what they did before there were exit polls — they would speculate and act as experts on the public mood without referring to the poll. This would create a very difficult situation for everyone, because they would have seen the poll. The networks would be asking their correspondents to report on the closeness of the election without referring to a poll they had seen.

The compromise was to ask each of the networks and other participants to use their best news judgment about when to report their analysis of the national election. To the best of the authors' knowledge, all networks did this responsibly and did not prematurely report national trends.

The Fishbowl

Throughout 1992 the networks each said they would try to keep the results of the election confidential until they broadcast them. They were not successful. Unfortunately, anyone who wanted to know the preliminary exit poll results could find someone to tell him or her. They were known to the politicians, they were known to the business community, including people at the stock exchanges, and they were known to most people in the media, including news organizations that were not primary participants.

The consequences of these elites having this information were readily observable. Leaks of unanticipated primary results on the day of the

New Hampshire primary caused the stock market to swing wildly. Phil Donahue announced leaked VRS primary results at 4:30 on the afternoon of the New York primary and got snotty when he was told the polls had not closed yet. He said he did not make an agreement with Congress or anyone else not to broadcast results before the polls closed. Early numbers caused President Bush's campaign to target get-out-the-vote drives when they learned at mid-day that their vote was less than expected. As long as the information was circulated to the networks and the other participants, there was no way to keep the information confidential.

For the authors, this was the biggest single change in exit polling since the days when the networks each did their own exit polls. In the old days, information was tightly held until it was suitable for distribution. In one primary years ago, the exit poll was never broadcast because of uncertainty about the quality of the results. However, VRS's work was done in a fishbowl where all participants could watch the results through every step in the process, from noon until the exit polls were final late at night. And, they were free to interpret complex statistical information, and sometimes did. This loss of control was responsible for a lot of preliminary data getting wide distribution to the political elites. It was not a healthy development!

Not for Air

There was a reporting problem with the analysis data that was particularly vexing. Crosstabs of the analysis data were made available to the participants on formatted computer screens. The screens were designed to show vote by demographics, issues and all other questions asked on the exit poll.

In 1992, VRS added a line at the top of these screens. It was an estimate of the popular vote percentages for each candidate produced at the same time as the exit poll cross tabulations. It was not intended to be VRS's most up-to-date best estimate. The estimate on the survey screen was there as a convenience with a big bold caption under it that said: "ABOVE %S NOT FOR AIR." It was expected that that was sufficient notice to keep people from reporting those percentages. It was a preliminary estimate, just as the exit poll analysis data was preliminary at that time. It reflected the data received up to the time the crosstabs were produced. It did not reflect new vote returns that were reported since the last update of the crosstabs. That could have been an hour for the national exit polls and longer for state polls. The NOT FOR AIR label disappeared when the survey was complete and the estimate was good enough to be broadcast or printed.

The best estimate came from a series of post-stratified ratio estimates that involved quality control and a few other refinements. It used all the data available at the time. The best estimate appeared elsewhere, after it had been evaluated and deemed to be a fairly precise estimate of the final outcome.

Nonetheless, the estimate that said ABOVE %S NOT FOR AIR found its way on air and into print. It became the source for critics who said the poll was off the mark. Of course it was off the mark. That was why it had a label on it that said NOT FOR AIR!

The solution is obvious. The overall estimate should not have been on the screen in its preliminary form. It should have been withheld until such time as VRS thought it was good enough for presentation to the public. This solution would not satisfy the curiosity of news producers and reporters. But VRS was in the business of making estimates based on events that had already transpired, not making predictions of things that had not yet happened. The preliminary estimate was not a forecast of the final result.

Evaluating the Exit Poll Estimates

This next section discusses some of the things that were learned about the quality of the data. An evaluation of the estimates, or the projections as they are called by the media, is the first topic.

State Estimates

On election night in 1992 projections were made on 133 statewide contests for President, Senator, Governor and a variety of propositions, referenda and other state contests of local interest. There were exit polls in 114 contests and none in 19 others.

As can be seen from Table 6.2, 67 contests were projected at poll closing time based on exit polls. The median presidential contest projected at poll closing time had an 11.5 point margin between the winner and his nearest opponent.

TABLE 6.2 State Election Projections, 1992

	Total	Projections at Poll Closing Time Based Only on Exit Polls
President	51	29
Senate	33	21
Governor	12	7
Other	18	10
	114	67

The median margin for the presidential contests projected after poll closing time was only 4.4 percentage points. They were all contests with smaller margins of victory for the winning candidate. The models for those other projections used either the actual vote returns in sample precincts or were made using the cumulative raw vote counts in counties. This chapter does not evaluate the estimates based on those other sources of data, except to say that VRS had the correct winning candidate with all the projections, including the exit polls. That included the primaries as well as the general election.

National Estimates

The national exit poll was used to make preliminary estimates at different times during the evening of November 3, 1992. The problem of premature reports of these estimates was discussed above. This section discusses how those estimates were made and their accuracy at different points in time. If the national exit poll data had just been weighted by the reciprocal of the probabilities of selection, it would have been an unbiased estimate. However, that would not have been the best estimate that could have been made. It was possible to do better. This is how it was done.

Forcing. In each state there was an improvement on simple unbiased estimates by taking advantage of the correlations with past election results. Without going into the details, VRS did this by making post-stratified ratio estimates in each state. All the data available in a state was used to make the estimate. Early in the day, only exit poll results were available. After poll closing, actual vote returns in sample precincts became available. Eventually, vote returns by county were used.

VRS combined the best estimates from each state to make subregional estimates. The national exit poll results within each subregion were then forced to those estimates. Without forcing, at the end of the night, the national exit poll would have overstated Clinton's margin over Bush by 5 percentage points.

National Estimates at Each Hour. What follows is an examination of the national estimates throughout election night. At 7 o'clock Eastern time the national estimate was based on incomplete exit poll returns from sample precincts in all time zones. (All times are Eastern Standard Time.) That was one of the reasons why VRS had that "%S NOT FOR AIR" message.

As the evening went on, the national exit poll gradually was completed. The results shown in Table 6.3 for midnight were the only results that included the completed exit polls. All estimates at earlier times were incomplete.

The table shows national estimates at each hour. Clinton actually won over Bush by just under 6 percentage points. At 7 o'clock — which is not presented in the table, as the data is not available — Clinton's margin over Bush was overstated; the margin was 11 points. At 8 and 9 o'clock VRS estimated a 10 point Clinton lead, then nine points at 10 o'clock, eight points at 11 o'clock and 7.5 points at midnight when the poll was completed. The difference between that final margin and the VRS esti-

TABLE 6.3   National Exit Poll Estimates, 1992

	Clinton	Bush	Perot	Clinton - Bush	Estimate -Actual
End of Night[a]					
U.S.	43.4%	37.5%	19.1%	5.9%	
EAST	47.1	34.8	18.1	12.3	
MIDWEST	42.5	36.9	20.7	5.6	
SOUTH	41.3	42.6	16.0	-1.3	
WEST	43.2	34.2	22.5	9.0	
8:10 p.m.[b]					
U.S.	46.2	35.9	18.0	10.3	4.4
EAST	50.0	32.9	17.1	17.1	4.8
MIDWEST	45.5	36.4	18.1	9.1	3.5
SOUTH	42.8	40.8	16.3	2.0	3.3
WEST	47.2	32.1	20.8	15.1	6.1
9:10 p.m.					
U.S.	45.6	35.5	18.9	10.1	4.2
EAST	48.6	33.2	18.2	15.4	3.1
MIDWEST	44.8	34.9	20.2	9.9	4.3
SOUTH	42.5	40.8	16.7	1.7	3.0
WEST	47.3	31.9	18.7	15.4	6.4
10:10 p.m.					
U.S.	44.8	36.1	19.1	8.7	2.8
EAST	47.6	34.1	18.3	13.5	1.2
MIDWEST	43.9	35.3	20.7	8.6	3.0
SOUTH	41.7	41.9	16.5	-0.2	1.1
WEST	47.1	31.7	21.2	15.4	6.4
11:10 p.m.					
U.S.	44.3	36.5	19.2	7.8	1.9
EAST	47.5	34.7	17.7	12.8	0.5
MIDWEST	42.9	36.3	20.8	6.6	1.0
SOUTH	41.6	41.9	16.6	-0.3	1.0
WEST	46.3	31.4	22.4	14.9	5.9
12:10 p.m.					
U.S.	44.2	36.7	19.1	7.5	1.6
EAST	47.4	34.8	17.8	12.6	0.3
MIDWEST	42.8	36.6	20.7	6.2	0.6
SOUTH	41.8	42.5	15.7	-0.7	0.6
WEST	45.9	30.4	23.6	15.5	6.5

[a]"End of Night" is based on the final unofficial News Election Service Vote Count, as of Thursday following the election.
[b]No national or regional estimates were saved for 7:10 p.m.

mate was 1.6 percentage points. VRS consistently overstated Clinton's lead all evening.

Regional Estimates by Hour. The regional results tell a similar story. All polls were closed in the East and South by 9 o'clock. An hour later at 10 o'clock the estimates for those regions had complete returns. The Midwest was an hour later. The last poll in the West, except for Alaska, closed at 11 o'clock. The exit poll was complete at the time of the 12 o'clock estimate. As can be seen, the estimates gradually improved as the data became more complete. This should surprise no one. (What surprised the authors were the reporters who thought VRS should have had the result to the last decimal point early in the evening, before the exit poll was completed.)

An examination of the regional estimates at each hour shows that they got better. At the end of the night, all but the Western region produced good estimates. The bad estimates in the West cannot be attributed to the large absentee vote in California. That was not the source of the problem.

Discussion

Overestimating the Democratic candidate was a problem that existed in the last two presidential elections. It is not nearly of as much concern at the national level; it is of great concern at the state level. It is believed that the problem was related to different response rates by supporters of the two candidates. The candidate with more enthusiastic supporters seems to have been overstated in the VRS exit polls. His supporters appear to have been more willing to respond to VRS's request for an interview.

The same problem existed in the New Hampshire Republican primary where VRS overestimated Patrick Buchanan's vote. The Buchanan problem continued into Georgia, which was the next primary where he campaigned vigorously. It disappeared after that as soon as he stopped campaigning.

Present research is under way looking for correlates between the questions on the exit polls and the over-reporting of candidates. Questions that differentiate voter enthusiasm for the candidates are expected to correlate with varying response rates. Other explanations are also being investigated.

Questionnaire Experiments

Two experiments were conducted that affected the presentation of questions on the exit polls. Ben Black, a young research associate, made a significant contribution to this work.

During the presidential primaries the importance of national issues to the voters, as measured by the exit polls, had an effect on the political agenda of the candidates. However, there was a problem with these data. The authors were aware that the order of presentation of issues in a list affected the degree of their selection by the voters. The magnitude of these order effects was unknown.

The authors also were concerned that the last question on the exit poll, which asked the respondent to "Check All That Apply" from among a list of up to nine items, was underestimating the proportion of voters who were members of a labor union or said they were gays and lesbians, etc. Experiments were conducted to evaluate these problems.

Order Effects

There were two similar questions on the exit poll questionnaire where the order of presentation of the choices could be a problem. One question asked respondents, "Which one or two issues mattered most in deciding how you voted today?" The other question asked, "Which one or two candidate qualities mattered most in deciding how you voted today?" There were up to nine possible choices listed for each question.

VRS conducted split-ballot experiments during the Pennsylvania and Oregon presidential primaries. There was very clear evidence of an order effect for the selection of issues by the voters. After observing the order effects in the Pennsylvania test where nine issues were listed, a shorter list was tried in Oregon. It was hoped that the shorter list would make it unnecessary to have two versions of every questionnaire with the choices in reverse order.

The length of the list did not matter. In both states, issues placed at the beginning of the list were selected more frequently.

There was no clear evidence of an order effect when it came to "candidate qualities." If anything, the results were counter-intuitive. Only one item in each state varied by a significant amount. All other items had smaller variations in the two orders.

The differences observed in the issues questions clearly required remedial action, as this question is so essential to the interpretation of an election. For the national poll in the general election, VRS created two versions of the questionnaire with the order of the issues and qualities reversed. Table 6.4 shows the effect of having the issues and qualities presented in different orders on the national exit poll.

Order effects existed in the national exit poll for both the issues items and the qualities. As can be seen, items listed early or late had the biggest response deviations. Items in the middle had negligible deviation. The order of presentation does influence the marginal percentage of selecting

TABLE 6.4   National Exit Poll, 1992: Question Order Effects

	VERSION		
	White	*Yellow*	*Difference*
ISSUES[a]			
Health Care	24	15	9
Federal Budget Deficit	25	17	8
Abortion	13	11	2
Education	12	13	-1
Economy/Jobs	41	44	-3
Environment	4	7	-3
Taxes	12	17	-5
Foreign Policy	7	9	-2
Family Values	10	20	-10
QUALITIES			
Has the right experience	22	15	7
Will bring about change	40	32	8
Is my party's candidate	5	5	0
Cares about people like me	14	13	1
Is honest and trustworthy	14	13	1
Has the best plan for the country	21	28	-7
Would have good judgement in a crisis	14	19	-5
His choice of Vice President	7	10	-3
Has strong convictions	13	15	-2

	Clinton	*Bush*	*Perot*
ISSUE			
Health Care			
White	67	19	13
Yellow	65	20	14
Deficit			
White	36	29	34
Yellow	35	23	42
Family Values			
White	15	75	10
Yellow	26	62	12

[a]White Version Order

an item. There doesn't seem to be much relationship to presidential preference, except for family values. Even so, analysis of these issues or qualities and their relationship to candidate preference is better done in relative terms, that is, one item has a stronger relationship to voting choice than another. The marginal percentage of the items may be distorted by order effects.

Response Category Format

There is a question that VRS has asked at the end of exit polls that is a catch-all for stray topics. It consisted of a list of factual and opinion items where the respondent was asked to "check all that apply." A voter either checked an item, or left it blank if it did not apply. An experiment was conducted in order to improve the response rate to this type of question and also to estimate the nonresponse rate.

It was suspected that all respondents did not check all items that applied to them. The way the exit poll data had been collected and tabulated, a nonresponse was considered the same as a negative response to the question, as the people not responding were included in the denominator. This made the marginal percentages saying "yes" an understatement.

A change of format was tested by providing both a "yes" and a "no" category for each item. The instruction was changed also. Respondents were asked, "please answer all questions." These changes were tested in the same primaries as the order effects. The old and new versions appeared on split-ballots.

The new format increased the affirmative responses on almost all items by an average of close to seven percentage points. What was still troubling was the rather high nonresponse to the items in the "yes-no" version. The last three items had a 14 percent nonresponse rate, which was four to eight points higher than the earlier items on the list. That included three percent who did not answer any of the questions.

As the marginal percentages for these items includes a large nonresponse rate in the denominator, the exit poll still understates the proportion of voters who identified with each item even with this change in format. When used as a description of the electorate, these marginals should include some adjustment for nonresponse or at least a mention that it is an understatement. Under these circumstances, the items in this list are most meaningfully used as independent variables and not as a measure of incidence.

Response Rates

Nonresponse in exit polls is very high. It averaged 42 percent in 1992, which compares to the 40 percent rate CBS had in 1988. Most of the nonresponse was a refusal to participate in the survey. However, one-fourth of the nonresponse was not refusals, but was due to interviewers missing voters who should have been included in the sample. This typically happened when too many voters left the polling place at the same time.

Those high nonresponse rates were the bad news. The good news was that the rate of nonresponse was not correlated with the deviation of the exit poll from the actual result.

As compensation for voters who did not participate, VRS made a noninterview adjustment to the weighting before it was forced to the subregional estimates that were described above. This was done separately by age, race and sex. The interviewers kept a count of these characteristics for all voters who did not participate. It included those who refused as well as those who were missed.

Nonresponse rates were about the same for men and women and voters in most age groups. They differed for whites and blacks and for older voters. The nonresponse adjustments by sex and race had no overall effect on the national estimate of the presidential vote. The adjustment by age did. It changed the margin by a little over one percentage point.

A related question was the effect on the marginal distributions of demographic characteristics as a result of the age-race-sex noninterview adjustments. The first two columns of Table 6.5 show the proportions of key demographic items before and after this adjustment for nonresponse. As can be seen, there was a significant effect on the proportion of older voters. However, none of the other demographics were changed.

The authors made this adjustment for nonresponse in the years prior to VRS when they did exit polls for CBS. The demographics had about the same adjustments then. The 1992 VRS material can most meaningfully be compared to the CBS exit polls for the years prior to 1990.

A related question was whether forcing the estimates to the final result misrepresented the demographics of the voters. For example, decreasing Clinton's share of the vote could also lower the estimated size of his major support groups. The third column of Table 6.5 displays the marginal demographic proportions after the nonresponse adjustment and forcing to the final result. Fortunately, there was almost no effect on these marginals from the forcing. There was a small effect on only one item, party identification, which was highly correlated with vote.

Demographics of Voters Compared with Other Surveys

There are two other reliable surveys that estimated voters' demographic characteristics. One is the National Election Study, carried out by the University of Michigan, and the other is the Current Population Survey (CPS), conducted by the Census Bureau. Table 6.6 shows a comparison of the marginal distributions of demographic characteristics from all three surveys.

The table shows about the same distribution for sex from all three surveys. For age, all three surveys have different distributions. The exit poll

TABLE 6.5   Effect of Weighting on Demographics

	Weighted But Not Adjusted	Age-Race-Sex Adjusted	Age-Race-Sex Adjusted And Forced
SEX			
Male	46	47	47
Female	54	53	53
RACE			
White	86	87	87
Black	9	8	8
Hispanic	3	2	2
AGE			
18-29	22	21	21
30-44	38	36	36
45-59	24	23	23
60 +	16	20	20
EDUCATION			
No HS degree	7	7	7
High school	25	25	25
Some college	29	29	29
College graduate	23	23	23
Post graduate	16	15	16
RELIGION			
Protestant/Christian	55	56	56
Catholic	27	27	27
Jewish	4	4	4
Something else	7	6	6
None	7	7	7
PARTY ID			
Democratic	39	39	38
Republican	33	33	35
Independent/other	28	28	27
INCOME			
Under $15,000	14	14	14
$15,000-$30,000	24	24	24
$30,000-$50,000	30	30	30
$50,000-$75,000	20	20	20
$75,000 or over	12	12	12

shows fewer older people even after the noninterview adjustment than the other two surveys. There was a difference between the CPS and the other surveys for the 25- to 44-year-old age group and there was a difference between the exit poll and both other surveys for older people. The other age groups are all comparable.

The biggest deviation was for education. The exit poll shows substantially more people with a college education or better participating in the election and fewer people not completing high school than the other surveys.

It is not known which survey provides the better estimates. It is known that in the validated National Election Study about seven percent of the vote was cast absentee and that it was primarily from older people. It was also the case that those older people had lower educational achievement levels. Obviously, absentee voters were not counted in the

TABLE 6.6   Comparison of Voter Demographics From Three Surveys, 1992

	NES[a]	CPS[b]	VRS[c]
SEX			
Male	47	47	47
Female	53	53	53
AGE			
18-24	7	9	11
25-44	47	42	46
45-64	28	30	30
65+	18	19	13
EDUCATION			
No HS degree	12	12	7
High school	33	33	25
Some college	27	28	29
College graduate	28	18	23
Post graduate		9	16

College- and Post-Graduates as a Percentage of Age Groups, 1992

	NES	VRS
AGE		
18-24	10	24
25-44	36	45
45-64	30	38
65+	17	26

[a]National Election Study
[b]Current Population Survey
[c]Voter Research & Surveys

exit poll. It is believable that absentees could account for part of the discrepancy, but certainly not all. At present, it is known that both NES and CPS overstated citizen participation in the election. It is not known how that affects their distribution of education.

Unfortunately, the distribution of race from the exit poll could not be compared to NES and CPS. The other surveys asked voters about race and Hispanic origin as separate questions. VRS asked about race and Hispanic identification in the same question.

Conclusion

This chapter discusses some of the exit poll problems that have been evaluated and others still in progress. It seems that this is a never ending job.

There is still a lot of research to do. Looking for correlates of differential nonresponse rates was a major research project for 1992. VRS also looked for more error-free methods of taking the vote into the computer and thinking about item imputation. There really are many research projects still to do.

All the research is a trade-off against the logistical complexity and the magnitude of the project. For example, it has been demonstrated in this chapter that there was an order effect for some of the items. The effect of not having House candidate names on the questionnaire also has been shown. To solve both problems VRS would have had to print and pad 1,200 separate versions of the national questionnaire. All this would have had to have been done during a one-week period before the election. But a longer lead time would have affected VRS's usefulness as a news organization, which was our raison d'etre.

Notes

1. VRS was terminated in 1993. It was replaced by Voter News Service. VNS performs all the functions formerly provided by VRS and by the News Election Service. The same four television networks and the Associated Press are the sponsoring networks of VNS. The AP had been a member of NES but was not a member of VRS. When VNS was formed, Robert Flaherty, formerly of NES, became the managing director and Murray Edelman became the editorial director. NES had been responsible for conducting a census of vote returns for the same political contests for which VRS conducted exit polls and made projections. The members believed a single political pool would result in more economical election coverage.

Warren Mitofsky left the networks when they merged VRS with NES. His new organization, Mitofsky International, was established to conduct exit polls for American and international clients. His U.S. clients thought it desirable to have a second source of exit poll analysis. In 1994, they included *The New York Times*, *The Washington Post*, *The Wall Street Journal* and National Public Radio.

2. In 1994, ABC News and the Associated Press exercised their right to make their own projections. ABC, using Voter News Service's data, was more aggressive and more willing to take risks than VNS, and hence was much quicker in some of their calls of winners. This may lead to more competition among VNS members in 1996.

7

Methods of Allocating Undecided Respondents to Candidate Choices in Pre-Election Polls

Robert P. Daves

Sharon P. Warden

The poll is out of the field. It's the first look at the horserace numbers. And one of the first questions is, "How will the undecideds split?"

Tough question.

It's tough because there is no fail-safe way (or at least not one discussed in the public domain) to divvy up undecided respondents among candidate choices in a pre-election poll. It's a question that those of us who do pre-election public opinion research always are asked. And one for which we rarely have a good, concrete answer. This chapter discusses ways — conceptional and pragmatic — to apportion undecided respondents in pre-election polls.

A week before the 1992 presidential election, Phil Meyer[1] challenged the nation's pollsters to be brave by polling up to the last minute and allocating undecided voters. He says public opinion research has advanced to the point that pollsters can afford to be brave rather than fall into the ranks of the wimpy. Wimpy pollsters, he says, bail out at the last minute or report the poll results with undecideds unallocated, giving them an "out."

He challenges pollsters to use a method of allocating undecided voters and report those figures — which could then, of course, be compared to the outcome of the election. If one picks up the gauntlet he throws down, the obvious question is, "Which is the best method of allocating those last remaining undecided voters?"

Virtually all pollsters have had to face the question before, usually because the candidate, party, editor or reporter wanted to know which way the undecideds would go. And virtually all have come up with the same dilemma: There is usually not enough known about undecided respondents in the waning days of the election for anyone to be comfortable apportioning them among candidate choices.

Pre-election polls are used to measure and analyze strength of support for a candidate, the depth of that support, the differences among candidates and the mood of the electorate in general. The most common method for measuring voter preference is to interview some sample of voters by telephone in advance of an election, usually asking a variant of the question, "If the election were held today, would you vote for Candidate X or Candidate Y?"

Measuring voting intent seems like a straightforward proposition until a random sample of voters is contacted. Then researchers find that some voters just don't seem to be decided about whom they will vote for, and others simply refuse to say. Five months before the 1992 presidential election, *The Washington Post*-ABC News poll found that eight percent of registered voters did not know how they were going to vote in November, or refused to say how they would cast their ballots. However, by November this figure dropped to about two percent when the trial-heat measure for registered voters included those who professed a choice for a candidate plus respondents who initially were undecided, and after probing said they leaned toward voting for a particular candidate. For the Gallup poll, the percentage of undecided respondents stayed relatively high right up to the election. The last Gallup pre-election poll showed six percent of respondents undecided.

Reducing Undecideds

The public and pollsters judge polls by how closely they reflect the outcome of the election and polls with high numbers of undecided or "no opinion" responses simply cannot accurately reflect election day results. Since non-voters are irrelevant, most researchers attempt to identify a likely electorate in their sample to help reduce the number of undecideds.

Some researchers, particularly in states where one must be registered weeks ahead of the election to be permitted to vote, interview only registered voters; most others usually go further and ask voters how likely they are to vote on election day.[2] Registered voters who are not likely to vote are excluded from the sample at this point. Some pollsters use additional criteria, such as voting history, to filter out people not likely to actually cast a ballot on election day.

In states such as Minnesota, which permit election day registration, researchers may not be able to use voter registration as the sole screening device — or even partition a sample into likely and unlikely voters. This may be a serious problem for the pollster in states such as Maine, Wyoming and Minnesota, if election day registration is substantial, as in the 1992 election when more than one in every six voters in Minnesota registered the same day they voted. Thus, the Minnesota Poll uses registration history and other likelihood-to-vote questions to construct a scale, and then weights respondents based on their position on the scale; very likely voters get a higher case weight and less likely voters get a lower weight.[2] This is similar to the way the *New York Times* poll treats likelihood to vote (Kagay, 1991, p. 43.)

Another technique for reducing the percentage of undecided respondents is to ask a "leaner probe" of those who initially said they "don't know" or refused to tell preferences. This probe once again asks them to choose among the major candidates. Those who choose a candidate on the first question are combined with those who choose a candidate from the "lean" question.

The result of these reduction techniques is a marked decrease in the number of respondents who say they don't know whom they will vote for on election day, or who refuse to give a response to the question. At this point the percentage of "don't knows" and "no opinion" may be as little as two percent of all potential voters, but could range into the double digits. For example, the June 7, 1992 *Washington Post*-ABC News Poll showed eight percent of registered voters responding "don't know" or "refused" when asked for whom they planned to vote in November. The eight percent were next asked whether they leaned more toward George Bush, Bill Clinton or H. Ross Perot. All but two percent of them chose one of the three candidates. Their choices were added to the votes of respondents who had already chosen a candidate, which resulted in only two percent of the sample who didn't know or did not want to give a choice.

Apportioning Undecideds

The challenge for public opinion researchers at this point is determining which candidate's camp voters who remain in the undecided and "no opinion" categories belong. Conceptually, many pollsters treat these "no opinion" voters as if they will not vote or will, "split as do the decided voters" (Crespi, 1988, p. 108). Operationally, these voters are sometimes excluded from the base of potential voters and candidate preferences are recalculated. The new base for calculations becomes respondents who are considered likely to vote on election day and are willing to choose a candidate at the time of the interview.

Another way to deal with "no opinion" voters is to exclude just "no opinion" voters from the sample. This method assumes that "no opinion" voters will not cast a ballot on election day. While this supposition may be accurate in many elections, it may not hold true for volatile elections. For example, during the 1992 presidential election, Ross Perot encouraged his followers not to tell pollsters how they intended to vote. Some researchers have suggested that members of an aging electorate who feel that how they cast their ballot is no one's business but their own may have decided how they will vote but refuse to tell an interviewer.

Crespi reported that undecided voters have been allocated by splitting the undecided percentage evenly among (or between) the major candidates (Crespi, 1988, p. 22). Some pollsters have allocated "no opinion" voters using statistical methods such as discriminate analysis (Fenwick, 1982, p. 383-391). Some researchers have reported that undecided voters also will end up going to the challenger (Crespi, 1988, p. 114; Panagakis, 1989, p. 1).

Panagakis advocates the concept that undecided voters will "end up with the challenger." He reported that in "127 cases out of 155, most or all of the undecideds went for the challenger" (Panagakis, 1989, p. 2). He has developed an "incumbent rule" that suggests that if the point spread between two candidates were 50 percent to 40 percent and 10 percent of respondents were undecided, then the likely outcome would be 52 percent to 48 percent on election day (Panagakis, 1989, p. 2). Panagakis reported that "it helps to think of undecided voters as undecided about the incumbent, as voters who question the incumbent's performance in office. Most or all voters having trouble with this decision appear to end up deciding against the incumbent" (Panagakis, 1989, p. 2). However, Panagakis prefers to call this a way of characterizing an outcome than one of actually allocating respondents. This "theory that undecided voters break for the challenger when an incumbent seeks re-election [has been followed in] state and local elections, but Gallup is the first to apply it to a presidential race" (Meyer, 1992, p. 7A). In 1992, Gallup chose to allocate all of the undecided vote to the main challenger because its "study of the other five incumbency races since 1956 shows strongly that Panagakis was right" (Meyer, 1992, p. 7A). However, Panagakis cautions against applying his "incumbency rule" to presidential races because "the intense media attention afforded by the primary campaign and the national conventions gives the challenger such wide recognition" (Panagakis, 1989, p. 3).

One of the reasons that Gallup utilized the "incumbency theory" method was that none of the allocation methods cited here have consistently produced accurate results, that is, results that mirrored the outcome of an election. One allocation method may work well for a two-way race between nominees of the two major parties. It may not work as well for a three-way race such as the 1992 election with an independent candidate like Ross Perot. Statewide, national, senate, house, gubernatorial and mayoral elections may each show very different results depending upon the number of undecided and "no opinion" voters and the kind of allocation method used to account for them.

Methods and Measures

To help understand more about allocating the undecided and "no opinion" groups in pre-election polls, pre-election poll results using four experimental methods of allocating these undecided potential voters were calculated, then the results were compared to determine which of the four methods produced the most accurate results.

For this examination, the four allocation methods were:

1. Repercentaging major candidate votes after taking out undecided and "no opinion" and allocating them proportionate to the trial heat support that candidates received in the poll
2. Repercentaging major candidates' support after removing undecideds and "no opinion" and allocating these respondents equally between or among the major candidates
3. Allocating all undecided and "no opinion" respondents to the challenger
4. Allocating undecided and "no opinion" respondents using discriminant analysis assignments.

For purposes of simplicity, let's define undecided respondents to include "don't know" and "no opinion" survey respondents combined. From this point on this group will be called undecided voters. Decided voters were those who told interviewers whom they would vote for — or leaned toward — on election day. Accuracy was defined as results that most closely paralleled the official outcome of the election.

The four methods of allocating undecided voters were tested using statewide and national polls:

1. An Oct. 27-30, 1992 *Star Tribune*/WCCO-TV Minnesota Poll of 1,104 likely voters in Minnesota
2. An Oct. 28-Nov. 1, 1992 *Washington Post*-ABC News poll of 722 likely voters nationwide
3. An Oct. 30-Nov. 4, 1988 *Star Tribune* Minnesota Poll of 1,200 likely voters in Minnesota

4. A Nov. 5-7, 1988 *Washington Post*-ABC News poll of 1,010 likely voters nationwide (known as the Fifty State Poll)
5. Three *Star Tribune*/WCCO-TV overnight polls conducted in Minnesota Nov. 1, 2 and 3 published after the election.

The first four polls were chosen because they were the last polls published by the *Star Tribune* and *The Washington Post* just prior to the 1988 and 1992 elections respectively. The overnight statewide polls were used to examine how levels of support changed during the final days of the election — important when a precise electorate can't be determined until quite close to election day.

Results from these surveys were compared to actual votes cast and to results of the four undecided voter allocation methods. The outcome of these experiments was used to investigate three main questions:

1. Which of four methods was best at apportioning undecided voters in pre-election polls?
2. Did the number of candidates in an election make a difference? And, if so, which was better for a three-way election and which was better for a two-way election?
3. Was one of the four methods better for national polls as opposed to statewide polls?

The four allocation methods analyzed in this research were chosen because they have been used by one or more news polling units or by political research firms (Crepsi, 1988, pp. 108-116; Meyer, 1992, pp. 224-226 and Panagakis, 1989, pp. 1-3).

Repercentaging—Two Techniques

Repercentaging assumes that undecided voters will allocate themselves to presidential candidates in the same proportion as decided voters as Crespi documented (Crespi, 1988, pp. 108-116). This method makes no assumptions about the demographic or political characteristics of undecided survey respondents. It does, however, assume that they will turn out on election day. Some researchers contend that respondents who are still undecided close to election day will not go to the polls and vote (Crespi, 1988, p. 112).

For calculation purposes, researchers used two repercentaging techniques. One allocated undecided voters proportionally to the percentage of the vote each major candidate received in the poll. The other repercentaged by dividing undecided voters equally between (or among) the candidates.

Challenger Gets the Undecided Vote

This method of allocating undecided voters in a pre-election poll assumes that, on election day, the challenger will take all or most undecided votes (Crespi, 1988, p. 114 and Panagakis, 1989, pp. 1-5).[3] Researchers usually need to make some assumptions about which candidate is the main challenger for a three-way race. No clear operational definitions exist for making this decision.

In an election such as 1988, where Vice President George Bush inherited the GOP blessing to take President Ronald Reagan's place, one could argue that he was not the challenger, and looked very much like an incumbent. In 1992, it was clear that he was the incumbent. One could argue that Bill Clinton, who won his party's nomination, was the main challenger while Ross Perot, the independent candidate, was the secondary challenger.

Discriminant Analysis

This is the most complex and methodologically rigorous of the three methods tested.[4] The potential advantage of using discriminant analysis as an allocation technique is that it allows researchers to account for the complexities of the voting process. Discriminant models do not assume that all undecided voters are alike, will all vote for one candidate, will split evenly between (or among) the major candidates, or will not vote. (It does assume that all the respondents in the sample will vote; hence the carefulness with likely voter screens and weights.) Discriminant analysis is based on the assumption that undecided voter behavior can be predicted from knowledge of, for example, the relationships between demographics and voter attitudes.

A wide variety of demographic and attitudinal variables can be included in models based on discriminant analysis. Research, however, suggests that undecided and "no opinion" responses are not random and are correlated to respondent demographics. Faulkenbery (1978) showed that "those classified as not having an opinion were found to be less educated and used mass media less" (p. 531). Francis (1975) found that "item nonresponse is systematically related to sex, age, education and household composition... region, city and occupation" (p. 207). Converse found that education was the "single best predictor of no opinion percentages" in Gallup and Harris data he analyzed (Converse, 1976, pp. 528-529). Crespi found that party identification was also an important predictor of voting behavior (Crespi, 1988, pp. 38-40).

Discriminant Analysis Procedures. The first step was setting aside cases for respondents who chose "other" in the poll (third party or minor candidates, usually one percent to three percent of the sample). These were brought back into the sample at a later stage.

Next the researchers generated discriminant functions for those who said they would vote for, or leaned toward, voting for a major candidate—in 1992, that was Clinton, Bush or Perot. Respondents who initially did not disclose their support but upon further questioning named a candidate they "leaned" toward were included as supporters of that candidate. These discriminant functions were used to classify undecided voters.

The last step was to calculate the percentage of total support for each candidate. This involved adding the number of cases for the decided, the re-classified undecided voters and "other" voters (set aside up to this point). Percentage of vote was calculated by dividing by the sample size (the "other" category should always be the same after this process as before).

The authors used the same independent variables in the discriminant analysis procedures where possible. However, there were two differences between the statewide and national polls. One difference was an abortion attitude question used in the statewide polls and discriminant function analyses. An abortion question of this kind was not asked in the national polls. The abortion item did not contribute significantly to the statewide discriminant functions, so this should have made little difference in comparability of discriminant methods used for the statewide and national polls.

The second difference between the national and state polls was the way likely voters were ascertained. National poll respondents were screened for registered voters, then a single, self-professed likelihood-to-vote question was used to determine likely voters. For the statewide polls, a 12-point index was computed based on four questions correlated with voting behavior and the data were weighted on likelihood to vote.

Predictor variables used for both national and statewide poll discriminant analyses were:

1. Six-way age: 18-24, 25-34, 35-44, 45-54, 55-64, 65 or older
2. Three-way education: High school graduate or less, some college, college graduate or more
3. Five-way party: Democrat, leaned Democrat, independent or not affiliated, leaned Republican, Republican
4. Gender: male or female
5. Four-way household income: Less than $20,000, $20,000-$29,999, $30,000-$49,999, $50,000 or more
6. Three-way abortion: Pro-life, middle of the road, pro-choice (used only in the Minnesota data)
7. Political ideology: Liberal, moderate, conservative.

As with nearly any survey, a small number of respondents refused to answer one or more demographic questions. For purposes of this study, those missing data were recoded to the median value for that question. This was done to assure that all undecided cases could be classified via discriminant analysis. There were no missing values for gender.

Discriminant analysis procedures are essentially the same for most statistical packages. For purposes of this research, the SAS discriminant program was used for the statewide data and the SPSS discriminant program was used for national poll data.

Analysis

To make interpretation of the results easier, Table 7.1 summarizes each of the experimental techniques in terms of the direction and percentage point difference from election results. Tables 7A.1-7A.4 in the appendix show results for each of the four allocation techniques applied to each of the four polls used for this study and the amount of error for each method.

Considering overall results after taking out the "other" vote served two purposes. First the data could be examined as though it were real election results in which very few voters (often less than one percent) actually voted for someone other than a major candidate. The most important thing, however, was that it helped mitigate a rounding error problem. Several of the allocation methods showed results adding to 101 percent because of rounding.

Statewide Poll—1988

The poll showed Michael Dukakis with 48 percent of the support, George Bush with 43 percent and nine percent undecided. Dukakis carried Minnesota (one of his few states) with a seven-point margin, 52 percent-45 percent; three percent voted for a long list of other candidates on the Minnesota ballot.

The proportional method of allocating undecided voters resulted in an overestimate for both Bush and Dukakis, and an underestimate for the minor candidates. Less the minor candidates, total error was three points for the proportional method.

Equal apportioning of undecided respondents resulted in no error for Dukakis, three points for Bush and three points for minor candidates. Less the minor candidates, total error was three points for the equal allocation method.

Allocating all undecided respondents to the main challenger —

TABLE 7.1 Percentage Point Differences Between Election Results and Experimental Methods of Allocating "No Opinion" Responses Among Candidate Choices

	Poll Results	Proportional	Equal	Main Challenger	Discriminant Analysis
1988					
Minnesota Poll					
Bush	-2	+2	+3	-2	+3
Dukakis	-4	+1	0	+5	0
Other	-3	-3	-3	-3	-3
No Opinion	+9				
Washington Post/ABC News National Poll					
Bush	-2	0	0	-2	0
Dukakis	-2	-1	0	+2	-1
Other	+1	+1	+1	+1	+1
No Opinion	+3				
1992					
Minnesota Poll					
Clinton	0	+4	+3	+9	+4
Bush	-4	-1	-1	-4	-1
Perot	-6	-4	-3	-6	-4
Other	+1	+1	+1	+1	+1
No Opinion	+9				
Washington Post/ABC News National Poll					
Clinton	0	+2	+2	+5	+2
Bush	-3	-1	-1	-3	-1
Perot	-3	-2	-2	-3	-2
Other	+1	+1	+1	+1	+1
No Opinion	+5				
1992 Minnesota Overnight Polls					
Saturday, Oct. 31:					
Clinton	+9	+11	+10	+13	+11
Bush	-6	-5	-5	-6	-5
Perot	-7	-6	-6	-7	-6
Other	0	0	0	0	0
No Opinion	+4				
Sunday, Nov. 1					
Clinton	-4	-1	-2	+4	-1
Bush	-4	-2	-2	-4	+2
Perot	-2	-1	0	-2	-3
Other	+2	+2	+2	+2	+2
No Opinion	+8				
Monday, Nov. 2					
Clinton	0	+3	+2	+4	+1
Bush	-2	0	0	-2	0
Perot	-5	-4	-3	-5	-2
Other	+1	+1	+1	+1	+1
No Opinion	+6				

Note: The signs may not sum to zero error because of rounding in the allocation.

Dukakis — resulted in 10 points of total error: a five-point overestimate for Dukakis, two-point underestimate for Bush, and a three-point underestimate for minor candidates. Less the minor candidate error, there were seven total error points.

When the discriminant function was applied to respondents who had chosen, nine of ten were classified correctly. Using discriminant analysis to allocate undecided respondents resulted in no error for Dukakis, three points for Bush and three points for minor candidates for a total of six points of error. Less the minor candidate error, discriminant analysis allocation resulted in three points of total error.

In the 1988 Minnesota data, discriminant analysis, equal apportioning, and proportionate allocation had the same amount of error, three points. The most amount of error came from assigning all undecided respondents to the challenger.

National Poll—1988

This poll is known to some as the recall poll from the 1988 Fifty State Survey. Data showed Bush with 52 percent of likely voters, Dukakis with 44 percent, "other" with one percent and undecided with three percent. This 1988 poll underestimated each candidate by two percentage points. Final election figures gave Bush a slim majority of 54 percent. Dukakis received 46 percent of the popular vote.

The proportional allocation method resulted in a correct prediction for Bush's support but underestimated Dukakis by one percentage point. The equal allocation technique resulted in a correct prediction — again, rounding was a problem. Equal allocation gave Bush 54 percent and Dukakis 46 percent of likely voters.

The technique of allocating all undecided voters to the main challenger resulted in Bush receiving only 52 percent of the vote. This underestimated his final vote total by two percentage points. The main challenger method overestimated Dukakis by two percentage points, assigning him 48 percent of voters. The discriminant analysis allocation technique was correct for Bush at 54 percent of the vote. But it underestimated Dukakis by one percentage point at 45 percent.

The discriminant analysis technique included sex, education, income, political ideology, age and party identification as independent variables. Discriminant analysis results indicated that these independent variables were better predictors for 1988 than for the 1992 poll results. When the discriminant function classification was applied to voters in 1988, nine out of ten Dukakis voters were correctly classified as Dukakis voters. Eight out of ten Bush voters were correctly classified.

Statewide Poll — 1992

This poll showed Bill Clinton with 44 percent of the support, George Bush with 28 percent, Ross Perot with 18 percent and minor candidates with one percent. Undecideds and no opinion responses amounted to nine percent. Clinton won the election with 44 percent of the vote, Bush had 32 percent and Ross Perot garnered 24 percent, one of the highest percentages in the nation.

All apportioning methods overestimated Clinton's support, all slightly underestimated Bush's support and all underestimated Perot's support. Less the minor candidate error, equal assignment of undecided respondents resulted in the least percentage point error, seven points, while assigning all to the main challenger — Clinton — resulted in the most error, 17 points. Proportional and discriminant assignment resulted in an equal amount of error, nine points.

It is clear for both statewide elections that assignment of all undecided voters to the main challenger resulted in the most error while the other three appear to be about equal in accuracy. It also is clear that allocation of undecided respondents was much more prone to error in the 1992 election than in 1988.

An example of the difficulty of allocating undecideds in 1992 is that discriminant analysis correctly classified fewer than seven in ten correctly.

National Poll — 1992

This poll showed Clinton at 43 percent, Bush at 35 percent, Perot at 16 percent, "other" at one percent, and undecided at five percent. The poll correctly captured Clinton's vote at 43 percent but it underestimated Bush and Perot by three percentage points. All poll results and allocation techniques underestimated the Perot vote.

Proportional allocation did not work as well for these 1992 data as it had for the 1988 poll. Proportional allocation overestimated Clinton's support by two points, underestimated Bush by one, and underestimated Perot by two points.

Equally allocating undecided voters among the candidates did not work as well in 1992 as it had in 1988. In this 1992 national poll, equal allocation overestimated Clinton by two points, underestimated Bush by one and underestimated Perot by two points.

Allocating all undecided voters to the main challenger resulted in the least accurate outcome. This method overestimated Clinton by five points, underestimated Bush by three and underestimated Perot by three points.

The discriminant analysis allocation technique did not work as well for the 1992 election as it had for the 1988 election. Discriminant analysis overestimated Clinton by two points, underestimated Bush by one, and underestimated Perot by two points. Overall, however, discriminant analysis, proportional and equal allocation showed the same error, six points. Clearly there was no single best allocation method for this 1992 election poll.

Discriminant analysis revealed similar classification patterns for both Bush and Clinton in the 1992 national poll. But, this technique worked more poorly at classifying Perot voters. Only one-quarter of Perot voters were correctly classified as Perot voters. This suggested that the independent variables used in this study may not have provided an adequate profile of the Perot voter. Some other set of variables including attitudes toward government or the state of the economy, for example, may have been better predictors of Perot voters.

Discriminant analysis for the 1992 national poll correctly classified 70 percent of Bush, Clinton and Perot voters. Classification predicted that 74 percent of Bush voters would vote for Bush and that 84 percent of Clinton voters would vote for Clinton. Classification was not as accurate for Perot, however. Only 26 percent of Perot voters were classified as Perot voters, 38 percent were classified as Clinton voters, and 37 percent were classified as Bush voters.

Statewide Overnight Polls — 1992

The *Star Tribune's* three overnight polls just prior to the 1992 election showed a wide swing in the strength of support for Bill Clinton, ranging from 53 percent on Saturday, just after the larger sample had been collected and before publication, to 40 percent on Sunday. If there's any point that these overnight polls drive home, it is the increase in accuracy the closer polls are taken to Election Day (despite the documented call-back problems with overnight polling).

The percentage of no opinion respondents fell to four percent on Saturday, rebounded to eight percent on Sunday and settled to six percent on Monday. (Table 7A.5 shows the overnight polling results compared to actual vote with undecideds not allocated; Table 7A.6 shows overnight polling results compared to actual vote with undecideds allocated.)

In the final poll on the Monday before the election, Clinton received 44 percent of the support, 30 percent went to Bush and 19 percent to Perot. These numbers were little different than the larger sample poll. The proportionate allocation of "no opinion" voters resulted in a seven-point total error, equal allocation resulted in a three-point error, the main-challenger method resulted in an 11-point error and the discriminant allocation resulted in a three-point error.

In the Monday poll, discriminant analysis allocated three of the six points to Perot, two to Bush and one to Clinton. While the discriminant method and the equal apportionment method had the same total error overall, the discriminant allocation of the undecideds came closest to estimating the outcome of the election, because it did a more accurate job of allocating the undecideds correctly to Perot.

Discussion and Conclusions

These data suggest that assigning undecided respondents in pre-election polls to a candidate is indeed a chancy business, no matter which method is used. But clearly the data suggest that assigning all undecided respondents to a challenger in a presidential election can result in the most error.

There was relatively little substantial difference among the proportional, equal and discriminant methods of allocating undecided voters, despite the larger degree of allocation error associated with the statewide polls.

The statewide poll in both the 1988 and 1992 election had more percentage points of error for all allocation techniques than the nationwide poll.

We believe one major reason is election day registration. Minnesota allows election day registration, which could potentially mean a large influx of undecided voters at the last minute. For example, 18 percent of voters in the 1992 election registered on election day, one reason why voter registration as a pre-election poll screen is not feasible in Minnesota.

The introduction of a major third candidate may increase the potential for error in allocating undecided respondents to a candidate's camps. One reason may be that in an election with an extremely high degree of voter alienation toward government, many voters may indeed support the independent candidate and call themselves "undecided," or refuse to tell interviewers how they plan to vote.

The development of discriminant functions using more than just demographic variables seems quite promising. In the 1992 election all allocation methods resulted in a larger estimate of error for both state and national polls and this election was characterized by a high degree of voter mistrust in government. Perceptions of how much efficacy an individual might have in government also dropped. Future research that includes variables such as these in discriminant functions might find promising results.

For those doing pre-election polls, it still is tricky to allocate undecided respondents among candidate choices. It may be advisable to allocate undecided respondents if for no other reason than to help understand where a candidate's support lies. If one allocates undecided respondents among the candidate choices, it would be advisable to use several methods, including discriminant analysis, particularly if issues salient to the specific election are included with demographics as predictor variables.

Notes

The authors wish to thank The Minnesota Poll's survey specialist, Denise Brownfield, and the Roper Center for their assistance in preparing and retrieveing data. This chapter is based on a paper the authors presented to the American Association for Public Opinion Research in St. Charles, Illinois, in May, 1993.

1. Philip Meyer was William Rand Kenan Jr. Professor of Journalism at the University of North Carolina at Chapel Hill when he served as public opinion polling consultant for *USA Today* during the 1992 presidential election. He has written articles about public opinion polling and presidential elections for *USA Today* and the *Miami Herald*.

2. In the 1988 presidential election, the *Washington Post*-ABC News election poll used the following registered voter filter, interest in the election, likelihood to vote and vote intent questions:

Q. Can you tell me whether you are registered to vote at your present address, or not?

Q. How closely are you following the 1988 presidential race: very closely, somewhat closely, not too closely, or not closely at all?

Q. Some people have busier schedules than others. Because of this, some people who plan to vote can't always get around to it on election day. With your own personal daily schedule in mind, I'd like you to rate the chances that you will vote in the 1988 presidential election next November: Are you certain to vote, will you probably vote, are the chances about 50-50, or don't you think you will vote in that election?

Q. The candidates in November's presidential election are George Bush and Dan Quayle, the Republicans, and Mike Dukakis and Lloyd Bentsen, the Democrats. Suppose the election were being held today, For whom would you vote: Bush and Quayle, or Dukakis and Bentsen?

During the 1992 presidential election, respondents were asked the voter registration question followed by likelihood of voter and then for whom they planned to vote:

Q. Are you registered to vote?

Q. Some people have busier schedules than others. Because of this, some people who plan to vote can't always get around to it on election day. With your own personal daily schedule in mind, I'd like you to rate the chances that you will vote in the 1992 presidential election next November: Are you certain to vote, will you probably vote, are the chances about 50-50, or don't you think you will vote in that election?

Q. If the 1992 presidential election were being held today, and the candidates were George Bush, the Republican candidate, Bill Clinton, the Democrat, and H. Ross Perot, the independent, for whom would you vote?'

In the 1988 and 1992 presidential elections the Minnesota Poll used a similar series of questions to take likelihood of voting into account. The questions were used to construct an index, with lower index values indicating less likelihood to vote and higher values indicating more likelihood to vote. Cases were weighted according to index scores with less likely voters given a lower weight and more likely voters given a higher weight. Weights ranged from 0.23 to 0.77. This was done partly because Minnesota permits Election Day registration. It was not judged practical to screen out unregistered voters in Minnesota because same-day registration is allowed. This was important in 1992, when same-day registration in the state was 18 percent of those who cast ballots. The index questions:

1988

Q. Generally, speaking, how much interest would you say you have in politics at any of the federal, state or local levels? Are you very interested, somewhat interested, slightly interested or not at all interested?

Q. Many people happen to be registered to vote while many others are not. How about you? Are you registered to vote where you live?

Q. People tell us that there are things that come up on the last minute that sometimes keep them from getting to the polls on election day, even if they are registered to vote. How much of a chance do you think there is that something will come up to keep you from voting in the November election, a fair chance, some chance, hardly any chance or no chance at all?

1992

Q. Are you registered to vote in the precinct or township where you live?

Q. Did you vote in the 1988 November general election or did something come up that kept you from getting to the polls that day?

Q. Generally speaking, how much interest would you say you have in the upcoming general election this November, a great deal, a fair amount, only a little or no interest at all?

Q. People tell us that there are things that come up on the last minute that sometimes keep them from getting to the polls on election day. How much of a chance is there that things will come up to keep you from voting on election day, a fair chance, some chance, ardly any chance or no chance at all?

Q. There will be several names on the presidential ballot this November. If the election were held today, would you vote for Republican George Bush, Democrat Bill Clinton, Ross Perot, or someone else?

3. Panagakis asserts that undecided voters may be taken by the challenger in local, statewide or U.S. House races but not necessarily in presidential elections (Crespi, 1988, p. 114 and Panagakis, 1989, p. 1).

4. "Discriminant analysis is a statistical technique which allows the researcher to study differences between two or more groups or objects with respect to several variables simultaneously" (Klecka, 1980, p. 7). "Discriminant analysis has been used by "political scientists who examine voting behavior among citizens...they attemp to isolate variables which descriminate among citizens who will vote for Democrats versus Republicans, for example... (Klecka, 1980, p. 5).

Procedures for conducting and analyzing discriminant analysis results can be found in a number of texts. The Sage series on quantitative applications in the social sciences by William R. Klecka provides a thorough explanation of the multivariate procedures called discriminant analysis. The SPSS/PC+ Advanced Statistics manuals have a good step-by-step explanation of procedures and analysis techniques.

The *Washington Post*-ABC News poll data were analyzed using SPSS discriminant analysis procedures for SPSS-PC+. Minnesota Poll data were analyzed using SAS discriminant analysis procedures for SAS Ver. 6.1.

Appendix

TABLE 7A.1 October 30-November 4, 1988 Minnesota Poll

		Experimental Assignment of Undecided Vote				
	Survey Results *n=1,200*	*Election Results*	*Proportional*	*Equal*	*Main Challenger*	*Discriminant Analysis*
Dukakis	48%	52%	53%	52%	57%	52%
Bush	43	45	47	48	43	48
Other	<1	3	<1	<1	<1	1
No Opinion	9	—	—	—	—	—
Total absolute p.p. error		6	6	6	10	6
Total, less "other" p.p. error		3	3	3	7	3

TABLE 7A.2 November 2-5, 1988, *Washington Post*/ABC News Poll — Likely Voters From the Recall Sample of the Fifty State Poll

		Experimental Assignment of Undecided Vote				
	Survey Results *n=1,010*	*Election Results*	*Proportional*	*Equal*	*Main Challenger*	*Discriminant Analysis*
Dukakis	52%	54%	54%	54%	52%	54%
Bush	44	46	45	46	48	45
Other	1	—	1	1	1	1
No Opinion	3	—	—	—	—	—
Total absolute p.p. error			2	1	5	2
Total, less "other" p.p. error			1	0	4	1

TABLE 7A.3 October 27-30, 1992: Minnesota Poll Likely Voters

| | Survey Results n=1,104 | *Experimental Assignment of Undecided Vote* | | | | |
		Election Results	Propor- tional	Equal	Main Challenger	Discriminant Analysis
Clinton	44%	44%	48%	47%	53%	48%
Bush	28	32	31	31	28	31
Perot	18	24	20	21	18	20
Other	1	<1	1	1	1	1
No Opinion	9	—	—.	—	—	—
Total absolute p.p. error			10	8	18	10
Total, less "other" p.p. error			9	7	17	9

TABLE 7A.4 Oct. 28 - Nov. 1, 1992 *Washington Post*/ABC News Poll — Likely/Registered Voters

| | Survey Results n=722 | *Experimental Assignment of Undecided Vote* | | | | |
		Election Results	Propor- tional	Equal	Main Challenger	Discriminant Analysis
Clinton	43%	43%	45%	45%	48%	45%
Bush	35	38	37	37	35	37
Perot	16	19	17	17	16	17
Other	1	—	1	1	1	1
No Opinion	5	—	—	—	—	—
Total absolute p.p. error			6	6	12	6
Total, less "other" p.p. error			5	5	11	5

TABLE 7A.5 1992 Minnesota Overnight Polling Results Compared to Actual Vote, Undecideds Not Allocated/Likely Voters

	Oct. 27-30	Saturday, Oct. 31	Sunday, Nov. 1	Monday Nov. 2	Actual Vote
Clinton	44%	53%	40%	44%	44%
Bush	28	26	28	30	32
Perot	18	17	22	19	24
Other (VOL)	1	<1	2	1	<1
No Opinion	9	4	8	6	—

TABLE 7A.6 1992 Minnesota Overnight Polling Results Compared to Actual Vote, Undecideds Allocated

Allocated	Saturday October 31				Sunday November 1				Monday November 2				Actual Vote
	PP^a	EQ^b	MC^c	DA^d	PP	EQ	MC	DA	PP	EQ	MC	DA	
Clinton	55	54	57	55	43	42	48	43	47	46	48	45	44
Bush	27	27	26	27	30	30	28	34	32	32	30	32	32
Perot	18	18	17	18	23	24	22	21	20	21	19	22	24
Other	>1	>1	>1	>1	2	2	2	2	1	1	1	1	>1
Total p.p. error	22	22	26	22	6	6	12	8	8	6	12	4	
Less "other" p.p. error	22	21	26	22	4	4	10	6	7	5	11	3	

[a]PP=proportional assignment of undecided voters
[b]EQ=equal allocation of undecided voters (undesirable when the percent undecided is even and the number of candidates is odd, because of the large rounding error involved)
[c]MC=undecideds go to the main challenger
[d]DA=assignment using discriminant analysis

PART FOUR

Media Polls in the 1992 Election

8

The 1992 Election and the Polls: Neither Politics Nor Polling as Usual

Richard Morin

In the politically unsettled winter of 1992, Democratic Rep. Barney Frank of Massachusetts spoke to the Washington Press Club Foundation's annual congressional dinner.

"Voters are angry with politicians like me," he told his audience. "And they're angry with you in the media.

"Well, let me tell you something: The voters are no bargains, either."

It was that kind of election year. Anger on the left. Anger on the right. And in the middle, the once-silent majority appeared neither quiet nor complacent.

Some of this anger was directed at the polls. And, in the perfectly revealing light of hindsight, the public had a right to be occasionally perturbed by the analytic and methodological antics of some polling organizations in 1992, including my own.

At the same time, I would argue that 1992 saw a maturing of the major media polls. In terms of technique and content, the polls were more sophisticated. Journalists in the major news organizations used polls more wisely and more cautiously than in the past. One unequivocal sign of this growing maturity was the willingness of news organizations to quote or display the results of each other's polls in stories about their own surveys. *The New York Times* and *USA Today* institutionalized this practice in 1992, regularly publishing in a chart the results of their own and other news surveys done about the same time.

- In 1992, more polls proved to be better than fewer polls. In fact, the presidential campaign offered compelling evidence that America has more to fear from too few polls, rather than too many. With the increase in the number of presidential polls, the risks have diminished that one sensational but incorrect or misleading result from a single poll will go unchallenged.

- The media remained overly fond of horse race polls, and remained too dependent on them to shape our coverage. But lay the blame where it squarely belongs: with editors and reporters, not pollsters or the polls.

- At the same time, journalists paid too little — not too much — attention to non-horse race survey results, and either ignored or lightly reported a number of significant and often prescient findings that challenged prevailing conventional wisdom. In my view, one of the headlines of 1992 is how nearly all of the most important stories were first told by the polls, often to a disbelieving press corps.

- Tracking polls and focus groups were more widely used than ever this year, with mixed results. Give a hammer to a five year old and suddenly everything in the world needs hammering. Well, 1992 was the year that the media added national tracking polls and focus groups to its toolbox — and let the world beware.

Still, I would argue that the quality of the polls and poll stories in America's newspapers, news magazines and on the air increased dramatically. In a year that was widely reported as anything but politics-as-usual, journalists plumbed the depths of the polling record to inform their view of the present.

This, of course, was helped by the simple fact that a number of the major media polls are emerging from childhood to adolescence and young adulthood. *The Washington Post*-ABC News polling partnership turned 13 in 1994. CBS News established its in-house polling unit in 1967, and *The New York Times* and CBS News have conducted national election projects together since 1976. Gallup has been polling on presidential elections for nearly six decades.

The study of polling history has its rewards. As the major polls accumulate more trend data, the more useful polling becomes to reporters. At the same time, more reporters were comfortable with polls, understood and explained their limitations and used them effectively as reporting tools. Still, the media remained *data-rich but analysis poor*, perhaps the biggest failing of the popular polls in 1992.

That said, how'd we do in 1992? My own biased view is that we "nutty" pollsters (thank you Ross Perot) did OK. Looking at one admittedly gross measure — how close the pre-election polls came to the final outcome — we did better than we had any right to expect.

The last pre-election presidential preference polls not only predicted the right winner — not always a sure thing, as those who remember the 1980 presidential polls might recall — but the final poll numbers actually came close to the election-day results. The exit polls, too, were reasonably well behaved in 1992, with a few notable and troublesome exceptions.

For pollsters, the day after election day was remarkably easy. The major media polls had predicted that Clinton would win, and several had hit Clinton's 43 percent share of the vote right on the button.

The Washington Post and Polling the 1992 Election: Past as Prologue

Polling at *The Washington Post* changed significantly in 1992, reflecting changes in the way that this newspaper and others covered the last presidential campaign in the wake of what was generally viewed by many journalists as a dismal performance in 1988.

The Post abandoned two major projects closely identified with our election polling: the 50-State Poll and daily tracking polls in the primary elections. Instead, the Post decided to do more large-sample "theme" polls, to do more focus groups linked to those polls, and to do a weekly horse race poll designed, perhaps paradoxically, to wean us away from horse race journalism.

These changes were the consequence of a serious re-examination of the way we polled, wrote and reported the 1988 presidential race. Late in the summer of 1991, as we began planning coverage and polling projects for the coming presidential race, it was clear that *Post* political reporters were still deeply troubled by the 1988 campaign.

There was a disquieting sense that the media had stumbled badly (cf. Lewis, 1991). "The evaluation of 1988 was that the politicians understood our business better than we understood theirs," said Dan Balz, the Post's chief political writer.[1] The candidates — more specifically, the candidates' handlers — had "led the coverage and controlled the agenda." In the process, he said voters' concerns were lost as journalists buried themselves in recounting "the ebb and flow of the campaign."[2]

David Broder, perhaps the country's most respected political writer, was more direct. He repeatedly argued for campaign coverage that would, in his words, "give this election back to the voters." He frequently expressed dismay at what he saw as the Teddy White "Making of the President" style of political reporting: Long on the mechanics of politics and election strategy, but increasingly distant from the real interests of the voters.[3]

Such expansive rhetoric was to be expected in planning meetings. But

Broder and Balz were serious and committed to avoiding the insider, horse race-dominated coverage that had characterized 1988, and each had the clout internally to force a change. *Post* polling in 1992 also changed, perhaps even more dramatically than the coverage. Each of those changes was an attempt to use polling and the 1992 election campaign as a window into the concerns of voters, and to de-emphasize the results of the candidate preference questions — the horse race — in our polling stories.

The Horse Race: More Is Less

We deliberately decided to de-emphasize the horse race by saturating the "market" within the Post newsroom with horse race results. This was done by contracting with Fred Soulas and ICR Research, a private research company, to add the candidate preference questions every week onto ICR's 1,000-sample EXCEL national omnibus survey, thereby producing a weekly horse race number. ABC also joined in this weekly tracking poll, which began the week before the Democratic convention in July.[4]

It appeared to have the desired effect. The view of *The Post* political staff, of which this writer is an ex-officio member, was that more horse race numbers had indeed produced less horse race-driven copy. Adding the ballot test questions substantially reduced the costs of obtaining a horse race result, which dampened down the "we paid big bucks for it, we've got to run it big" mentality that too often forces horse race results into the paper and onto page one.

In fact, we decided not to do separate horse race poll stories, but to include the weekly results in the day's political story and run the numbers inside, almost always with a graphic that displayed the trend.

Unlike other coverage decisions, this pledge to downplay the horse race was generally kept. The notable exception was on September 22, when *The Post* and ABC's weekly tracking poll result showing Clinton with a 58 percent to 37 percent lead. The 21-point margin was included in the headline of the story that led the September 22 front page of *The Washington Post*. Other polls at this time suggested that Clinton held a more modest 10 to 15 percentage point lead at that time. In fact, the following week's tracking poll showed a nine-point Clinton advantage— but this result ran in a story inside the paper.

Playing the big Clinton lead on the top of the front page and the smaller Clinton advantage inside the paper led some to question the paper's objectivity. In fact, the newsroom received so many calls that the Post's Ombudsman, Joann Byrd, did a pointed but fair column noting that the disparity "was the perfect formula for fueling all the assumptions that the Post is supporting Bill Clinton for president."[5]

What happened? In my opinion, we made at least two mistakes. Highlighting the 21-point margin in the headline was bad journalism for two reasons. First, it was horse race journalism at its worst. The second mistake was to focus on the lead rather than the marginals in the headline. In any poll the margin difference between two results—Clinton's 21-point lead in this case—is a highly unreliable number, since a one-point shift in vote share in a two-candidate race translates into a two-point change in the lead. In short, it's a hype number, and journalists are seduced by it because it's a shorthand way of expressing the results and because it tends to overstate one candidate's advantage over another.

Reporters, in my view, should never highlight the lead in stories. If "leads" are used at all, they should be reported after the marginal results of the poll (Clinton was favored by 58 percent of those interviewed and Bush by 38 percent) and after the survey's margin of sampling error are reported. And the lead should never—not ever—appear in a headline, a practice that persists in the media.

But not at *The Post*, not anymore. As Executive Editor Leonard Downie noted in Byrd's Ombundsman's column, "We decided immediately the next day that we should not have, and never again will use a poll number in the headline."

What about that 21-point spread? Two possible explanations. First, the survey had a margin of sampling error of plus or minus four percentage points for registered voters at the .95 confidence level. Factor margin of sampling error into the 58 percent to 37 percent result, and the range for Clinton would have been 62 percent on the high end and 54 percent on the low end (plus or minus 4 percentage points about the point estimate of 58), while Bush's range could have been as high as 41 percent or as low as 33 percent. That means, given our confidence level, the margin likely was somewhere between 13 points (which others were reporting) or 29 points, which nobody was finding. Since the horse race result dropped immediately in the following week's survey, my own view is that the September 22 result was a "sport," or one of those times in which by chance alone you are left with results at the outer edge of the expected range.[6]

But that September stumble wasn't the only time that *Post*-ABC News survey results may have overestimated Clinton's strength. During July and early August, the weekly tracking survey produced a Clinton number that was consistently three to five points higher than other survey organizations. A subsequent review of those surveys identified the problem: An apparent over-sampling of black respondents. While blacks represented about 8 percent of the electorate in 1988, the percentage of blacks in our sampling of registered voters ranged between 10 to 15 percent. Since blacks overwhelmingly are Democrats, any skew in the black proportion added or subtracted directly from Clinton's share of the vote. When we switched after Labor Day to reporting results based only on those most likely to vote, the black proportion of the likely sample dropped back to 1988 levels.

Daily Tracking Polls

The Post and ABC News pioneered the media's use of daily tracking polls in 1984, when we correctly caught the shift to Gary Hart in the New Hampshire Democratic primary. Eight years later, The Post decided to go out of the daily tracking poll business.

The Post dropped daily tracking polls in 1992 because we had lost our stomach for horse race polls, and a tracking survey is the ultimate horse race poll.

It also appeared on the basis of our considerable experience that we bought very little for our money. A tracking poll costs about $2,000 to $5,000 a day to collect 250 to 500 interviews a night. And what did we get? In 1988, surprisingly little. My review of our 1988 election coverage found that each day of a week-long tracking poll typically produced a paragraph or two in the next day's newspaper.[7]

Tracking poll numbers also are about as perishable as fresh fish. The Post's deadlines (7 p.m. for our first edition) mean that we would report the latest tracking results two days after the interviews were done, taking the bloom off the numbers.

As it turned out, in 1992 other news organizations filled in the void left by The Post, with generally good results.

The 50-State Poll

One of the first tough decisions we made in 1991 was to abandon the Post's 50-State poll. It was a decision that was not lightly made; this project, which involved surveys in each of the 50 states and the District of Columbia, had been a featured part of our election coverage since 1984.

The 50-State poll was easily the single most controversial polling project of the 1988 campaign. In 1988, the project had involved separate horse race surveys in each of the 50 states and the District of Columbia. It cost nearly $100,000 to complete. It also was a panel-back project: respondents were interviewed over a two-and-a half-week period in late September and early October, then re-interviewed the week before the

November election to provide a final estimate of the vote as well as a look at who had switched their votes.[8]

Since we collected samples in each state, we and ABC could estimate the electoral vote by allocating each state to Dukakis, Bush or to the "tossup" column on the basis of the survey results in that state.

The results of the first round of interviewing were published two days before the second Bush/Dukakis debate and suggested that Dukakis trailed Bush badly. Perhaps because of the scope of the project and the prominent display of the results on ABC and in *The Post*, the poll fueled media speculation that absent a miraculous performance by Dukakis in the second debate, a Bush victory was inevitable.

The survey results and the timing of its release enraged Dukakis staffers, who shared their anger with reporters. ABC was singled out for more criticism than *The Post* — unfairly, in my view — largely because *The Post* chose to allocate states to Bush or Dukakis not merely on the results of the 50-State survey results, but on interviews by reporters with knowledgeable political observers in each state, as well as other polls done in that state.[9]

Less partisan critics noted that the sample sizes in some states were small: Fewer than 50 registered voters were interviewed in a few states that were safely in the Bush or Dukakis column, like Utah and the District of Columbia. And they noted that interviewing for the survey took three weeks to complete, increasing the possibility that the survey could be overtaken by events.

But the decision by *The Post* to abandon the 50-state project was not based on the small sample sizes in some states. Quite frankly, how large a sample do you need in the overwhelmingly black and Democratic District of Columbia to allocate its electoral votes to the Democratic candidate?[10]

Criticism of the three-week interviewing period was, however, less easy to ignore. But even that problem might have been surmounted simply by spending more money to put more interviewers on the telephone lines, thereby shortening the field period.

In the end, the 50-State poll was killed by credibility problems inside as well as outside the *Post* newsroom. The considerable cost of the project outweighed the benefits. And since reliable polls are increasingly available in most of the states, the 50-State project is history at *The Post*.[11]

Focus Groups

Two key decisions made in the fall of 1991 involved focus groups. The first was to dramatically increase the number of focus groups that *The*

Post did. In fact, the $47,000 that *The Post* spent in 1988 as its half share of the costs for the 50-State Project was earmarked for focus groups in 1992.

A second decision, prompted by now-managing editor Robert Kaiser, was to overhaul the way that *The Post* conducted focus groups. Kaiser shared my objections to the informal way that *The Post* had been conducting focus groups.

In the past, groups were organized by the research aide for the national desk. He or she typically would be directed by reporters to call community organizations — churches, PTAs or service clubs — and ask for the telephone lists of members or for recommendations as to who might be "good" in a group. Recruits would then gather in a hotel room to talk to *Post* reporters.

The results of that conversation were reported in great depth. In my view, these discussions came to be used as mini-polls to characterize the views of interesting slices of the electorate: undecided voters, Reagan Democrats or as was done in one case, "typical Iowans."

And the general perception was that focus groups had worked well for *The Post*. Reporters loved the voices and the nuanced discussion that these directed discussions produced.

But by 1991, doubts about what we were doing had surfaced. Criticism grew within *The Post* that we were using focus groups recklessly. Some staffers also were uncomfortable with the way we recruited participants. In the 1988 campaign, for example, haphazard recruiting resulted in a Post focus group in St. Louis being packed by members of Phyllis Schlafly's Eagle Forum.

Yet if 1992 really were to be the Year of the Voter at *The Washington Post*, we decided that focus groups, and the chance to engage real people in directed discussions, should play a more prominent role in our political coverage.

But these groups would be different. We contracted with Chilton Research, the national firm that does the field work for *Post*-ABC News surveys, to oversee recruiting of group participants. We decided to use professional focus group facilities. We would always link focus group projects to large random-sample surveys, to avoid mischaracterizing public opinion on the basis of what was said in our focus groups.[12]

The Post did 16 separate focus group/polling projects in 1992, including a group that explored the attitudes of Republicans who were voting for Clinton, another of non-voters and a third on Baby-boomers.

In my opinion, these groups generally served us well. The directed discussion provided the voices, while the surveys provided the quantitative foundation on which to characterize the attitudes of all Americans — not just group members — to the issues being discussed (see Traugott, Chapter 4).

But *The Post* still doesn't have it exactly right. I believe we're still overly addicted to heartfelt blather, no matter how unrepresentative or wrong. Sometimes poll results ended up being pushed out of a story entirely and into an accompanying graphic.[13]

And too often *The Post* worked backwards: First doing the poll and then convening a group to discuss interesting results, rather than doing a group first and then translating interesting or unexpected insights from participants into survey questions.

Other Media Polls

Despite our successes, *The Post* and America's media polling organizations have much to be modest about in 1992. Once again, news coverage in the final two weeks of the campaign was dominated by horse race journalism, largely because of the availability of daily tracking polls during the final weeks of the campaign.

In 1988, there was only one tracking poll, and it was being conducted by the Hotline, a daily news digest that's a must-read for the political community. Four years later, there were three tracking polls—four if you count the CBS-*New York Times* election-weekend poll.

The Hotline was still in the tracking business, beginning their three-day moving average early in the fall campaign. Gallup for CNN and *USA Today* began a two-day moving average tracking poll of registered voters in September, switching to likely voters in late October.

ABC News, *The Post*'s polling partner, independently did a tracking poll. ABC had not planned to do tracking, but the CNN-*USA Today* tracking poll spooked ABC, and they quickly pieced together a tracking poll of their own.

The sheer number of surveys offered the opportunity to do a daily "grand mean" of the polls to gauge the state of the campaign, particularly when the comparison included more rigorously done large sample surveys done at about the same time.

But I would argue that the flood of numbers also proved too seductive to daily reporters, and after a campaign in which many news organizations had successfully downplayed horse race journalism, we all fell off the wagon, and the coverage, particularly during the final week of the campaign, came to be dominated by the horse race polls.

In the high anxiety of the final week of the campaign, we at *The Post* nearly undid our decision not to join ABC's tracking, particularly when a Gallup tracking poll reported that Clinton and Bush were virtually deadlocked. In the end, we did not join ABC or cobble together something of our own, but only because we already were over-budget.

These widely followed tracking polls were able to correct for some of the problems that tracking polls inherently face. In order to turn around daily samples of between 800 and 1,000 voters, shortcuts had to be taken, including abandoning or severely modifying callback schedules.

Most organizations tried to compensate by building in at least one callback to numbers that had not been reached the previous night, but, as Gallup has acknowledged, every reported result of their tracking poll was based on a sample that disproportionately contained respondents reached on the first attempt.

As those who have done tracking polls know, among the bigger problems with tracking polls is that when the numbers are most important, the results are the least reliable. I'm talking about interviews done the weekend before the election on the very worst days for interviewing: Friday night and Saturday.

In 1992, some organizations acknowledged this problem and, like the Hotline Poll and campaign polls, did not interview on Fridays or Saturdays. Others did, with unsatisfactory results. *The New York Times*, for example, noted in its election-day story that the results of Saturday and Sunday interviews showed Clinton holding an 11-point lead over George Bush, a margin that I would suggest from experience might have had more to do with the problems of capturing a good sample on the weekends than on the attitudes of the electorate.

Gallup had other, more troublesome problems with their tracking poll for CNN and *USA Today*. Gallup decided to wait until the week before the election to begin basing its results on likely voters, not merely all registered voters.

One result was that Clinton's double-digit lead instantly and mysteriously vanished. Then, over the election-eve weekend, Clinton's lead in the Gallup tracking poll grew from two points to eight on Monday and then magically to 12, as Gallup decided to allocate virtually all of the undecided vote to challenger Clinton.

Gallup officials argue that the changes in Clinton's lead over the weekend reflected real shifts in the electorate. But they also agree that their decision to allocate all the undecided vote to Clinton may have, in retrospect, been unwise.

Gallup may have been trying to be too bold. Undecideds at the end of the campaign are admittedly messy (see Daves & Warden, Chapter 7); "undecided" isn't a choice in the voting booth. To eliminate them, Gallup decided to allocate the undecided vote on the basis of their analysis of previous presidential elections.

That analysis suggested virtually all undecided voters in presidential elections go to the challenger, which they believed would be Clinton.

Said Larry Hugick, who directed the Gallup poll: "What seems to have occurred is that voters who traditionally had swung to the challenger in the end, swung to a different kind of challenger, Ross Perot."

Election-day exit polling by Voter Research & Surveys, the television network consortium, fared reasonably well in its first presidential test.

One obvious slip-up: An early miscall of Georgia for Clinton. VRS first gave Georgia to Clinton early on election night after its state exit poll showed, incorrectly as it turned out, a big Clinton win by about eight points. When early vote counts indicated a much tighter race, VRS changed their decision, saying the race was too close to call. Later, after most of the votes had been tallied and Clinton was maintaining a modest lead, they again called Georgia for Clinton.

Some VRS subscribers also wondered why the national exit poll results suggested that Clinton held an 11-point lead nationally when the final vote was much closer.

But as VRS warned, the numbers during the day were only for guidance (see Mitofsky & Edelman, Chapter 6). Warren Mitofsky of VRS told everybody not to be surprised if they changed, "based on the results of later voting and other adjustments."

Those are important caveats. But they should not distract from the underlying problem, namely that the national exit poll appeared to have been off, and by a considerable margin.

One little appreciated fact about the national presidential exit polls is that they are weighted to election outcomes late on election night or soon thereafter, and that the actual results of the polls often are relatively far from the mark. Unweighted results of the ABC exit poll in 1988, for example, suggested George Bush and Michael Dukakis in a virtual dead heat.[14]

And in 1992, the early edition of *The New York Times* on the day after the election suggested a big Clinton win because it was based exclusively on exit poll results.

Of course *The Times* was not alone. Several months earlier, *The Washington Post* jumped offside based on a VRS exit poll. Early exit poll results through the afternoon on primary day in the New Hampshire suggested that Republican Pat Buchanan was within 10 percentage points of Bush, prompting a massive deployment of reporters—and an early-edition story line suggesting a symbolic upset—that vanished when the votes actually were counted.

And that's how the year ended, somewhat badly for the polls. And the sour taste of those surveys may linger longer than the good work done by America's pollsters in 1992.

But a more benevolent view—a more accurate view, I argue—emerges when one looks across the whole of 1992 to see how both quantitative and qualitative research tools were used to help understand the 1992 presidential election.

Predicting the "Unpredictable"

By February or early March of 1992 , it was abundantly clear that it
would be a singular year in American politics. Perhaps a watershed year.
It already was being characterized in print as an "unpredictable" year.
Not true. Not even close. I believe that election year 1992 was anything but "unpredictable." Most of the major surprises of 1992 were no
surprise to dedicated poll watchers. In fact, a review of polling done in
the winter of 1991 and early in 1992 suggests that, if anything, the political press corps might have paid too little—not too much—attention to the
polls.

Consider what the polls were telling us early in the campaign.

Trust in government was at an all-time low, and nearly everyone was
worrying about the economy.[15] The early primary exit polls showed that
eight out of 10 Democrats and Republicans believed the economy was in
trouble. Unemployment yo-yoed during the winter and spring, and consumer confidence as revealed in the polls had plummeted to new lows.

As a result, George Bush had become the Limbo President, with
Beltway insiders wondering how low his job approval rating would go.[16]
The Democrats, meanwhile, were trying hard to decide between Elmer
Fudd—Paul Tsongas—or Elmer Gantry—Bill Clinton—or they were
ignoring the primaries altogether. And three out of four Republicans in
the early primaries were casting their votes for someone other than
George Bush.

A sour economy. An unappealing set of candidates in both parties.
And growing disenchantment with government and politics-as-usual.
The stage was set for a challenge from outside mainstream politics. Enter
Ross Perot, right on cue, though no one at the time treated him seriously.

"Treated him seriously"—those are words to linger over. It was the
voters, of course, who discovered Perot and made him into a viable candidate. But I would also argue that it was the polls that legitimized Perot
as a president candidate, forcing the political establishment to treat Perot
and his message seriously.

Only then, and very late in the game, was Perot taken to be a serious
candidate by the political press corps. Certainly at *The Post*, political
reporters tended, in my view, to be either indifferent or actively antago-
nistic toward Perot even as his popularity rose in the polls. Said political
editor Bill Hamilton of *The Washington Post*: "Before he moved way up in
the polls, we didn't take him seriously. The polls made Ross Perot."

The Democrats Love New York

I grew up only a few blocks from the beach in sunny Southern California. That perhaps explains why I've only loved New York once in the many times I've been there. It was at the Democratic convention last July. The city was clean. Police were everywhere.

And everyone, even the Democrats, were smiling.

Particularly Bill Clinton. Consider what happened during Bill and Al's excellent adventure in New York.

Thanks to a world-record convention bounce, Clinton soared over a hapless President Bush to take a stupendous lead in everybody's post-convention polls. Perot conveniently quit on Thursday of convention week, and the polls told us that almost immediately three out of four Perot supporters shifted to Clinton.

A week after the convention, a *Post*-ABC News poll showed Clinton leading President Bush by a 58 percent to 29 percent margin among registered voters. And we were soon eclipsed by a Harris survey that reported a 30-point lead.

What a bounce. What a lead. A close election? Hardly. But that was wrong. Beneath the froth of the bounce, the real election was beginning to emerge, and I believe journalists were remarkably diligent in 1992 in reporting the transience of these post-convention bounces and identifying the real factors that ultimately would make the election reasonably close.

Confused voters back then rightfully were asking, how can it be close in November with Clinton now ahead by 29 percentage points?

Actually, it was easy. James Campbell, a political scientist at LSU who's studied post-convention bounces, noted as did others that about half of the first-convention bounce dissipates by the second convention. And, he said, the typical first convention bounce further erodes at an average rate of about three points a month to election day.[17]

So by Labor Day, the traditional start of the campaign season, Campbell and others were widely quoted as predicting that Clinton would have about a 10-point lead on Labor Day—within striking distance for Bush. Which is about what happened.[18]

The way journalists handled the "bounce" stories this year was one small but important sign of how journalists were far more likely this year to correctly interpret as well as merely report survey results.

In 1988, the bounce was reported much differently. A number of newspapers, including *The New York Times*, reported how the middle class had moved in mass back to the Democrats and Dukakis after the Democratic convention in Atlanta. Unfortunately for the national press corps and Dukakis, those voters bounced right back after the Republican Convention and stayed with Bush through the campaign.

The Bush Collapse

As the Republicans gathered in Houston, pollsters and reporters who were busily plumbing the depths of polling trend reports were noting that, less than two years after his triumph in the Gulf War, President Bush had staggered into Houston as arguably the most unpopular incumbent president ever to seek re-election in the past five decades.

The Gallup trend was ominous for the GOP: Compared to every president since Franklin Roosevelt, Bush had set new standards of under-performance for a sitting president, all of which was lavishly reported in the major national newspapers. Among his dubious statistical achievements, as reported in *The Post*, *The Times* and *The Wall Street Journal*, among others:[19]

- One of the biggest sustained drops in popularity ever. Bush's approval rating dropped 57 points in *Post*-ABC News polls between the conclusion of the Gulf War and the GOP convention. Harry Truman, the Gallup record-holder, saw his popularity plunge by 55 points in a 15 month period after World War II.
- Lowest job approval rating of any president at a similar point in their presidency. In fact, only three presidents since World War II had lower approval ratings than Bush at any time in their administrations, much less 10 weeks away from an election.
- Highest disapproval rating of any incumbent president standing for re-election. And it was even worse than that: In terms of job performance, Bush arguably was as unpopular with the American people as Richard Nixon was in the worst days of his failed presidency.

Bush also came to Houston on the wrong side of another modern-era first. Democratic nominee Bill Clinton's 26-point lead in *Post*-ABC News polls was the biggest advantage a challenger has ever enjoyed over an incumbent president seeking re-election at a similar point in the campaign. In the past six decades, only Barry Goldwater was further behind in the summer polls.

The Final Weeks

During the final five weeks of the campaign, it was becoming increasingly clear that there was little that could be done by Bush to avoid defeat.
Bush's hopes for re-election were growing bleaker by the day. Even the GOP's own polls detected no shrinkage in Bill Clinton's lead. With five weeks to go, many journalists attempted to use polling data to examine what Bush could do to close the gap. Remarkably, the numbers suggested that he could do very little.
Here's what was left for Bush and first-pal James Baker to play with as the race entered the home stretch:

- Five more weeks of the campaign, and the possibility that a truly masterful effort might erase the gap between Bush and Bill Clinton. Unfortunately for the Republicans, the polling record was rather clear about what little impact "good" campaigns have on the vote. Yet as even a cursory review of polling data from earlier campaigns suggests, campaign wizardry alone doesn't work when the economy is sour, voters are angry and your candidate sleeps in the White House.
- They could rely on advertising, millions of dollars of it — particularly negative advertising designed to cool the voters' infatuation with Bill Clinton and bring these prodigal voters back to Bush. But as surveys in the final weeks of the election disclosed, negative campaigning, which the Republicans used artfully four years ago, wasn't what it used to be in 1992. And Willie Horton, the poster boy of the 1988 campaign, arguably worked against Bush in 1992.[20]
- The presidential debates. Presidential debates historically have had little impact on voting decisions — including the 1960 presidential debate that convention wisdom holds turned the tide of the election toward John F. Kennedy. The remarkable series of presidential and vice presidential debates may have had somewhat more of an impact, boosting Perot's share of the vote , surveys suggest that while they may have boosted Perot's share of the vote, they merely, they had little substantive impact again in 1992.

Those were somewhat contrarian notions when I and others wrote them. In my opinion, too many political journalists need to believe that campaigns push votes around. But the evidence in presidential races suggests otherwise. In most presidential elections, the polls typically remain remarkably stable through most of the post-Labor Day campaign season—as they did again in 1992.

In fact, with few exceptions, the candidate who leads in the June Gallup pre-convention polls, ultimately wins the race. Democratic pollster Peter Hart says he pays close attention to first polls in September, arguing that they're a remarkably reliable guide to who will win in November.

What about 1992? Perot's early October entry complicates the analysis, but an examination of *Post*-ABC News trend data suggests relatively little movement after Labor Day. In fact, the *Post*-ABC News weekly survey ending on September 13 found that in a three-way contest, Clinton was the choice of 45 percent of those interviewed, while Bush was preferred by 33 percent and Perot by 16 percent.

Even given the vagaries of sampling error and the unsettled nature of the campaign itself, the stability of the 1992 campaign is apparent. In the 26 *Post* and ABC News polls during the last two months of the campaign (including ABC tracking), Clinton always led, though occasionally by statistically insignificant margins; Bush always came in second, and Perot third. In those polls, Clinton's share of the projected vote varied between 41 percent and 50 percent. Bush's vote ranged between 30 percent and 38 percent, while the Perot total ranged from a low of 6 percent in early September to a high of 21 percent after the debates.

Polling and the 1992 Debates

The polling record also was clear on the impact of the 1992 presidential and vice-presidential debates, which were riveting television—perhaps the single most memorable feature of the last campaign.

A review of *Post* and ABC News trend data suggests that Perot's showing in the debates boosted his projected share of the likely vote from the 12-15 percent range before the debates to 21 percent in late October. But this post-debate bounce appeared to dissipate somewhat, while Clinton and Bush's share of the vote remained largely unchanged during the debates and immediately after. (*Post*-ABC News and other polls suggest that Bush may have closed slightly in the final 10 days of the campaign).

Those results should not be surprising. Three decades of polling suggests that relatively few presidential debates — and perhaps only one — have really been felt on the bottom line on election day, and the debate that really mattered did not occur in 1960.

The "decisive" debate in presidential campaign folklore, and the one that I believe still overly influences the media's view of the power of presidential debates, was the first Nixon-Kennedy debate in 1960, the first presidential debate to be televised. Conventional wisdom has it that a young, vibrant John F. Kennedy won the election on national TV by creaming a sickly, disheveled and unshaven Richard Nixon in the country's first televised debate.

The truth is somewhat less dramatic. What's typically ignored is the fact that Kennedy held a 50 percent to 46 percent advantage over Nixon in the June Gallup survey, months before Nixon stepped onto the stage, a fact that was sporadically reported. Even in late August, after the convention bounce and bounce-backs but before the first debate, Kennedy held a statistically insignificant 48 percent to 47 percent lead over Nixon in Gallup polls, about equal to his final margin over Nixon.

And reviews of survey data from the 1960s suggest that the debates had little impact on the overall vote. A post-election Gallup survey in 1960 found that only one percent of the electorate said the debates were a major factor in determining their vote—and among this admittedly small group, the two candidates divided the vote.

There was, however, one presidential debate that may have moved around a significant number of votes. According to Andrew Kohut, director of the Times Mirror Foundation Center for the People and the Press, the only debate that really has matter occurred in 1980: the second debate, when Ronald Reagan went to Cleveland behind in the polls, moved ahead by four points after the debate and surged to 10 by election day.

Forward to 1996

At *The Post* and, I strongly, suspect, at other major news organizations, planning for the 1996 campaign began almost immediately after election day 1992.

The lessons of 1992 that *The Post* learned were not forgotten. Our attempt to reign in horse race coverage were viewed internally as a qualified success. "We did a better job in 1992 with the horse race," Balz said. "It's not that we switched 180 degrees; after all, telling people who's ahead and why is something that's important to our readers. But I felt more comfortable about the balance between horse race and other kinds of coverage." The combination of focus groups and national surveys also, in my view, worked well to characterize responsibly public attitudes in an engaging, approachable way. The 50-State project and daily tracking polls were not missed.

Yet the most intriguing polling projects in 1992 were not done by *The Post* or other national newspapers or the television networks. It was the work of *The Charlotte Observer*, which built on an earlier experiment by another Knight Ridder newspaper, *The Wichita Eagle*.

Briefly characterized, *The Observer* experiment attempted to use qualitative and quantative research techniques to identify voter's concerns, and inform voters of the candidates' positions on those issues. Polls, focus groups and community meetings organized by the newspaper worked together to determine the "voter's agenda," and that agenda directly shaped coverage. Other techniques like regularly running brief summaries of each candidate's position on the major issues attempted to increase voters' knowledge of issues and the candidates. It was, in part, a mature and more rigorous and sophisticated version of what we at *The Post* had somewhat haphazardly attempted to do in 1992.[21]

In my view, the Charlotte experiment represents a glimpse into the future of political reporting, a future in which coverage decisions are shaped and informed by rigorous research, producing truly issue-driven coverage that will finally and forever put horse race driven journalism out to pasture.[22]

Notes

1. Balz was *The Post*'s national editor in 1988 and oversaw the newspaper's election coverage with then-political editor Ann Devroy.

2. National political columnists Jack W. Germond and Jules Witcover offered a critical analysis of both the performance of the press and the presidential candidates in 1988 in their book *Whose Broad Stripes and Bright Stars: The Trivial Pursuit of the Presidency*. They argued that the election was "decided on the basis of technique and not issues."

3. Broder also pleaded publicly for issues-based campaigns and for reinventing political coverage, notably in an October, 1990 op-ed column in *The Post* that was appropriately headlined, "Sick of Issueless Campaigns," and in a longer piece in the Sunday opinion section of *The Post* that same year.

4. *The Post* and ABC had added the "horse race" questions to weekly ICR polls in the fall of 1988; the success of that experiment prompted both organizations to commit to an expanded effort in 1992.

5. Byrd's column ran Oct. 10, one of several critical but fair columns on the misuse of survey results by *Post* reporters during the 1992 and 1993 election seasons.

6. In fact, as you do more horse race polls, the odds increase that one of the polls will, by chance alone, produce a result that's outside the margin of sampling error.

7. Sometimes tracking results were misused. In the week before the 1988 Illinois Democratic primary, a *Post* writer cited as evidence of increasing support

for Jesse Jackson a one-point increase in Jackson's proportion of the vote.

8.   A total of 10,118 self-described likely voters were interviewed in the first phase of the project.

9.   Two of that project's most responsible critics, political scientists Thomas E. Mann and Gary R. Orren, noted in their 1992 book *Media Polls in American Politics* that the controversy over the 50-State project in 1992 was mainly "political, that the timing of the poll's release may have cost Dukakis the election." They also raised questions about the small sample sizes and relatively long field period.

10.   Only 45 registered voters were interviewed in the District, with Dukakis the choice of 77 percent of those surveyed and Bush favored by 18 percent. Some critics ignored, however, the fact that those small samples were drawn in states where the election was not in doubt like the heavily black and Democratic District of Columbia. For example, the margin of sampling error for the D.C. sample is large, but the Dukakis percentage is big enough to conclude at the .95 confidence level that Dukakais led Bush when the survey was taken. Dukakis eventually won 83 percent of the vote in D.C.

11   ABC News operated a redesigned version of the 50-State project in 1992 independent of *The Post*.

12.   These changes dramatically increased the cost of focus group projects. In 1988, the typical direct cost of a focus group was less than a thousand dollars (one cost $74 to rent the meeting room and provide snacks to participants), not including travel costs for reporters and staff time to recruit participants. In 1992, the Post paid between $2,500 to $4,000 to do a focus group, which included recruitment costs, renting the facility, recording and transcribing the group. We also paid each participant $25 to $35, the standard participation fee.

13.   The problem: the now-numberless "survey" story moves over the news wires and is reprinted by other newspapers. But technical limitations of the wire prevents the computer-generated graphic from moving with the story. The result: The survey results end up being lost to all but local readers.

14.   *The Post* ran a detailed demographic breakdown of ABC's unweighted 1988 exit poll results in its first post-election editions, breakdowns that suggested to several perceptive callers that the election had ended in a virtual tie.

15.   In a *Post*-ABC News poll in late October 1991, 63 percent of those interviewed said they trusted the government in Washington "to do what is right" only some or none of the time; 71 percent said the country was headed in the wrong direction and 56 percent believed the economy was getting worse. And in subsequent months, each of those results worsened.

16.   According to *Post*-ABC surveys, 45 percent of those interviewed in January, 1992 approved of the way Bush was handling the presidency. In March of 1991 after the end of the Gulf War, his job approval rating stood at 90 percent; in August of 1992 it had sunk to 33 percent.

17.   The Post conducted a special series of three polls to measure the "bounce" phenomenon. Those surveys were conducted before, during and after the Democratic Convention in July, 1992.

18.   In a survey of registered voters completed September 13, Clinton was the choice of 45 percent of those interviewed, Bush 33 percent and Perot, who would re-enter the race in October, 16 percent.

19. An expanded analysis of presidential approval ratings in the post-World War II period appeared in *The Post* under this writer's byline in the Aug. 17, 1992.
20. Ellen Hume, a media analyst at the Shorenstein-Barone Center for Media Studies at Harvard University and a former *Wall Street Journal* reporter, said in October of 1992: "Journalists were used in 1988 because they amplified the propaganda by passing it through without critiquing it. This year, people have been much more sophisticated....They are not simply repeating the advertisement. The Willie Horton case, above all taught reporters this lesson."
21. And yes, the media, including *The Post*, still have far to go. Witness the evauluation of Maxwell E. McCombs, professor of jounrnalism at the University of Texas, who sugggested in the Winter, 1992 Journalism Quarterly that "despite numerous promises" by the media to emphasize the issues, all Americans learned from the 1992 presidential election coverage "is that Gennifer is spelled with a 'G'!"
22. Some journalists consider certain aspects of Charlotte experiment to be potentially troubling intrusions by the media into the political process. In particular, some object to newspapers organizing and then covering community meetings to discuss political issues.

9

The Evolving Use of Public Opinion Polls by *The New York Times*: The Experience in the 1992 Presidential Election

Michael R. Kagay

Throughout 1992, *The New York Times* used public opinion polling to aid its reporters, editors, and readers in understanding how the American electorate was reacting to the personalities, issues, and events of the Presidential election campaign. The polls included six major types in 1992:

1. Frequent national telephone polls to measure how voters' perceptions and attitudes shifted as the primary and general election campaigns progressed from January to November.
2. A regional poll in the South early in the campaign cycle when local electorates there were "ahead" of the rest of the country by virtue of the primary election campaigns conducted in their region.
3. Statewide exit polls of voters leaving voting places on primary election day in states having major presidential primaries from February through June.
4. Polling of delegates to the national party nominating conventions (*The Times* polled Democratic delegates; CBS News polled the Republican delegates).
5. Statewide telephone polls in the autumn in Florida, Texas, Ohio, Illinois, and New York to see how the national contest was playing out in individual battleground states.
6. A national exit poll of voters leaving voting stations across the

country on Election Day in November, including additional exit polling in several key states.

Our telephone polls were conducted mostly with our polling partners, CBS News. The exit polls we analyzed were conducted by Voter Research and Surveys, the agency created in 1990 by ABC News, CBS News, CNN, and NBC News (see Mitofsky & Edelman, Chapter 6). These polls were used in several ways. First, in the 12 months running up to the election, they formed the basis of 50 news articles in *The Times* that relied heavily on polling data, usually including graphic or tabular presentations of detailed results. Second, they were incorporated to a lesser extent into another 150 articles that integrated one or more particularly relevant polling results with more traditional reportorial materials. Third, they also resulted in free-standing graphics. Fourth, they indirectly helped to inform reporting and editing during the election year by permitting reporters and editors to check hunches, to test the claims of candidates and pundits, and to avoid being manipulated.

The Times has been involved in directly conducting its own public opinion polls by telephone since 1975 in New York City and 1976 nationwide (cf. Kagay, 1991). In 1992, as in previous years, the questionnaires were developed jointly with CBS News from topics suggested by correspondents, editors or producers in both organizations, winnowed and developed by the two organizations' polling directors and their staffs. CBS News drew the samples and took responsibility for the data processing. *The Times* oversaw the field work, including the recruiting, training, and monitoring of interviewers. One change from prior election years was that in 1992 we utilized a C.A.T.I. system (Computer Assisted Telephone Interviewing), located at CBS News, in which our interviewers read poll questions from a computer screen and entered responses using a computer keyboard. Once the data were ready, each news organization had independent access to the data sets, and each interpreted and reported its findings independently. Extra zest is added to our joint operation in my view because every poll receives two simultaneous but independent analyses by separate research teams, each of which takes satisfaction in discovering some more subtle finding than the other. The actual data sets of all our polls have been archived both in the Roper Center for Public Opinion Research at the University of Connecticut and in the Inter-university Consortium for Political and Social Research at the University of Michigan.

In 1992, as in previous election years, *The Times* conducted a systematic program of polling research designed to cover the American public's reactions to the campaign. We viewed the campaign as a year-long process in which the public could take the measure of those who would lead, and our polls were designed to find out what the public learned and concluded. Drawing on examples from our polls, the following sections discuss our major goals in this program, many of the particular devices we used in pursuit of those goals, and some of the most important conclusions we reached. At each point we also indicate the headline, byline, and publication date of the articles in the newspaper that reported our findings and conclusions. The chapter is organized into sections, according to the type of use we made of polls.

Understanding the Political Setting and Mood
as the 1992 Campaign Year Began

Every Presidential election year opens with a unique political setting that confers on each political party an initial balance of advantages and disadvantages. Such initial conditions do not necessarily determine the ultimate outcome of the election, of course; they can subsequently be modified by the candidates who come forward, the campaign strategies they pursue, the issues that catch fire, the events — domestic and foreign — that transpire during the course of the year.

On the international scene during the years leading up to 1992 the American public witnessed the collapse of Communism in Eastern Europe, the breakup of the Soviet Union, the end of the Cold War, and the allied victory in the Persian Gulf War. In the spring and summer of 1991 the national euphoria that followed the Gulf War made George Bush's re-election seemingly certain. Such appearances can have consequences. One important consequence was that several major Democratic politicians decided to pass up 1992, declining to run for their party's nomination.

On the domestic scene, Americans experienced 11 years of Republican control of the White House, a "Reagan revolution" that had probably run most of its course, a mounting federal budget deficit that constrained the government's ability to undertake new programs, and a downturn in the economy as the boom of the '80s ended and recession set in. For much of 1990 and 1991 the Persian Gulf crisis and war had focused the public's attention on dramatic events abroad, but by the autumn of 1991 Americans were shifting their gaze and their priorities back to the nation's domestic problems.

The Times employed several polling devices to inform its reporters, editors, and readers about the political setting and public mood as the 1992 election year approached. These allowed us to probe the strengths and vulnerabilities of George Bush as he sought a second term as President and to examine some of the early indicators of his likely electoral fate in the year to come. The signs, we reported at the time, pointed to a more competitive election year than had previously seemed likely or even possible.

A Continuing Referendum on the Incumbent's Stewardship

Throughout the President's tenure in office, the *Times*/CBS News Poll regularly measured his job performance rating by asking the question: "Do you approve or disapprove of the way George Bush is handling his job as President?" Introduced by George Gallup in the 1930's, this question permits a continuing public referendum on an incumbent's stewardship between elections. Two additional questions get more specific — probing the President's handling of foreign policy, and of the economy, in particular.

By November, 1991, a year before Election Day, the spectacular boost in ratings George Bush received from the Gulf War had clearly faded. Table 9.1 shows the dramatic surge and decline. Before the Gulf war — at the end of October, 1990, two years prior to Election Day — overall approval of Mr. Bush stood at 52 percent. That shot up to 79 percent after the bombs began to fall on Baghdad in January 1991, as Americans rallied around their flag, their troops, and their Commander-in-Chief. The President's approval rating peaked at 88 percent in early March immediately after the quick ground assault ended successfully for the allies. This spectacularly high level matched, or came within an inch of matching, the two historic high-water marks recorded in Gallup polls during the past 50 years, both set by Harry S. Truman as fighting in World War II ended in Europe during the spring of 1945 (when Truman got 87 percent approval) and in the Pacific during the summer of 1945 (when Truman got 92 percent approval).

But after the Persian Gulf War, euphoria and victory parades could not be sustained indefinitely, and Mr. Bush's ratings began to ebb during the summer and fall of 1991. By late November Mr. Bush received 51 percent approval, returning him to the level that existed a year earlier, before the war began.

Mr. Bush's overall job rating would not rise above 50 percent again before Election Day. In fact, it did not even level off, but continued to decline, drifting downward through the 40's during the first quarter of 1992, and hovering in the mid-to-high- 30's during the remaining months before the election. President Bush's total slide from his peak to his nadir was more than 50 percentage points. This was an ominous sign: since scientific polling began, Harry S. Truman in 1948 was the only incumbent President who had been re-elected with ratings so low during an election year.

TABLE 9.1 A Continuing Referendum on George Bush's Stewardship[a]

Dates of Poll	*His Job as President[b]*	*Foreign Policy*	*the Economy*	*Percent Saying the National Economy Is Very Good or Fairly Good*
	Percent Approving of the Way George Bush Is Handling . . .			
Oct. 8-10, 1990	60	63	36	30
Oct. 28-31, 1990	52	58	30	33
Jan. 27-28, 1991	79	74	43	38
March 4-6, 1991	88	83	42	45
April 1-3, 1991	80	76	38	42
June 3-6, 1991	75	68	41	42
Oct. 15-18, 1991	67	69	33	32
Nov. 18-20, 1991	51	57	25	24
Jan. 6-8, 1992	48	59	23	17
Jan. 22-25, 1992	44	44	21	21
Feb. 19-20, 1992	42	51	18	17
Feb. 26-March 1, 1992	40	47	19	17
March 26-29, 1992	41	50	18	19
April 20-23, 1992	39	44	21	24
July 8-11, 1992	36	47	18	21
Aug. 11-14, 1992	38	48	14	21
Sept. 9-13, 1992	42	56	19	20
Oct. 2-4, 1992	37	54	16	19
Oct. 20-23, 1992	40	54	20	23
Oct. 27-30, 1992	37	52	18	23

[a]Based on all adults in 19 *New York Times*/CBS News polls and one CBS News poll (Jan. 27-28, 1991).
[b]The four questions were: "Do you approve or disapprove of the way George Bush is handling his job as President?", "Do you approve or disapprove of the way George Bush is handling foreign policy?", "Do you approve or disapprove of the way George Bush is handling the economy?", "How would you rate the condition of the national economy these days? Is it very good, fairly good, fairly bad or very bad?"

Mr. Bush's more specific ratings on handling foreign policy and the economy enabled us to look beneath the surface and understand more of what was happening. During the two years charted in Table 9.1, the public always gave George Bush higher marks on foreign policy than on the economy. Ominously, by November 1991, a year prior to the election, his economic rating sank into the 20's, and it spent much of 1992 in the teens. Such a low level had not been recorded since 1979 when Jimmy Carter's Presidency also was endangered by economic difficulties, including in his case double-digit inflation.

Fatefully for George Bush, as the nation's attention turned from victory in the Persian Gulf to the country's economic problems at home, the public's priorities were shifting from an area of Bush's strength to an area of Bush's vulnerability. By the end of 1991 and the beginning of 1992 the trend in the President's job performance ratings offered warning signs for all who cared to see. These signs and their implications for a competitive election year were analyzed by the _Times's_ national political correspondent, Robin Toner, in two front page articles: "Casting Doubts: Economy Stinging Bush" on November 26, 1991, and "Poll Shows Price Bush Pays for Tough Economic Times" on January 10, 1992.

Gloomy Perceptions of the Economy and the Nation's Prospects

Times/CBS News polls normally include a question specifically intended to chart the public's perception of the country's economy: "How would you rate the condition of the national economy these days? Is it very good, fairly good, fairly bad, or very bad?" Table 9.1 shows the readings we obtained over the two years from October 1990 to October 1992. Throughout all of 1992 the percentage of people saying very good or fairly good hovered in the low 20's or high teens. The troubled feelings about the economy were apparent even a year before the election — reported in the paper of October 22, 1991, by Richard L. Berke under the headline "America Grows Gloomier on Economy, Poll Shows." Social scientists have confirmed that such subjective perceptions about the economy — even when they are objectively inaccurate — take on a life of their own and have consequences. Consumer confidence, for example, affects the way people make purchasing decisions even if that subjective level of confidence is uninformed or unjustified. And econometric forecasting models, designed by social scientists to predict election results from _objective_ economic conditions, tend to have improved accuracy if they also include _subjective_ measures of how voters _think_ the economy is doing. Thus, although in retrospect it turned out that economic recovery actually began in the fourth quarter of 1992, it was not perceived at the time and Bush received no credit for it.

It is also important to know what priority the public gives to the economy at any given time compared to other problems facing the nation. The question we used to gauge the public's priorities, invented decades ago by George Gallup, is: "What do you think is the most important problem facing this country today?" By late 1991 and early 1992, it was clear that the public's number-one problem was indeed the economy. References to the economy in general, plus unemployment and recession specifically, had come to swamp all other topics. I reported this finding and analyzed seven years of shifting "number-one problems" — from

nuclear war, to illegal drugs, to the Persian Gulf crisis, to the economy —
in an October 20, 1991 article in *The Times's* Week in Review, headed "As
Candidates Hunt the Big Issue, Polls Can Give Them a Few Clues."
We also studied the national mood via yet another device, and found sentiment to be the gloomiest we had measured in 13 years. Periodically we
ask respondents to rate "the way things are going in the United States,"
using a scale of one to ten, with one being the worst possible situation
and ten being the best, and we then compute the average value of these
perceptions across all respondents in the poll. We also ask them to give
additional ratings to the situation five years in the past, and again five
years in the future, so that we can put their rating of the current situation
into perspective.

When we included these questions on a January 1992 *Times*/CBS
News poll we found that not since 1979, when Jimmy Carter hit bottom
during the period of "malaise," had the current situation looked so poor
to Americans and the country's future prospects seemed so dim. It was
clear that concerns over the economy were infecting Americans' outlook
about the entire national scene. Robin Toner reported these results in her
page-one article on January 28, 1992, under the headline "Bad News for
Bush as Poll Shows National Gloom."

Bush in a Close Race Against an "Unnamed" Democrat

Perhaps the most direct evidence that President Bush could be in trouble in his re-election bid was his slipping performance in trial heats
against a generic, unnamed Democratic opponent. As Table 9.2 shows,
by November 1991 Bush had fallen from a strong advantage into a virtual tie in such trial heats. By January and February 1992 Bush began to
lose by a small margin to a generic Democratic opponent.

At that early point in the election year, of course, the actual prospec-
tive Democratic nominees were not very well known, so an "unnamed"
Democrat ran better against Bush than did any of the actual Democratic
candidates who were seeking their party's nomination. But the warning
sign for the President was clear: the public was increasingly willing to
entertain the idea of a Democratic replacement for Mr. Bush. The 1992
election year had the prospect of being genuinely competitive.

Charting the Dynamics of the Campaign Year

We approached 1992 as a year-long cycle of events that was bound to
take some surprising turns. We therefore tried to design a program of
research that would be responsive, flexible, and adequate to the task.

TABLE 9.2 Preferences of Registered Voters for George Bush vs. an Unnamed
Democratic Opponent [a]

Dates of Polls	Prefer Bush[b]	Prefer Democratic Candidate (Unnamed)	Bush Advantage
March 30-April 2, 1990	36	26	+ 10
Aug. 16-19, 1990	41	26	+ 15
Jan. 27-28, 1991	43	28	+ 15
March 4-6, 1991	52	21	+ 31
April 1-3, 1991	51	23	+ 28
May 7-8, 1991	51	21	+ 30
June 3-6, 1991	46	22	+ 24
Aug. 18-22, 1991	42	29	+ 13
Oct. 15-18, 1991	49	28	+ 21
Nov. 18-20. 1991	39	37	+ 2
Jan. 6-8, 1992	41	38	+ 3
Jan. 22-25, 1992	36	44	- 8
Feb. 19-20, 1992	40	45	- 5
Feb. 26-March 1, 1992	40	44	- 4
March 26-29, 1992	43	41	+ 2

[a]Based on registered voters in 14 New York Times/CBS News polls and one
CBS News poll (Jan. 27-28, 1991).
[b]The question, beginning with the October 1991 poll, was "If the election for
President were held today, would you probably vote for George Bush or would
you probably vote for the Democratic candidate?" Prior to October 1991 the question was: "If George Bush runs for re-election in 1992, do you think you will
probably vote for George Bush or probably vote for the Democratic candidate?"

That required frequent polls with many time-series questions to be asked
again and again to capture the dynamics of the campaign process. One
such device used to record the twists and turns of 1992 was to ask registered voters whether their opinion of each of the major candidates was
"favorable," "not favorable," "undecided," or if they "hadn't heard
enough" about particular candidates yet to form an opinion. We asked
this series of questions on a frequent basis throughout the year, starting
with a large slate of candidates, gradually winnowing the names as particular candidates formally dropped out, and adding Ross Perot's name
in the spring once it was clear he was to be taken seriously.

A valuable feature of this question format is that it does not require
respondents to choose among the candidates; at any given time a respondent is free to like all of the candidates, or none of them, or some but not
others. Each candidate, in effect, runs against himself in an effort to generate more favorable than unfavorable impressions in the public mind.

This feature is particularly useful early in the season when the public often has quite different levels of familiarity with various candidates. Furthermore, by offering two ways for a respondent to admit that he or she has not yet formed any clear opinion of certain candidates ("undecided" in addition to "haven't heard enough"), these questions gave us a good handle on "non-opinions" about candidates at any given time, helping us chart the pace of "crystallization" of public opinion regarding several candidates who started the year as virtual unknowns.

Voters' Shifting (and Growing) Opinion of Bill Clinton

Table 9.3 presents registered voters' reactions to Bill Clinton over the year-long campaign cycle. A year before Election Day he was almost unknown to the general public: 88 percent were undecided or hadn't heard enough about Clinton as of October 1991. But those who had formed an opinion of Clinton were, on balance, positive in their early impression of him, a balance that increased slightly by the first month of 1992.

But allegations of past philandering and of manipulating his draft status during his youth were leveled at him just as the spotlight of publicity in the New Hampshire primary campaign was making Clinton better known to voters. By late February and early March about half the registered voters nationwide had come to hold some opinion of Clinton, but it was on balance negative. This continued throughout the spring and early summer, even as Clinton won many state primary elections and pulled ahead of, first Paul Tsongas, and then Jerry Brown.

During the primary election phase, of course, it is more important how a candidate is viewed by voters of his own party than by all registered voters. Among just Democratic voters Clinton's image retained a positive balance throughout this period. But even among them his negatives were high and rising as more people came to know him. Our polling aided Robin Toner in her close analysis of Clinton's image problem in her page one article on April 1, "Clinton Dogged by Voter Doubt, Poll of U.S. Says." She concluded that, although Clinton had clearly broken from the pack of Democratic hopefuls, he continued to confront a cloud of doubts and reservations about his character, even within his own party.

We studied Clinton's image problem not only in our national surveys but also in numerous statewide exit polls of voters leaving voting stations in the primary election states. In general, we found, Democratic primary voters seemed unswayed by the allegations regarding Clinton's character. Even in the first primary, in New Hampshire, just after the allegations surfaced and figured most dramatically in the news, only six percent of Democratic primary voters said allegations about Bill Clinton's

TABLE 9.3 Registered Voters' Shifting Opinion of Bill Clinton[a]

Dates of Poll	Favorable Opinion[b] (%)	Not Favorable Opinion (%)	Net Balance: Favorable Minus Not Favorable	Uncrystallized Opinion: Undecided or Not Heard Enough Yet
Oct. 15-18, 1991	7	5	+ 2	88
Jan. 6-8, 1992	11	6	+ 5	83
Feb. 19-20, 1992	24	26	- 2	49
Feb. 26-March 1, 1992	20	31	- 11	48
March 26-29, 1992	24	41	- 17	36
April 20-23, 1992	26	40	- 14	34
May 6-8, 1992	24	37	- 13	38
May 27-30, 1992	15	40	- 25	46
June 17-20, 1992	16	40	- 24	44
July 8-11, 1992	20	31	- 11	48
DEMOCRATIC PARTY CONVENTION AND PEROT WITHDRAWS				
Aug. 11-14, 1992	36	24	+ 12	39
REPUBLICAN PARTY CONVENTION				
Aug. 23-24, 1992	36	28	+ 8	35
Sept. 9-13, 1992	32	29	+ 3	39
Sept. 25-27, 1992	35	31	+ 4	33
PEROT RE-ENTERS CONTEST				
Oct. 2-4, 1992	34	35	- 1	30
Oct. 12-13, 1992	41	36	+ 5	23
Oct. 20-23, 1992	33	39	-6	28
Oct. 27-30, 1992	37	40	- 3	22
Oct. 29-Nov. 1, 1992	39	40	- 1	19

[a]Based on registered voters in 17 *New York Times*/CBS News polls and two CBS News polls (May 27-30 and Sept. 25-27).
[b]The question was: "Is your opinion of Bill Clinton favorable, not favorable, undecided or haven't you heard enough about Bill Clinton yet to have an opinion?"

character were a very important factor in their vote. By comparison, 58 percent said the economy and jobs were among the issues that mattered most in deciding their vote. This was our first evidence that Clinton's image problem, while bothersome to some, might not in itself be disqualifying in many voters' minds. Most voters seemed to be saying there were more important things to worry about. These findings were reported in text and graphics in Robin Toner's front page article on February 19 under the banner headline "Bush Jarred in First Primary; Tsongas Wins Democratic Vote." Clinton's second-place showing in New Hampshire could be interpreted as a considerable achievement since winner Paul Tsongas was from a neighboring state.

Likewise, in the next important test for Clinton, the Georgia primary which first indicated how the South would vote, the draft issue didn't seem to hurt Clinton much, even in a state with a strong military tradition. Again, the economy and jobs swamped all other considerations in voters' minds. Peter Applebome reported these exit poll findings in his March 4 article, "Clinton Draft Issue Doesn't Sway Most in Georgia."

As the primary season wore on, we also kept our eye on another exit poll question asked in many states: "Do you think Bill Clinton has the honesty and integrity to serve effectively as President?" But the pattern of results, while intriguing, was not conclusive: in general, states that gave Clinton a strong vote in their Democratic primary tended to answer "yes," while states that gave him a harder time by voting in larger numbers for Tsongas or Brown tended to divide more closely on Clinton's honesty and integrity with many answering "no." We acknowledged the parallelism, but never felt we were seeing clear-cut causality, and we suspected that disparaging Clinton's character might simply be a rationalization by some voters who preferred one of Clinton's opponents on other grounds. Obviously, enough Democratic voters were sufficiently untroubled by the "character" issue that Clinton continued to win primaries and to accumulate convention delegates. We published these state-to-state comparisons on several different occasions, including in a graphic with Jeffrey Schmalz's March 26 article, "Despite Denials, Many Hesitate About Clinton," and in another graphic with Robin Toner's page one article on April 29, "Clinton Appears to Ease Doubts on Character as Brown Fades."

Throughout the spring and early summer Clinton continued to evoke a negative balance of opinion among all registered voters nationwide. This balance became somewhat less negative as the Democratic Party nominating convention approached and Clinton seemed to regain some momentum. Then the balance dramatically reversed as the convention concluded. Clinton was propelled to a positive public image for the first time since January by his official nomination as his party's standard bearer, the images of a united party broadcast during the smooth convention, his well-received choice of Senator Al Gore as Vice President, and their joint bus trip from New York City to St. Louis following the convention. He was also aided by the sudden withdrawal of Ross Perot from the Presidential race on the very day Clinton gave his acceptance speech, a withdrawal that left Clinton as the only realistic alternative for change-oriented voters who wanted to replace George Bush in the White House. Robin Toner reported that Clinton had essentially managed to tie George Bush in voter preference among all registered voters on the eve of the convention in her front page story July 13, "Democrats Display a New Optimism, Reflected in Poll." And afterwards R. W. Apple, Jr. reported on the biggest nomination "bounce" in 50 years of polling history in his page one article July 18, "Poll Gives Clinton a Post-Perot, Post-Convention Boost."

During August and September Clinton's positive balance of images gradually faded until, by early October, 34 percent of registered voters held a favorable impression of him and a statistically identical 35 percent held an unfavorable impression. For the rest of the campaign this balance remained approximately even — sometimes slightly negative, sometimes slightly positive. By Election Day the challenger who had started the year almost unknown had become known to eight out of ten voters. By the end, the size of uncrystallized opinion regarding Clinton had become as small as it had been all along regarding President Bush.

Voters' Shifting Opinion of George Bush

But, for Clinton, maintaining merely an even balance of public sentiment, or just a slightly negative balance, would prove sufficient to defeat George Bush. As illustrated in Table 9.4, public impressions of Bush remained clearly negative from the spring through Election Day. After Bush declined to offer any dramatic medicine for the ailing economy in his February State of the Union speech — and subsequently failed to receive any lift from that widely anticipated speech — and after Patrick Buchanan unexpectedly challenged the President for his own party's nomination in the early primaries, voters' opinion of Bush faded from a clearly positive balance in January, to an even balance in February and March, to a clearly negative balance beginning in April. The Republican Party nominating convention did not succeed in reversing this deficit, and throughout the fall campaign Mr. Bush evoked from registered voters between 10 and 20 points more negative than positive reactions. Andrew Rosenthal and Joel Brinkley analyzed the Bush record and the Bush re-election predicament in their page one article June 25, "Bush in a World Remade: Will the Old Compass Do?"

The failure of Bush to receive a lasting boost from his nominating convention will be remembered as one of the crucial turning points of the 1992 campaign. If Bush had experienced the kind of post-convention bounce that Clinton did — and that most nominees of both parties in the past have been able to count on — the fall campaign would surely have been much closer. As one explanation, some observers have pointed to the atmosphere of the convention which emphasized a theme of "family

TABLE 9.4 Registered Voters' Shifting Opinion of George Bush[a]

Dates of Poll	Favorable Opinion[b] (%)	Not Favorable Opinion (%)	Net Balance: Favorable Minus Not Favorable	Uncrystallized Opinion: Undecided or Not Heard Enough Yet
Oct. 15-18, 1991	56	20	+ 36	23
Jan. 6-8, 1992	47	33	+ 14	19
Feb. 19-20	40	41	- 1	19
Feb. 26-March 1	41	41	0	17
March 26-29	42	41	+ 1	17
April 20-23	35	44	- 9	20
May 6-8	36	43	- 7	19
May 27-30	30	43	- 13	25
June 17-20	29	44	- 15	26
July 8 11	30	43	- 13	26

DEMOCRATIC PARTY CONVENTION AND PEROT WITHDRAWS

Aug. 11-14	28	47	- 19	24

REPUBLICAN PARTY CONVENTION

Aug. 23-24	31	46	- 15	23
Sept. 9-13	31	44	- 13	23
Sept. 25-27	29	47	- 18	22

PEROT RE-ENTERS CONTEST

Oct. 2-4	29	49	- 20	20
Oct. 12-13	34	47	- 13	18
Oct. 20-23	35	45	- 10	20
Oct,. 27-30	32	50	- 18	17
Oct. 29-Nov. 1	34	50	- 16	16

[a]Based on registered voters in 17 *New York Times*/CBS News polls and two CBS News Polls (May 27-30 and Sept. 25-27).
[b]The question was: "Is your opinion of George Bush favorable, not favorable, undecided or haven't you heard enough about George Bush yet to have an opinion?"

values" that might have been effective in some other election year but that was simply out of sync with the public's agenda of high priority issues in 1992.

At first we thought Bush actually was in the process of receiving the traditionally expected bounce. CBS News polls on two nights during the

Republican convention seemed to show Bush closing the gap with Clinton, and when *The Times* joined CBS News for a third night of polling, we were not surprised to find the gap closing a bit more. Andrew Rosenthal reported these results, along with the caveat that results of polls taken during or immediately after dramatic events can be fleeting, in his page one August 22 piece, "Bush Pulls Close in Poll, but Not With Women."

And fleeting they were. When we polled again a couple days after the convention ended it became clear that any gain for Bush had dissipated — or perhaps had been artificial in the first place. Adam Clymer reported our findings that the "family values" gambit had flopped and that Bush received no lasting boost from his convention in a front page article August 26, "Bush's Gains from Convention Nearly Evaporate in Latest Poll." Later in the fall, with added hindsight, Robin Toner further analyzed the poorly used Republican convention along with four earlier missed opportunities, including the State of the Union address, in her October 11 article in *The Times's* Week in Review, "How Bush Lost Five Chances to Seize the Day."

Voters' Shifting Opinion of Ross Perot

But there was another factor that complicated George Bush's task in seizing the day from Clinton and winning re-election. The independent challenge of Ross Perot, the flamboyant billionaire from Dallas, who campaigned via TV talk shows on the issues of deficit reduction, job retention, and political reform, managed to keep George Bush off balance or on the defensive at key junctures.

During the spring and early summer, in particular, Perot drew the spotlight, fascinating the public as well as the pundits, and made the economic case against the Bush Administration at a time when Clinton was relatively weak due to the rough primary season. If Bush had been as free to mount an attack against Clinton in June and July of 1992 as he had been during the comparable period of 1988 when he opened up on Michael Dukakis, the 1992 contest might have turned out differently. Instead, there stood Ross Perot — little known at first, but in April, May, and June the only candidate of the three who was able to elicit a more positive than negative impression among the public — effectively criticizing the economic stewardship of George Bush, while having little to say at all about Bill Clinton. Robin Toner analyzed Perot's early effect on the contest in her page one article April 26, "Poll Shows Perot Gaining Strength to Rival Clinton's."

As the public began to learn more about Perot, however, they also heard of his allegedly authoritarian ways, his pattern of having people investigated ("Inspector Perot"), and his seeming need for centralized control of his local volunteer supporters. Perot himself later attributed some of this negative information to a Republican "dirty tricks" department. As shown in Table 9.5, public opinion of Perot crystallized into an unfavorable balance by early July and remained negative for the rest of the campaign. We followed Perot's rise and fall closely, starting in late March after it was clear he was a force to be reckoned with, and the series of favorable/unfavorable ratings was one of our chief tools in doing so.

TABLE 9.5 Registered Voters' Shifting Opinion of Ross Perot[a]

Dates of Poll	Favorable Opinion[b] (%)	Not Favorable Opinion (%)	Net Balance: Favorable Minus Not Favorable	Uncrystallized Opinion: Undecided or Not Heard Enough Yet
March 26-29, 1992	16	8	+ 8	77
April 20-23	21	9	+ 12	69
May 6-8	24	11	+ 13	64
May 27-30	22	15	+ 7	63
June 17-20	26	20	+ 6	54
July 8-11	19	27	- 8	54
DEMOCRATIC PARTY CONVENTION AND PEROT WITHDRAWS				
Aug. 11-14	23	40	- 17	37
REPUBLICAN PARTY CONVENTION				
Aug. 23-24	19	38	- 19	43
Sept. 9-13	21	39	- 18	39
Sept. 25-27	13	48	- 35	38
PEROT RE-ENTERS PRESIDENTAL CONTEST				
Oct. 2-4	7	59	- 52	33
Oct. 12-13	18	35	- 17	46
Oct. 20-23	29	32	- 3	38
Oct. 27-30	23	41	- 18	35
Oct. 29-Nov. 1	24	42	- 18	34

[a]Based on registered voters in 13 *New York Times*/CBS News polls and two CBS News polls (May 27-30 and Sept. 25-27)
[b]The question was: "Is your opinion of Ross Perot favorable, not favorable, undecided, or haven't you heard enough about Ross Perot yet to have an opinion?"

An example is Robin Toner's front page article on June 23, "Bush and Clinton Sag in Survey; Perot's Negative Rating Doubles," which featured fever lines on page one graphing each candidate's positives and negatives. After Perot announced he was withdrawing from the campaign on July 16, we continued to track his image even in his absence, and we found it turned more negative yet. When Perot later changed his mind and announced on October 1 that he was re-entering the contest, his image had sunk to a balance that was 52 percentage points more negative than positive. But his subsequent participation in the fall TV debates and his expensive half-hour TV "infomercials" worked to his advantage. By Election Day Perot's image had improved, but to a level that was "only" 18 points more negative than positive, or about what it was after he dropped out in July. He never managed to get back to the positive image he enjoyed in the spring.

It can be argued that in his second campaign in the fall, like his first in the spring, Ross Perot affected the atmosphere and the dynamics of the 1992 campaign in important ways. Perot's presence in the fall again served to keep George Bush on the defensive and to blunt his message; Perot represented a second voice criticizing Bush's economic stewardship and calling for change. Perot made it all that much harder for Bush to refocus the public's attention on Clinton's "character," the issue of "family values," or other themes like "trust" that were preferred by the Bush campaign. Yet, Ross Perot perplexed many people during the 1992 campaign; even at the end, fully one-third of the voters held uncrystallized views of Ross Perot.

The Times published the trends for each candidate's favorable/unfavorable rating on several additional occasions during the campaign, including on the front page on October 6 with Robin Toner's article "Poll Finds Hostility to Perot and No Basic Shift in Race" and on October 25 with her piece "Contest Tightens as Perot Resurges and Clinton Slips."

Putting Major Campaign Events into Perspective

Another use of polling by *The New York Times* during 1992 was to put events into perspective and to make abstract processes more concrete. Two examples are given here.

A Composite National Democratic Party Primary Electorate

In 1992 *The Times* analyzed voting patterns in many individual state primary elections, utilizing exit polls of voters leaving voting stations conducted by Voter Research and Surveys. In our week-to-week polling analysis during the primary season we were interested both in what was unique about each state and in the underlying patterns that were common across states. But the news necessarily emphasized the individual victories and defeats of the candidates with the resulting impact on political "momentum" from state to state, and gave somewhat less prominence to the recurrent patterns that emerged. At the end of the primary season, therefore, it seemed useful to remind our reporters, editors, and readers of some of the voting patterns that had persisted across both time and geography in the Democratic primary battles.

To synthesize a national Democratic primary electorate for 1992, Table 9.6 combines vote totals and exit poll percentages from 29 states where exit polls were conducted in Democratic primaries from February to June. Each state influences the total table according to its share of all votes cast. A graphic containing these results ran in the paper of July 12 with Robin Toner's article, "While Others Shrank from Race, Clinton Clung to Dream of Presidency."

Clinton won half of all votes cast in the Democratic primaries, while Brown and Tsongas each won about a fifth — Tsongas garnering most of his share in the earlier primaries and Brown mainly in the later ones. Clinton tended to win greater support from blacks, the elderly, those people with lower income and lesser education, those who said they were worse off financially than four years earlier, and from ideological moderates and regular Democrats.

Support for Brown and Tsongas tended to be a mirror image of Clinton's. Both Brown and Tsongas tended to draw more support from whites, people under age 60, college graduates, higher income people, people who were better off than four years earlier, and political independents. In addition, Brown tended to attract more Catholics and liberals, while Tsongas attracted more support from Jews, conservatives, and the few self-identified Republicans voting in Democratic primaries. But these are tendencies and nuances; perhaps the most striking thing about the table is Clinton's considerable support within *every* demographic category listed. The breadth of Clinton's appeal would prove important in his fall campaign against the Republicans.

The Spectrum of Political Choice

In 1992 *The Times* used the device of a "spectrum" to portray the range of political choice available to voters. Candidates sometimes hide or misrepresent their views on contentious issues, but we have found over the years that delegates to the two party conventions are usually candid in revealing where they and their party stand. In 1992 *The Times* polled

TABLE 9.6 The Primaries Seen as a Whole: How Democrats in 29 States Voted[a]

Portion of Primary Voters	Voting Group	Percentage of Each Group Voting for		
		Clinton	Brown	Tsongas
100%	Total, all 29 states	50%	21%	20%
47	Men	50	22	20
53	Women	51	20	21
80	White	47	23	25
14	Black	70	15	8
4	Hispanic	51	30	15
12	18-29 years	47	24	19
33	30-44	45	26	22
25	45-59	51	19	20
30	60 and older	59	15	18
50	Protestant	55	14	21
30	Catholic	44	24	24
6	Jewish	45	15	33
8	No high school diploma	67	14	10
27	High school graduate	61	17	15
27	Some college	48	23	18
20	College graduate	42	24	26
18	Post graduate education	38	23	28
	Family income:			
15	Less than $15,000	62	17	13
25	$15,000 to $29,999	55	19	18
30	$30,000 to $49,999	48	23	21
18	$50,000 to $74,999	45	23	25
11	$75,000 and over	38	23	29
	Those who identify as:			
35	Liberal	47	26	20
45	Moderate	54	18	19
20	Conservative	48	17	23
67	Democrat	57	19	17
29	Independent	36	25	27
4	Republican	34	18	32
	Say family's financial situation today is:			
14	Better than 4 years ago	44	24	22
39	Same as 4 years ago	50	20	20
45	Worse than 4 years ago	53	20	18
(18.0)	TOTAL VOTES (millions)	(9.0)	(3.8)	(3.5)

[a]This table, which constructs a composite Democratic primary electorate for the nation, combines vote totals and exit poll percentages from 29 Democratic primary states from February to June. Vote totals are from secretaries of state. Exit polls were conducted by Voter Research and Surveys. Each state influences the total table according to its share of all votes cast. Other candidates, who received 1.7 million votes combined, or 9 percent of the total, are not shown.

Democratic delegates, while CBS News polled Republican delegates, and we jointly asked many of the same questions of rank-and-file members of each party in our national polls of voters. This enabled *The Times* to construct a graphic showing the "ideological center of gravity" of various groups, illustrating where each stood on a left-to-right liberal-conservative spectrum. The location of each group was derived by subtracting the percentage in the group who called themselves liberal from the percentage who called themselves conservative. Thus, higher numbers toward the right end of the graphic represent a greater surplus of conservatives over liberals in the group, while larger numbers to the left end of the graphic represent a greater surplus of liberals over conservatives in the group.

There are several striking patterns revealed by this exercise. The ideological center of gravity for the entire adult population is near the middle of the road, just slightly right of center. Thus, the American public as a whole tends to be moderate or centrist. Democratic voters and Republican voters are distinctly separated on opposite sides of this overall center of gravity, and roughly equidistant from it. Each party's activists and leaders, as represented by convention delegates, are more ideological than their rank-and-file voters, i.e. the politicos stand much farther out on their respective sides of the spectrum. But none of the groups ever strays out toward the farthest extremes of the spectrum; this means that even the activist leadership groups are a mixture of views rather than being ideologically pure.

A free-standing graphic similar to the top half of Figure 9.1 ran in the paper of August 21, headed "A Spectrum of Political Views." The bottom half of Figure 9.1 is added here, based on the views of actual Clinton supporters, Perot supporters, and Bush supporters as determined in the Election Day exit poll in November. As one would expect, Clinton voters and Bush voters are distinctly separated to the left and the right side of the overall center of gravity. But perhaps the most interesting feature is the location of people who ended up voting for Ross Perot.

As a group Perot voters are near the middle of the road, the closest of all the groups illustrated to the overall national center of gravity of the total adult population. This is additional confirmation of a finding we repeatedly came across in our 1992 polling: Perot drew supporters from both sides of the political and ideological fence, siphoning off supporters from both directions. Since Perot voters were a diverse group, they looked centrist as a whole. Perot's appeal lay in his style ("let's just do it, folks," "it's that simple") and his message of change, fiscal responsibility, and political reform — not in any ideological purity — and that appeal cut across the standard political categories in the U.S.

Polarization was sufficient in 1992 so that there were clearly distin-

162

FIGURE 9.1 A Spectrum of Political Views: Where Eight Groups Stand on the Liberal-Conservative Dimension

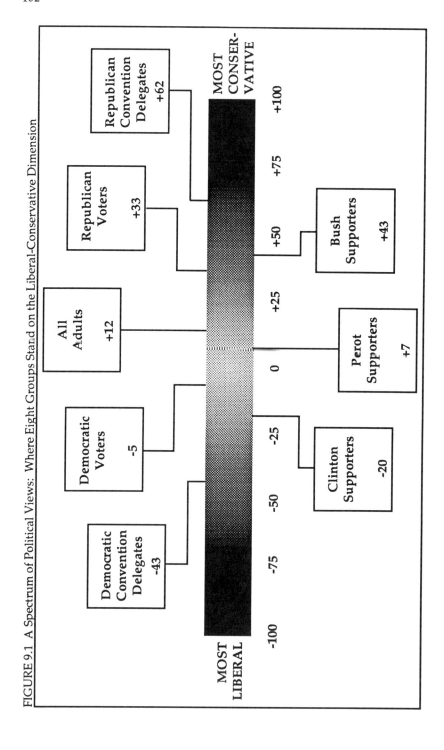

Question: "How would you describe your views on most political matters? Generally, do you think of yourself as liberal, moderate, or conservative?"

The ideological center of gravity of eight groups is expressed above as the difference between the percentage in each group who described themselves as liberal and the percentage in each group who described themselves as conservative. Higher numbers to the left indicate a larger surplus of liberals over conservatives. Higher numbers to the right indicate a larger surplus of conservatives over liberals. For example, 45 percent of Republican registered voters described themselves as conservative and 12 percent described themselves as liberal. Subtracting 12 from 45 leaves a conservative surplus of 33 percent among Republican voters.

Source: Data for 1,091 Democratic convention delegates are from a CBS News poll. Data for 921 Republican convention delegates are from a *New York Times* poll. Data for all adults and for the rank-and-file registered Democratic and Republican voters are pooled from four *New York Times*/CBS News polls conducted from April to July. Data for supporters of Clinton, Bush, and Perot are from the Voter Research and Surveys exit poll of 15,236 voters on Election Day.

guishable political choices available to any voter who was looking for them. Of course, the terms "liberal" and "conservative" can be vague and sometimes confusing; they certainly oversimplify a multi-dimensional political world by reducing numerous political battlelines to a single left-right continuum. But the above analysis can also be repeated using a host of specific issues of public policy — with similarly clear results. American voters had relatively clear choices available to them in 1992.

Analyzing Key Factors in the Campaign

During the 1992 election cycle we viewed the electorate as being influenced by forces of three different types — some of long duration, some of middling permanence, and some of short-lived intensity. We made polling efforts to study each type in order to explain *why* the election was developing as it was. The examples below include one factor from each category.

Long-Term Party Identification

"Party identification" is the electorate's underlying partisan allegiance. It normally changes only gradually as generations enter or exit the population or as long-term secular developments such as industrialization, suburbanization, or population migration work their social and political consequences. Only rarely does party identification undergo more rapid shifts, typically accompanying major historic junctures like the Civil War or the Great Depression.

Thus, the balance of party loyalty exerts a long-term force on any given election year, constraining the election, even if not fully determining it. Typically, it gives one party a starting advantage, which it must work to keep or expand, while it gives the other party an initial disadvantage which it must work to overcome. The Times and CBS News measure party identification in every poll, using the question originated by the National Election Studies at the University of Michigan: "Generally speaking, do you usually consider yourself a Republican, a Democrat, an independent, or what?" In Table 9.7, based on 257,566 respondents in 173 of our national polls, we have pooled our data within each year and show the party allegiance of Americans annually from 1976 through 1993.

A briefer version of Table 9.7, covering the years 1980 to 1991, was published with Adam Clymer's piece on July 14, 1991, "Poll Finds G.O.P. Growth Erodes Dominant Role of the Democrats," which took a close look at the state of the political parties six months before the campaign

TABLE 9.7 Shifts in Party Identification, 1976-1993: All Adults[a]

	Percentage of All Adults Identifying with Each Party		Democratic Advantage
Year	Republican[b]	Democratic	
1976	20	40	+20
1977	20	39	+19
1978	19	40	+21
1979	22	39	+17
1980	24	41	+17
1981	25	36	+11
1982	24	38	+14
1983	24	40	+16
1984	27	37	+10
1985	30	36	+ 6
1986	28	36	+ 8
1987	30	38	+ 8
1988	29	37	+ 8
1989	32	36	+ 4
1990	30	34	+ 4
1991	31	34	+ 3
1992	29	35	+ 6
1993	28	36	+ 8

[a]Based on 173 polls by *The New York Times* and CBS News, which have been pooled for each year, totaling 257,566 respondents.
[b]The question was: "Generally speaking, do you usually consider yourself a Republican, a Democrat, an independent or what?"

year opened. The fuller version of Table 9.7 not only updates the time-series through 1993 but also extends it back to 1976, the year the *Times*/CBS News Poll began nationally.

During the decade and a half leading up to the 1992 election, the long-term Democratic advantage that had existed since the Great Depression and the New Deal was in the process of dissolving. The Republicans, once the clear minority party, had been successfully closing the gap. From 20-point underdogs among all adults in the Ford and Carter years, the Republicans managed during the Reagan-Bush era to reduce their deficit significantly, so that by 1991 the gap was merely three percentage points.

The table shows a pattern of surge and partial decline that seems to have occurred after four of the last five Presidential elections. In 1981, 1985, and 1989 the Republican share of party loyalists increased and the Democratic share decreased — probably in response to the Republican victory in the previous year's Presidential election — only to revert partially in subsequent years until another G.O.P. White House victory reenergized it. We have described this pattern as a series of two-steps-forward-one-step-back motions for the Republicans throughout the 1980's.

With the addition of data forward to 1993 and backward to 1976 — two periods with Democratic victories — the fuller table puts this 1980's pattern into a broader context. It appears that the pattern was not consistently pro-Republican throughout the whole time period, but rather depended on who was winning the White House. In 1977, the year following Jimmy Carter's win, both parties' share of party identifiers remained virtually steady with no clear Republican gain. And during 1993, the year after Bill Clinton's victory, it appears that the reverse pattern happened: the Democratic share went up slightly, while the Republican share sagged a bit — perhaps in response to the Democratic recapture of the White House. A graphic based on the enlarged table ran in The Week in Review on February 20, 1994.

The gradual Republican gains over the previous decade and a half stalled by election year 1992, and the momentum the Republicans had enjoyed for years apparently ran out — at least temporarily. Not only did the gap in party loyalty among all adults never close completely, but by 1993 the Democrats succeeded in modestly reopening that gap in their favor. The net result by 1993 was an eight percentage point advantage for the Democrats among all adults — not as huge as it once was, but at least a rebound back to the level that existed in the mid-to-late 1980s before the Bush Administration.

The Middle-Term Impact of the Economy on the Vote

The link between the condition of the national economy and the vote on Election Day is an example of a middle-term factor that *The Times* focused much attention on in 1992. Middle-term or middle-run seems an appropriate designation, since the economy can change more rapidly than a long-term factor like party identification, but not nearly so fast as some of the truly short-term factors in the campaign like the candidates' personal images.

Electorates in the U.S. as well as other countries have long been observed to reward or punish incumbent governments on the basis of economic performance. Polling throughout the year-long election cycle left us in no doubt that this force was strongly at work in 1992. When we asked voters in the autumn what single issue they wanted the Presidential candidates to talk about most, the economy and unemployment beat all comers: 46 percent cited the economy or unemployment in our early September poll, while eight percent said health care, seven percent said education, six percent said the federal deficit, five percent said taxes, and all other issues received less than five percent each; "family values" for instance received just one percent. Robin Toner reported those results on September 16 and described Bill Clinton as riding a wave of economic discontent in her page one article, "Clinton Retains Wide Lead in Latest Survey."

But the strongest evidence linking the economy and the vote came from the exit poll of voters as they left voting stations across the country. Table 9.8 presents four tests we conducted of this relationship on Election Day. First, voters on November 3 gave highest priority to the economy and jobs. When asked to pick among nine issues the one or two that mattered most in deciding how they voted, 42 percent chose economy/jobs — twice as many as picked either of the next two most important issues (the deficit and health care). Furthermore, these voters who picked economy/jobs voted heavily for the Democratic candidate: Clinton received 52 percent of their vote, compared to 25 percent for Bush and 24 percent for Perot. Thus, three-quarters of those most concerned about the economy voted against the incumbent President.

Second, Americans voted as if they were rewarding or punishing the incumbent Administration according to their perception of the national economy. Those who pronounced the economy "excellent" or "good" voted overwhelmingly for Bush (80 percent). Those who said the economy was "not so good" split more evenly with 43 percent for Clinton and 37 percent for Bush. And those who perceived the economy as "poor" voted strongly for Clinton (64 percent). But the size of the group seeing poor economic health (32 percent of all voters) was half again larger than the size of the group who perceived an excellent or good economic performance (19 percent of all voters). So the advantage in total votes went to Clinton.

Third, these same patterns existed when it came to Americans' own personal financial situation. Voters acted as if they were rewarding or punishing the incumbent President according to whether their own family's financial situation was better or worse than four years earlier. Those who reported a "better" financial situation split their vote strongly toward Bush (62 percent). Those who said their family's situation was "about the same" split evenly: 41 percent for Clinton and 41 percent for Bush. And those who reported a "worse" financial situation split strongly toward Clinton (61 percent). Such a pattern would have produced a virtual tie vote overall if each group had been of similar size. But in 1992 the size of the group experiencing a worsened financial situation (34 percent of all voters) was sufficiently larger than the size of the group enjoying an improved situation (25 percent) that the advantage in total votes went to Clinton.

TABLE 9.8 The Economy and the Candidates: Four Tests[a]

Percent of All Voters Who Fall Into Each Category (% Add Vertically)		Percentage of Voters in Each Category Who Voted for: (% Add Horizontally)		
		Clinton	*Bush*	*Perot*

PRIORITY GIVEN TO THE ECONOMY: Which one or two of these nine issues mattered most in deciding how you voted?

42	Economy/Jobs	52	25	24
21	Federal budget deficit	36	27	37
20	Health care	67	20	14
15	Family values	22	67	12
14	Taxes	26	57	18
13	Education	60	25	16
12	Abortion	36	55	9
8	Foreign policy	8	87	5
5	Environment	72	14	13

PERCEIVED CONDITION OF NATIONAL ECONOMY: Do you think that the condition of the nation's economy is:

19	Excellent, good	10	80	10
47	Not so good	43	37	20
32	Poor	64	12	24

TREND IN FAMILY'S OWN FINANCIAL SITUATION: Compared to four years ago, is your family's financial situation:

25	Better today	24	62	14
41	About the same	41	41	18
34	Worse today	61	14	25

RATING OF GEORGE BUSH'S ECONOMIC STEWARDSHIP: Do you approve or disapprove of the way George Bush has handled the economy?

35	Approve strongly or somewhat	8	82	10
24	Disapprove somewhat	43	32	25
40	Disapprove strongly	74	3	24

[a]Based on questionnaires completed by 15,232 voters leaving polling places in 300 precincts nationwide on Election Day, conducted by Voter Research and Surveys.

Fourth, voters at the end of the long campaign acted in accordance with their retrospective judgment of the incumbent's economic stewardship. Those who said they "strongly approved" or "somewhat approved" of the way George Bush had handled the economy split their vote overwhelmingly in the President's favor (82 percent). Those who said they "disapproved somewhat" split more toward the Democratic challenger: 43 percent for Clinton and 32 percent for Bush. And those who said they "disapproved strongly" went strongly for Clinton (74 percent). And, just as we observed all year long, on Election Day the size of the two disapproving groups (nearly two-thirds of all voters) was much larger than the size of the two approving groups (slightly more than one-third of all voters). So, again, the advantage in total votes went to Clinton.

Thus, the election outcome could be seen heavily, though not solely, as a referendum on the nation's economic situation and on the incumbent President's stewardship. Both Bush and Clinton drew strongly from the economic constituencies they "ought" to have attracted. But in 1992 there were simply more economically dissatisfied people than satisfied people on Election Day.

These exit poll findings linking the economy and the vote informed many of the graphics and articles *The Times* published on November 4 and November 5 following Election Day. In his November 4 page one analysis, "The Economy's Casualty," R. W. Apple, Jr. concluded that "In the end it was the faltering economy, which had bedeviled him all year, that did George Bush in." Eight major graphics based on the exit poll — one for each geographical region each day — titled "Behind the Vote" on Wednesday and "Close-Up" on Thursday — documented that same conclusion.

Short-Term Personal Images of the Candidates

Much journalistic activity (and much polling, for that matter) concentrates on assessing the effects of shorter-term phenomena that occur during the course of any campaign. These include the propaganda and advertising efforts of each side, major speeches and issue appeals by the candidates, comparative performances in face-to-face TV debates, and dramatic events that happen along the campaign trail. These shorter-term factors occupy such attention, of course, because they are new since the last news story or since the previous poll, and because they are most likely to account for any week-to-week or month-to-month fluctuations in the standings of the candidates.

The matters that any campaign organization has direct control over are also — necessarily — the shorter-term aspects. A campaign organization cannot do much about either the long-term forces it faces or the middle-term conditions it has to contend with, except to try to exploit them when favorable and, when unfavorable, to attempt to distract people's attention toward other topics that have more potential. By contrast, campaigns spend enormous sums in attempts to create, and then to reinforce, positive images of their own candidate and negative images of their opponents.

Table 9.9 displays some personal images of the three candidates that *The Times* and CBS News monitored in 1992. In cases where a question was asked several times during the year, the results shown are for the poll closest to the election. In general, Clinton succeeded in being perceived, as he sought to be, as the candidate of change, the candidate with new ideas to get the country out of the recession. He bested both Bush and Perot on these dimensions. The public was somewhat less sanguine that Clinton would actually succeed in improving the economy, but he still bettered Bush on this expectation, too.

George Bush, for his part, succeeded in being perceived, as he sought to be, as the more trustworthy choice. He bested both Clinton and Perot in inspiring confidence in his foreign policy abilities and (somewhat less so) in his being able to deal with all the problems a President has to deal with. Bush also bettered Clinton when voters were asked whether or not they had "doubts" about each candidate's general "trustworthiness"; this question presumably tapped any lingering effects of the "character" issue that had raised doubts about Clinton among some voters all year long.

Table 9.10, from the Election Day exit poll, shows the priority voters actually gave, in the end, to nine candidate qualities. The striking thing about the table is that the theme of "change" tops all others on the voters' priority list, and that the theme of a better plan for the country and its economy is second. These were a challenger's themes rather than an incumbent's themes — Clinton's themes, also amplified by Ross Perot. Both these ranked higher in importance than Bush's themes of experience, judgment, and honesty/trustworthiness which ranked third, fourth, and fifth.

Clinton and Bush clearly did benefit from the themes each sought so hard to connect with his image. Those who put a priority on change and better plans split strongly toward Clinton, while those who gave priority to experience, judgment and honesty/trustworthiness split strongly toward Bush. It was just that by the end of the 1992 campaign the challenger's themes turned out to have greater resonance with the public than did the incumbent's themes.

Notice in Table 9.9, there were also some themes on which Ross Perot did particularly well, managing to tie either Bush or Clinton or both — like trust, caring, and being tough enough to make the hard decisions

TABLE 9.9 Some Images of the Candidates in the Fall Campaign[a]

Percent who say:	Regarding CLINTON	Regarding BUSH	Regarding PEROT
CLINTON ADVANTAGES			
The candidate has offered specific ideas to get the United States out of the recession. (a)	52	27	28
The candidate would bring about the kind of change the country needs, if elected. (b)	43	27	31
The economy will get better if the candidate is elected President. (c)	35	19	N.A.
BUSH ADVANTAGES			
Have confidence in the candidate's ability to deal wisely with a difficult international crisis. (d)	27	6?	10
The candidate can be trusted to deal with all the problems a President has to deal with. (b)	39	48	24
PEROT'S AREAS OF STRENGTH			
The candidate cares about the needs and problems of people like the respondent. (e)	65	48	66
The candidate is tough enough to make the hard decisions necessary to reduce the federal budget deficit. (a)	46	42	51
Have no doubts about the candidate's trustworthiness. (f)	33	49	46
MUTUAL WEAKNESSES			
The candidate is likely to raise the respondent's taxes if elected. (e)	82	61	80
The candidate says what he really believes most of the time. (a)	35	32	40

[a]Based on registered voters in four *New York Times*/CBS News polls and two CBS News polls during the fall campaign. After each question in the table the letter in parentheses indicates the dates of the poll, as follows: (a) Oct. 2-4; (b) Oct. 27-30; (c) Sept. 25-27 by CBS News; (d) Sept. 9-13 for Clinton and Bush, but Oct. 2-4 for Perot; (e) Oct. 20-23; and (f) Nov. 2 by CBS News. A question appeared on two or more polls in some cases; the results from the joint poll nearest the election were selected for presentation in the table. Note that each question was asked separately about each candidate, so that each candidate's image ranges between zero and 100 on each item.

TABLE 9.10 The Priority of Nine Candidate Qualities: What Mattered Most on Election Day[a]

Percentage of All Voters Who Fall Into Each Category[b] (% Add Vertically)	Candidate Qualities	Percentage of Voters in Each Category Who Voted for: (% Add Horizontally)		
		Clinton	Bush	Perot
36	Will bring about needed change	67	5	28
24	Has the best plan for country	58	17	25
19	Right experience	7	84	9
16	Good judgment in a crisis	8	88	4
14	Honest, trustworthy	14	63	23
14	Strong convictions	27	45	28
13	Cares about people like me	64	11	25
8	His Vice-President	85	13	2
5	My party's candidate	56	42	2

[a]Based on questionnaires completed by 15,232 voters leaving polling places in 300 precincts nationwide on Election Day, conducted by Voter Research and Surveys.
[b]The question was "Which 1 or 2 (of 9 listed) candidate qualities mattered most in deciding how you voted for President?"

necessary to reduce the federal budget deficit. And there were still others on which all the candidates had a poor image — such as not saying what they really believe, and being likely to raise taxes if elected.

Such poll findings about candidate images informed many of our campaign stories in 1992. A few examples are Robin Toner's page one political articles on August 17, "Fractured G.O.P. Meets as Public Voices Disfavor," and on September 7, "If Voters Won't Love Bush, He Hopes They Fear Clinton," and Elizabeth Kolbert's October 26 piece, "Bush Campaign Settles on a Sustained Message."

Documenting Voter Decision-Making and the Outcome of the Election

At the end of the 1992 presidential campaign cycle, *The Times* used public opinion polling to document voter decision-making and to record who voted for whom as the American public rendered their judgment on the men who sought to lead the nation. We also measured how the public evaluated the campaign itself and the extent to which voters felt involved in the campaign.

A Campaign that Engaged More Voters

Most voters felt involved in the 1992 Presidential campaign (see Kohut & Hugick, Chapter 11). As shown in Table 9.11, by the end of October, 80 percent of registered voters described the campaign as "interesting," while only 17 percent called it "dull." That was a marked change from public reaction to the 1988 Bush/Dukakis contest; at the end of that campaign a majority of 52 percent pronounced it "dull," while only 42 percent called it "interesting."

As a result of greater engagement, public attention to the 1992 campaign increased dramatically throughout the year and hit a level by the end that was far higher than in 1988. During the winter and spring primary election season, as Table 9.12 illustrates, the attention level in 1992 was roughly the same as recorded in 1988, but during the second half of the campaign year the public's attention level in 1992 continually outpaced the level measured at equivalent points in 1988. At the end of the campaign 69 percent said they were paying a lot of attention to the 1992 campaign; in 1988 the equivalent figure was only 45 percent. Partly as a consequence, voter turnout in the U.S. increased in 1992 by about five percentage points over 1988; this was the first increase since the election of 1960.

It is tempting to attribute much of this increased engagement to the unique presence of Ross Perot in the 1992 contest, and no doubt the novelty and quirkiness of his campaign did cause some voters to pay more attention than usual. But, as Table 9.12 makes clear, even during the months of August and September, when Perot had withdrawn from the contest, attention to the 1992 campaign was running at a much higher level than it had in the equivalent period of 1988. One has to give much of the credit for the increased interest to other factors, such as the higher stakes perceived by many voters in 1992 due to the bad economy. Indeed, 74 percent of registered voters in our final pre-election polling said the 1992 election for President was "more important" than previous Presidential elections. Another factor was the increased likelihood from August onward of a party turnover in the White House after Clinton catapulted out of his convention into the lead. The public's interest naturally perks up in a competitive contest with a possibility of party turnover.

It is useful for both journalists and campaigners to realize that the audience for election-year messages varies dramatically in size over the

TABLE 9.11 Voters Evaluate the 1988 and 1992 Campaigns[a]

	Views of Registered Voters	
	In 1988	*In 1992*
THE 1992 CAMPAIGN WAS SEEN AS MORE INTERESTING "Would you be more likely to describe the (year) Presidential campaign as interesting or dull?"		
Interesting	42	80
Dull	52	17
AND AS SOMEWHAT LESS NEGATIVE IN TONE "Compared with past presidential campaigns, do you think the campaign has been more positive this year, more negative this year, or about the same?"		
More positive	7	22
More negative	61	40
About the same	28	34
BUT VOTERS DID NOT SEE ANY DRAMATIC INCREASE IN THE DISCUSSION OF ISSUES, AT LEAST PRIOR TO THE TV DEBATES "Compared with past presidential campaigns, do you think there has been more discussion of the issues in this campaign, less discussion of the issues, or about the same amount of discussion?"[b]		
More discussion	8	12
Less discussion	46	38
Same amount	41	47
AND MANY WOULD HAVE PREFERRED OTHER CANDIDATES TO CHOOSE AMONG, THOUGH NOT SO MANY AS FELT THAT WAY IN 1988 "With (names of candidates) running for President this year, are you satisfied choosing among them, or would you want other choices?"		
Satisfied	34	49
Want other choices	64	48

[a]Based on registered voters in four *New York Times*/ CBS News polls — Oct. 1-4 and Oct. 27-30 in 1992, and Oct. 21-24 and Nov. 2-4 in 1988.

[b]The question about the amount of issue discussion in 1992 was asked prior to the televised Presidential debates. In the Oct. 27-30 poll, after the debates were completed, another question with modified wording suggested that perhaps the public saw more issue discussion in 1992 after all. In answer to the question "Compared with the 1988 Presidential campaign, when George Bush ran against Michael Dukakis, do you think there has been more discussion of issues in this campaign, less discussion of the issues, or about the same amount of discussion?", 50 percent said more, 16 percent said less and 29 percent said the same amount. However, there is no equivalent question asked in 1988 comparing that year's campaign with the 1984 campaign in particular, rather than previous campaigns in general.

So we cannot rule out the possibility that the seeming increase in perceived issue discussion in 1992 could be an artifact of the modified question wording which asks respondents to make a retrospective comparison with a particular campaign four years earlier.

TABLE 9.12 Registered Voters Paying "A Lot of Attention" to the Campaign[a]

Dates of Poll	Percentage Paying "A Lot of Attention" to 1992 Campaign[b]	Number of Registered Voters in 1992 Poll	Attention Level from 1988 Poll Nearest to Same Date
Jan. 6-8, 1992	17	1,068	—
Jan. 22-25	20	991	15
Feb. 19-20	30	820	27
Feb. 26-March 1	33	1,257	—
March 26-29	35	1,238	34
April 20-23	37	1,151	—
May 6-8	38	940	30
May 27-30	33	1,017	—
June 17-20	39	1,029	—
July 8-11	40	1,032	24
Aug. 11-14	45	1,022	26, 33
Sept 9-13	50	1,006	29
Sept. 25-27	51	1,861	32
Oct. 2-4	54	994	34, 39
Oct. 20-23	61	1,467	31
Oct. 27-30	67	1,912	—
Oct. 29-Nov. 1	69	2,248	45

[a]Based on registered voters in 15 New York Times/ CBS News polls and two CBS News Polls (May 27-30 and Sept. 25-27). The final two polls share respondents on two overlapping days.
[b]The question was "How much attention have you been able to pay to the 1992 Presidential campaign—a lot, some, not much, or no attention so far?"

course of the year. In 1992 the proportion paying "a lot" of attention quadrupled from January to November. But the size of that audience exceeded the majority threshold only by September. Thus, appeals from candidates made early in the campaign year may not reach some voters until late in the contest when they finally tune in. And the audience for news coverage and analysis by journalists also expands enormously as Election Day approaches to include many people who are innocent of earlier news reports.

Many Voters Remained Dissatisfied with the Tone and Content of the Campaign

While the public found the tone of the 1992 campaign to be somewhat less negative than usual, that was not a ringing endorsement: voters were still more likely to perceive negative overtones than positive ones. Four years earlier in 1988 a 61 percent majority of registered voters said that year's campaign was "more negative" compared with past presidential campaigns. In 1992 a smaller 40 percent — but still a plurality — rendered that same judgment on the Bush/Clinton/Perot contest. Nor, as shown in Table 9.11, were voters impressed with the level of issue discussion in the campaign, at least at the time we measured it just before the televised debates. Only 12 percent said there had been more discussion of the issues in the 1992 campaign compared with past campaigns.

Moreover, about half the voters in 1992 said they were not satisfied choosing among the three candidates running for President and would have preferred "other choices." This level of dissatisfaction was lower than that registered in 1988, when about two-thirds of voters wanted other choices, but the 1992 level was about the same as we recorded in 1984 and 1980. There may be something inherently confining about the choices produced by a two-party system that inevitably frustrates many voters — even in years like 1980 and 1992 when an independent candidate manages to offer a third alternative. Our findings about the public's evaluation of the 1992 contest informed a number of articles in *The Times*, including Jeffrey Schmalz's November 1 piece in the Week in Review, "Americans Are Sadder and Wiser, But Not Apathetic."

Head-to-Head Trial Heats

The measurement of the "horse race" has always been a secondary consideration in polls sponsored by *The Times*. Our first priority has always been to measure the public's reactions to issues, personalities, and events and to try to understand the public's political attitudes. But we did include trial heat questions on most of our 1992 polls to chart the tentative decisions voters were making as the campaign progressed. Table 9.13 reports the results of our three-way trial heats among Bush, Clinton and Perot, as well as the results of our two-way trial heats between just Bush and Clinton. We found that both trends were needed due to the on-again-off-again candidacy of Ross Perot.

From February through August the results are based on all registered voters. From September through November the results have been weighted to reflect a "probable electorate." As explained in the "Method Box" that accompanied most major poll articles, this technique uses responses to questions dealing with voter registration, past voting history, attention to the campaign, and intention to vote in 1992 as an indicator of the probability of particular respondents voting in the Presidential election. The technique weighted registered respondents from 0.11 to 0.88 according to their likelihood of actually turning out to vote on Election Day. The average of all these weights, including the zero weights given to unregistered people, indicates the percentage of the voting age population that our probable electorate model predicted would turn out to vote on Election Day. That figure in 1992 ran about five percentage points ahead of the equivalent figure generated in 1988.

When *The Times* reported trial heat results, it made a practice of not allocating undecided voters who, in answer to a subsequent question, said they "leaned" toward one of the candidates (cf. Daves & Warden, Chapter 7). When CBS News reported trial heats, it usually allocated these leaners. This accounts for occasional slight discrepancies between figures broadcast by CBS News and those published by *The Times*.

Table 9.13 shows that the preference of voters throughout the yearlong campaign broke into three distinct periods. In the first period of the year George Bush held an advantage over Bill Clinton that began in double digits and then shrank over a period of months as Clinton emerged from the pack of Democratic hopefuls and as Ross Perot arose and increased the pressure on Bush. By early July, prior to the Democratic convention, Bush's advantage over Clinton had melted to zero in the two-way trial heat and to just three percentage points — statistically indistinguishable from zero — in the three-way trial heat.

The second distinct period of the campaign year lasted from after the Democratic convention in July through August as Clinton leapt into a 13-point lead in three-way trial heats and to a slightly larger lead in two-way trial heats. This dramatic rebound then faded slightly after Labor Day as the traditional fall campaign season opened and things settled down.

But perhaps the most striking feature of Table 9.13 is the relative stability of the standings during the third period of the year — across the entire autumn phase of the campaign. Although individual voters may have switched back and forth or wavered, and although many voters said they might yet change their minds, the net outcome of all the individual voter decisions resulted in very stable aggregate standings for Bush and Clinton. In five successive *Times*/CBS News polls taken after Labor Day the preference of the "probable electorate" for Bill Clinton stood within plus or minus three percentage points of 43 percent (in three-way trial heats). In the same five polls, the preference of the "probable electorate" for George Bush remained within plus or minus two percentage points of 36 percent (in three-way trial heats). Graphics showing trend lines for the three-way trial heats were published several times during the autumn, including with Robin Toner's page one article on October 15, "Clinton, Fending Off Assaults, Retains Sizable Lead, Poll Finds" and again with her October 25 page one piece, "Contest Tightens as Perot Resurges and Clinton Slips."

Results in the four two-way trial heats we conducted in the autumn were similarly stable. Clinton's support stood within plus or minus one percentage point of 51 percent, while Bush's support remained within plus or minus two points of 40 percent.

TABLE 9.13 Voters' Preferences for President in Trial Heats, Both Three-Way and Two-Way[a]

Dates of Polls	Three-Way Trial Heats[b]				Two-Way Trial Heats[c]		
	Prefer George Bush (%)	Prefer Bill Clinton (%)	Prefer Ross Perot (%)	Clinton's Advantage over Bush	Prefer George Bush (%)	Prefer Bill Clinton (%)	Clinton's Advantage over Bush
Feb. 19-20, 1992	NA	NA	NA	NA	51	40	-11
Feb. 26-March 1	NA	NA	NA	NA	50	40	-10
March 26-29	44	31	16	-13	49	40	-9
April 20-23	38	28	23	-10	46	40	-6
May 6-8	36	30	25	-6	47	41	-6
May 27-30	35	27	26	-8	45	38	-7
June 17-20	32	24	30	-8	45	40	-5
July 8-11	33	30	25	-3	43	43	0
Aug. 11-14	32	45	12	+13	35	52	+17
Aug. 23-24	31	44	15	+13	36	51	+15
Sept. 9-13	35	42	13	+7	38	50	+12
Oct. 2-4	38	46	7	+8	41	51	+10
Oct. 20-23	35	40	15	+5	*	*	*
Oct. 27-30	34	43	15	+9	41	52	+11
Oct. 29-Nov. 1	35	44	15	+9	42	52	+10

aBased on registered voters in 14 *New York Times*/CBS News polls and one CBS News poll (May 27-30). Beginning with the poll of Sept. 9-13 the respondents were weighted to reflect a "probable electorate." This technique uses responses to questions dealing with voter registration, past voting history, and the intention of voting in 1992 as a measure of the probability of particular respondents voting in November 1992. Not shown are those who were undecided, some of whom, in answer to a subsequent question, said they currently leaned toward one candidate or another.

bThe three-way trial heat question, beginning with the Oct. 24 poll was: "If the 1992 Presidential election were being held today, would you vote for George Bush for President and Dan Quayle for Vice President, the Republican candidates, or for Bill Clinton for President and Al Gore for Vice President, the Democratic candidates, or for Ross Perot for President and James Stockdale for Vice President, independent candidates?" In prior polls, the Vice-Presidential candidates were not mentioned.

"NA" denotes the two polls in February and early March in which the three-way trial heat was not asked at all.

cThe two-way trial heat question, beginning with the Aug. 11-14 poll, was: "If the 1992 presidential election were being held today, would you vote for George Bush for President and Dan Quayle for Vice President, the Republican candidates, or for Bill Clinton for President and Al Gore for Vice President, the Democratic candidates?" Prior to that August poll, the names of the Vice-Presidential candidates were not included.

Asterisks (*) denote the Oct. 20-23 poll as the only poll in which the two-way trial was not asked of all registered voters. In that poll, it was asked only of those voters who supported Ross Perot in the three-way trial heat. An estimated preference can be derived or constructed by allocating those Perot supporters and adding their strength to voters who already preferred Bush or Clinton in the three-way trial heat; this method yields 42% for Bush and 47% for Clinton. However, this estimated result for a two-way contest is not necessarily the same as what might have been obtained had the two-way trial heat actually been asked of all voters in the poll. *The Times* did not include such an estimated result in its time-trends, but simply the figures on how Perot supporters said they would vote.

Such relatively small fluctuations were within the sampling error of most of these polls. Although the slight jiggles measured in support for Clinton and Bush in Times/CBS News polls were probably real and meaningful, one cannot rule out the statistical possibility that there was no movement at all in the standings of the two major party candidates once the autumn phase of the campaign began.

Why, then, did it seem at the time as if things were more fluid? Some of this impression was due to the sudden re-entry of Ross Perot, announced on October 1. Perot's re-entry, initially greeted with widespread hostility, and his subsequent partial comeback in voters' estimation after his participation in the televised debates and his half-hour "infomercials," created a lot of commotion and had the potential to reshuffle the entire electoral situation during October. Had Perot managed to win back the 30 percent of the voters that he attracted at his peak in June, the outcome in November might have been quite different.

Many pollsters and political scientists were not at all sure they understood exactly how voters would react inside the voting booth if an independent candidate looked poised to come in first or a close second, and if a major party candidate seemed likely to come in third in a three-way contest. Standard polling methods at the Presidential level in the U.S. have developed over decades of two-party contests, and have confronted only the occasional (and typically weak) efforts of third parties or independent candidates. But, in the end, Perot only reclaimed about half the strength in our October trial heats that he had at his peak in June, and he never seemed within realistic striking distance of either of the major party candidates as Election Day approached. So the adequacy or inadequacy of modern polling techniques to measure voter decision-making in a truly tight three-way contest was not put to the ultimate test in 1992.

Another reason for the impression of fluidity in the fall was the widely publicized period ten days to two weeks before Election Day, just after the debates were over. At that time Ross Perot temporarily attained what would prove to be the highest level of favorability he would reach in our autumn polling and his resurgence coincided with a six-point drop by Clinton and a three-point drop by Bush in our trial heats, momentarily bringing the Clinton-Bush gap to the narrowest margin we measured in the autumn — five percentage points. At that same time some other polling organizations registered an even narrower gap separating Clinton and Bush (The Gallup Organization reported just one percentage point) that received much publicity and raised Republican hopes. In situations like this, the poll with the narrowest gap tends to get the most attention in the news even when it is obviously an outlier from a larger group of polls. Since some degree of tightening was registered in several (though not all) polls, it was probably real rather than a fluke. But, if so, it proved transient: within a few days of that apparent tightening, the gap reopened again.

Still another factor contributing to the impression of fluidity in the fall was the *way* many trial heat results were reported in the news. Many journalists found it convenient to focus on the size of Clinton's lead over Bush (i.e. the magnitude of the gap) rather than on each man's individual level of support. Such a focus by its nature magnifies any movement and can make small jiggles look like an ominous swing. For example, the net result of the relatively small fluctuations in support for Clinton and Bush in our five autumn polls produced a range in the size of Clinton's lead over Bush (in three-way trial heats) that went from a five-point advantage at its minimum to a nine-point advantage at its maximum. But, psychologically speaking, whether Clinton was at any given moment at the high end or the low end of that range generated quite different impressions: a five-point lead looked rather fragile and could give the other party hope, while a nine-point lead began to look like a blowout in the making, demoralizing to the other party. And small jiggles for the individual candidates could easily drive the gap anywhere between five and nine from one poll to the next. (In retrospect, Clinton's lead now seems as if it continuously hovered at around seven points, give or take two percentage points.)

If a journalist wants to emphasize the gap or lead, then he or she ought at the same time to mentally double the normal margin of sampling error in reporting the results, because each of the two numbers from which a lead or gap is calculated is individually subject to sampling error. That was not often done by journalists or, if done mentally, its implication was not often communicated to readers and viewers (see Mitofsky, Chapter 5).

Final Pre-Election Polling

In the penultimate pre-election polling conducted by *The Times* and CBS News on October 27 to 30, the candidates stood at 43 percent of the "probable electorate" preferring Clinton, 34 percent preferring Bush, and 15 percent preferring Perot, with eight percent undecided. These were the figures reported by *The Times* in the paper of November 1, on the Sunday before the election in a page-one story by Robin Toner under the headline "Polls Say Clinton Keeps Lead Despite Furious G.O.P. Fire."

But, as extra precaution against last-minute shifts, *The Times* participated with CBS News in one more round of pre-election polling, and CBS News by itself participated in yet a further round. We added new interviews taken October 31 and November 1 to those taken October 29 and

30, at the same time dropping the older interviews from October 27 and 28. This resulted in what might be termed a semi-new poll, based on a half-refreshed sample, logically akin to what is done in "tracking" polls of longer duration. *The Times* reported the results briefly on the morning of Election Day, in the paper of November 3, as part of broader article on page one by Michael Kelly, "Clinton and Bush in a Sprint as Race for White House Ends," and as part of a large graphic inside the paper which rounded up final polls from many organizations. But our refreshed results were virtually unchanged: 44 percent for Clinton, 35 percent for Bush, and 15 percent for Perot, with six percent undecided.

CBS News then continued by itself to poll one additional night (November 2), adding those results to the October 31-November 1 interviews, and dropping the older October 29-30 interviews. But, again, there was little change. Allocating leaners, CBS News broadcast its final figures on the morning of Election Day: 45 percent for Clinton, 37 for Bush, and 15 for Perot, with three percent undecided.

Actual Outcome Compared with the Polls

On Election Day, November 3, 1992, the actual outcome of the balloting across the country, according to returns compiled by *Congressional Quarterly*, was: 43.0 percent of the popular vote for Clinton, compared to 37.4 percent for Bush, and 18.9 percent for Perot. That represented about a six-point victory for Clinton, just slightly narrower than the nearly eight-point victory Bush had won over Dukakis four years earlier. Ross Perot's showing was the best for an independent or third party candidate since 1924 (when Robert M. LaFollette got 17 percent of the popular vote); Perot ran stronger than George Wallace in 1968 (14 percent) or John Anderson in 1980 (7 percent).

The 1992 election year was a good year for all the major national polls in the United States. The results of all the major polls at the end of the campaign were tightly bunched together, converging on roughly the same estimates which turned out to be quite near the true outcome of the election. On the morning of Election Day *The Times* published its last round-up of "Recent Polls" showing that six national polls by different organizations had estimated Clinton's support ranging between 43 and 44 percent, Bush's support ranging between 35 and 38 percent, and Perot's support ranging between 14 and 17 percent. On the day after the election in the paper of Wednesday, November 5, B. Drummond Ayres, Jr. assessed how the polls as a group fared in his article headed "Despite Some Puzzling Readings, '92 Polls Came Through at End."

In estimating the vote of the two major party candidates it would be hard for the polls as a group to be much more accurate or more tightly bunched than they were in 1992. If there was any difficulty the polls experienced it was that several (but not all) of them slightly underestimated Ross Perot's share of the vote in their final pre-election poll.

Of course, it could also be the case that many American voters themselves were experiencing a little difficulty in making up their minds about Ross Perot at the end of the 1992 campaign. In particular, one suspects that those who pronounced themselves "undecided" in the final pre-election polls may have split disproportionally towards Perot once they got in the voting booth. Some of them, eager for change and sensing that Bush would lose but feeling uneasy about Clinton as an alternative, may have felt free to send a message by voting for Perot. If pollsters have occasion to gain more experience with three-way contests for President, they should eventually be able to improve their methods to take better account of such calculations by voters. The degree of closeness of final pre-election poll estimates to the actual outcome of an election constitutes a natural "acid test" of the methods used in opinion polls, and creates a very visible and powerful built-in incentive for pollsters to constantly refine and improve their techniques.

Who Voted for Whom?: The "Portrait of the Electorate"

Use of polling by *The Times* in 1992 came to a climax when we analyzed the Election Day exit polls conducted by Voter Research and Surveys both nationally and in key states. Results of these polls informed several graphics and articles in the Wednesday and Thursday papers. On November 4 these included the two pieces by Robin Toner and by R. W. Apple, Jr. on page one under the banner headline "Clinton Captures Presidency With Huge Electoral Margin; Wins a Democratic Congress," and Jeffrey Schmalz's article inside, "Clinton Carves Wide and Deep Path Through Heart of Reagan Country." On November 5 they included Steven A. Holmes's page one news analysis on Ross Perot, "An Eccentric But No Joke," and Jeffrey Schmalz's piece inside the paper, "Gay Areas Are Jubilant Over Clinton."

The Times's most intensive use of polling data appeared in the Thursday paper when we printed the "Supertable" that was a full page deep and two-thirds of a page wide, showing how 106 different subgroups of the population voted in the Presidential elections of 1976, 1980, 1984, 1988, and 1992. Table 9.14 presents about half the contents (the top half) of that "Supertable." The bottom half, not shown here, contained an additional 60 lines of data such as race by age, sex by age, race by region, race by sex, sex by education, party identification by political philosophy, etc., exploiting the huge sample of more than 15,000 respondents by slicing it more finely than is possible in standard surveys of smaller size.

Our goal in preparing and publishing the Supertable is to share with readers some of the rich exit poll data that we pore over on election night and during the days afterwards, much of which would otherwise never make it into the newspaper. Publishing the data systematically as a Supertable enables the material to be utilized by a much wider audience.

The Supertable invites the reader to pursue his or her own analysis of the vote. One can compare different groups with one another within a given election year (vertically), or compare the same groups over time (horizontally), or both. For instance, when comparing the votes of men and women, one can see that a "gender gap" of five percentage points existed in 1992, with women giving the Democratic candidate a greater share of their vote than men did. At the same time one can see that a similar gender gap of six to eight points also existed in the three previous contests. One has to go back to the 1976 election to find men and women in close agreement.

In the demography of the 1992 vote one can discern the faint outlines of the old New Deal coalition. Clinton did particularly well among lower income Americans, less educated people, union voters, Catholics, Jewish voters, and liberals, as well as blacks.

But the big news was that Clinton also did well among independents, moderates, middle-income groups, and suburbanites — groups that Democratic candidates have had trouble capturing in recent elections. And Clinton managed to evenly split the South with Bush, another achievement unseen since Jimmy Carter in 1976.

Another important contributing factor to the Clinton victory was that for the first time in this five-election period, the Democratic candidate won as much loyalty from Democratic voters as the Republican candidate did from Republican voters. In the past, the pattern had been for self-described Republicans to be more loyal, while self-described Democrats suffered more defections to the other camp.

Also apparent in the Supertable are the outlines of the traditional Republican coalition. Bush did particularly well among white Protestants, college graduates, higher income-voters, and conservatives.

Ross Perot did particularly well among independents and among young men, but he received strikingly little support from blacks. One gains the impression that Perot tended to do well with people in the middle ranges of income and education. Perot also did fairly well with people who said their family's financial situation was worse off than four years earlier — but not nearly so well as Clinton did among this group.

TABLE 9.14 Portrait of the Electorate[a]

% of 1992 Total		1976		1980			1984		1988		1992		
		Carter	Ford	Reagan	Carter	Anderson	Reagan	Mondale	Bush	Dukakis	Clinton	Bush	Perot
100%	TOTAL VOTE	50	48	51	41	7	59	40	53	45	43	38	19
46	Men	50	48	55	36	7	62	37	57	41	41	38	21
55	Women	50	48	47	45	7	56	44	50	49	46	37	17
87	Whites	47	52	56	36	7	64	35	59	40	39	41	20
8	Blacks	83	16	11	85	3	9	90	12	86	82	11	7
3	Hispanics	76	24	33	59	6	37	62	30	69	62	25	14
1	Asians	—	—	—	—	—	—	—	—	—	29	55	16
65	Married	—	—	—	—	—	62	38	57	42	40	40	20
35	Unmarried	—	—	—	—	—	52	47	46	53	49	33	18
22	18-29 years old	51	47	43	44	11	59	40	52	47	44	34	22
38	30-44 years old	49	49	55	36	8	57	42	54	45	42	38	20
24	45-59 years old	47	52	55	39	5	60	40	57	42	41	40	19
16	60 and older	47	52	54	41	4	60	40	50	49	50	38	12
6	Not H.S. grad	—	—	46	51	2	50	50	43	56	55	28	17
25	H.S. graduate	—	—	51	43	4	60	39	50	49	43	36	20
29	Some college	—	—	55	35	8	61	38	57	42	42	37	21
40	College grad or more	—	—	52	35	11	58	41	56	43	44	39	18
24	College grad	—	—	—	—	—	—	—	62	37	40	41	19
16	Post-graduate	—	—	—	—	—	—	—	50	48	49	36	15
49	White Protestant	41	58	63	31	6	72	27	66	33	33	46	21
27	Catholic	54	44	50	42	7	54	45	52	47	44	36	20

(Continues)

TABLE 9.14 (Continued)

% of 1992 Total		1976 Carter	1976 Ford	1980 Reagan	1980 Carter	1980 Anderson	1984 Reagan	1984 Mondale	1988 Bush	1988 Dukakis	1992 Clinton	1992 Bush	1992 Perot
4	Jewish	64	34	39	45	15	31	67	35	64	78	12	10
17	White born-again Christian[b]	—	—	63	33	3	78	22	81	18	23	61	15
19	Union household	59	39	44	49	6	46	53	42	57	55	24	21
	Family income[c]												
14	under $15,000	58	40	42	51	6	45	55	37	62	59	23	18
24	$15,000–$29,999	55	43	44	47	7	57	42	49	50	45	35	20
30	$30,000–$49,999	48	50	53	39	7	59	40	56	44	41	38	21
20	$50,000–$74,999	36	63	59	32	8	66	33	56	42	40	42	18
13	$75,000 & over	—	—	63	26	10	69	30	62	37	36	48	16
	Family's financial siutation is:[d]												
25	Better today	30	70	37	55	7	86	14	—	—	24	62	14
41	Same today	51	49	46	47	7	50	50	—	—	41	41	18
34	Worse today	77	23	66	25	8	15	85	—	—	61	14	25
24	From the East	51	47	47	42	9	53	47	50	49	47	35	18
27	From the Midwest	48	50	51	41	7	58	41	52	47	42	37	21
30	From the South	54	45	52	44	3	64	36	58	41	42	43	16
20	From the West	46	51	53	34	10	61	38	58	46	44	34	22
35	Republicans	9	90	86	9	4	92	7	91	8	10	73	17
27	Independents	43	54	55	30	12	63	36	55	43	38	32	30
38	Democrats	77	22	26	67	6	25	74	17	82	77	10	13

Liberals	21	71	26	25	60	11	28	70	18	81	68	14	18
Moderates	49	51	48	49	42	8	53	47	49	50	48	31	21
Conservatives	29	29	70	73	23	4	82	17	80	19	18	65	17
Employed[e]	68	47	51	54	37	7	60	39	56	43	42	38	20
Unemployed	6	65	34	39	51	8	32	67	37	62	56	24	20
First time voter	11	—	—	—	—	—	61	38	51	47	48	30	22
Congressional Vote:													
For Democrat	54	75	23	22	69	7	23	76	27	72	74	11	15
For Republican	46	13	86	83	11	5	93	7	82	17	10	71	18

aBased on exit polls of voters leaving polling places around the nation on Election Day. The 1992 data were collected by Voter Research and Surveys with questionnaires completed by 15,490 voters in 300 random precincts. The 1976 data were based on a survey conducted by CBS News with questionnaires from 15,300 voters. Data for other years were based on surveys of voters conducted by The New York Times and CBS News: 15,201 voters in 1980; 9,174 voters in 1984; and 11,645 in 1988. Those who gave no answer are not shown. Dashes indicate that a question was not asked or a category was not provided in a particular year.

b"Born-again Christian was labeled "born-again Christian/fundamentalist" in 1992 and "fundamentalist and Evangelical Christian" in 1988.

cFamily income categories in 1976 were: under $8,000, $8,000-$12,000, $12,001-$20 000, and over $20,000. In 1980 the categories were: under $10,000, $10,000-$14,999, $15,000-$24,999, $25,000-$50,000, and over $50,000. In 1994 and 1988 the categories were: under $12,500, $12,500-$24,999, $25,000-$34,999, $35,000-$49,999, and $50,000 and over.

dFamily financial situation is compared to one year ago in 1976 and 1980; four years ago in 1984 and 1992; the 1976 and 1984 numbers for family financial situation are from NBC News.

Note that the version of this table that appeared in The New York Times on November 5, 1992 was approximately twice as long as the version above and contained an additional 60 lines; most of the additional groupings were formed by multiple criteria, such as race and age, sex and age, race and region, etc.

eIn 1976 and 1980 "employed" referred to the head of the household.

Testing Hunches and Claims

In addition to contributing directly to news articles, our polling allowed reporters and editors to check hunches, to test claims, and to avoid being manipulated.

What If Perot Had Not Been in the Contest?

Probably the most frequent puzzle we were asked to solve during 1992 was "Is Perot hurting Bush more or Clinton more?" or "Who would benefit more if Perot stays in/drops out/gets back in/drops out again?" Using polling data we repeatedly made attempts to answer the question at different junctures of the campaign. In tackling the question, we were usually looking for an answer in terms of votes: from whom does Perot siphon more votes, or to whom would Perot's supporters go if Perot were not a candidate?

As Table 9.15 shows, the answer in five separate tests from June through November was always similar: Perot drew heavily from *both* Clinton and Bush and, accordingly, his supporters would shift to Clinton and Bush in roughly *equal* proportion if Perot were out of the picture. In the first three tests Clinton would gain a few more Perot voters than Bush would if Perot were gone, and thus Clinton could be said to be hurt slightly more than Bush by having Perot in the contest. But by the last two tests — including the one that really counted on Election Day — the advantage or disadvantage to the two major party candidates was almost exactly equal.

In the Election Day exit poll 38 percent of Perot's actual voters said they would have voted for Clinton, while 37 percent said they would have voted for Bush. Steven A. Holmes drew on these findings in his November 5 page one article, "An Eccentric But No Joke."

Yet, of course, Ross Perot's effect on the 1992 contest was not limited to the 19 percent of the popular vote he drew. As argued earlier, Perot kept George Bush on the defensive in the spring at a time when Clinton was relatively weak, and Perot's re-entry into the campaign in the fall altered the dynamics of the Presidential debates and the balance of TV political advertising. Perot's presence doubled the criticism of the Bush Administration, and intensified the call for change. This made it harder for Bush to score his points or to turn Clinton's character, rather than Bush's own record, into the chief issue of the 1992 campaign.

TABLE 9.15 What if Ross Perot Were Not in the Race? What Perot's Supporters
Said on Five Occasions[a]

Dates of Poll	What Perot Supporters in a Three-Way Contest Say They Would Do in a Two-Way Contest Between Clinton and Bush	
IN JUNE WHEN PEROT WAS AT HIS PEAK OF 30 PERCENT SUPPORT		
June 17-20	Would vote for Clinton	39%
	Would vote for Bush	33%
	Undecided	7%
	Would not vote	21%
IN JULY A WEEK BEFORE PEROT WITHDREW FROM THE CONTEST		
July 8-11	Would vote for Clinton	40%
	Would vote for Bush	33%
	Undecided	13%
	Would not vote	14%
IN OCTOBER AFTER PEROT RE-ENTERED THE CONTEST AND PARTICIPATED IN DEBATES		
Oct. 20-23	Would vote for Clinton	49%
	Would vote for Bush	45%
	Undecided	5%
	Would not vote	2%
IN FINAL PRE-ELECTION POLLING WHEN PEROT'S SUPPORT STABILIZED AT 15%		
Oct. 27-30	Would vote for Clinton	39%
	Would vote for Bush	39%
	Undecided	8%
	Would not vote	12%
ON ELECTION DAY IN EXIT POLL WHEN PEROT GOT 19% OF THE VOTE		
Nov. 3	Would vote for Clinton	38%
	Would vote for Bush	37%
	Undecided	6%
	Would not vote	14%

[a]Based on four nationwide telephone polls by *The New York Times* and CBS
News, and the Election Day exit poll by Voter Research and Surveys.

What If All American Adults Had Voted?

We were also able to answer the question of whether the election results would have remained the same or been different if everyone had voted in 1992. This was an interesting question because non-voters have been approximately half the adult population in recent Presidential elections. In our our late pre-election polling we asked all adults the trial heat questions, rather than skipping unregistered voters over the trial heats as we had in all earlier polls. We found that Clinton would still have won, and by the same margin of victory over Bush, but that Perot would have gained another two percentage points if all adults had turned out to vote.

But, of course, this way of estimating it can only answer the question of how the campaign that was actually waged in 1992 would have ended if all non-voters had at the last minute been magically converted into voters. It cannot answer the potentially more interesting question of how that campaign itself might have changed if the parties and candidates had expected everyone to vote — including the poor, the young, the alienated, and others who usually have low rates of turnout. The kind of candidates who stepped forward might have been different, the electoral strategies those candidates pursued might have been revised, and the issue appeals and themes they emphasized might potentially have been transformed.

Conclusion

The major polling lesson reaffirmed by *The Times*'s experience in 1992 is that any program of opinion research must be designed so that it is responsive, flexible, and adequate to the task it faces. Because the election is a year-long process, it is necessary to design a 12-month (or longer) series of polls that can provide a setting to and offer perspective on the individual phases of the electoral cycle. Because public reactions to personalities, issues, and events can change during the year, it is important to repeat a core of trend questions time after time in order to capture the dynamics of the campaign. Because long-term, middle-run, and short-lived forces can each affect the outcome, it is important to build in devices to study all three types of factors. Because American Presidential elections are finally decided by 50 separate state elections, it is important to poll in some of the crucial battleground states to see how the national contest is playing out in different locales. Because last-minute shifts in voter preference can and sometimes do occur, it is important to poll as close as is practical to Election Day with pre-election polling, then to document actual voter decision-making through exit polling on Election Day itself, and then to be prepared to call back the pre-election respondents afterwards in the event there are surprises in the election outcome. Because voter turnout can be critical, it is important to develop and improve ways to estimate the likelihood that individuals will vote. Because nonvoters are almost half the voting age population, it is important to find ways to hear their voices too. And because the quality of the polling data is crucial to all subsequent interpretation and reporting, it is important to invest in properly drawn samples, high-quality interviewing, and an experienced staff for question writing and data analysis. Finally, when it comes to the ultimate reporting of poll results, it is a boon and a pleasure to have so many fine correspondents, editors, and graphics artists on your team!

Notes

Many thanks to the staff members of the News Surveys Department at *The Times* who originally computed, checked, and organized most of the numerical data presented in this chapter, and who contributed mightily to the paper's polling analysis during 1992: Marjorie Connelly, Janet Elder, and Deborah Hofmann. The correspondents and reporters who most frequently wrote the poll articles in 1992 brought to the polling effort a seemingly endless supply of ideas, hypotheses, and insightful interpretations: R.W. Apple, Jr., Richard L. Berke, Adam Clymer, Andrew Rosenthal, Jeffrey Schmalz, and especially the national political correspondent, Robin Toner. It was also a pleasure working with the editors most frequently involved with our 1992 polling: Soma Golden Behr, John M. Lee, Richard J. Meislin, Howell Raines, Dennis Stern, and Philip Taubman. Also many thanks to our partners in telephone polling, our colleagues at CBS News: Kathleen Frankovic and Martin Plissner. And finally, we much appreciated the exit polling expertise at Voter Research and Surveys: Murray Edelman and Warren Mitofsky. None of these individuals necessarily agrees with all the interpretations in this chapter.

10

Problems of Character: Was It the Candidate or the Press?

Michael W. Traugott
Jennifer Means

News organizations are increasingly attracted to the use of quick turn-around polls to support their coverage of breaking news events. Their presentation of survey results is typically limited to marginal frequencies for single questions, whether for the entire sample or by major subgroups defined by demographics. In campaign coverage, other politically relevant characteristics such as party identification, candidate preference, and likelihood of voting are important factors in interpreting the meaning and significance of political attitudes. Poll–based coverage often makes significant sacrifices for the sake of journalistic brevity and simplicity: infrequent discussion of complicated relationships that reflect the nuances of public opinion on an issue. Without seriously addressing the problems created by simplistic explanations, news organizations may misinform voters and encourage public misunderstanding of critical issues and events.

This dilemma becomes more acute as news organizations increase their use of public opinion polls in news stories. Many national newspapers, often in partnership with the television networks, now sponsor their own public opinion polls. They routinely survey the attitudes and opinions of the public to learn how Americans feel or think about a variety of issues, personalities, and events. The result of such polling has generally been accurate and reliable indicators of public sentiment; but in some circumstances, alternate interpretations of data could have moved the development of a story in an entirely different direction.

Public opinion must be interpreted cautiously because we live in a complex society and therefore our opinions are just as multifarious.

News organizations sometimes overlook these issues when they try to beat their competitors on a fast breaking story. As a result, news stories based on quick turnaround poll results are often written in an unrefined manner with the frequent consequence that intricate relationships in the data are lost in this hurried process. In the extreme case, there is the possibility that conclusions initially reached by journalists may in fact prove to be misleading or incorrect.

Many news organizations and journalists do not believe that there are any serious problems with the way in which poll results are generally reported. They claim that their readers do not want to be subjected to news stories that explore multivariate relationships in poll findings. This may have been more true in the past, but the 1992 presidential campaign suggests that the public wants a more detailed treatment of important issues facing this nation and can absorb such information. This is a reasonable standard to set for the reporting of public opinion results, and the news media should learn to deal better with the innate complexity of public opinion. If they do not, news organizations face two potential problems. They run the risk of superficial reporting, and their deficient scenarios may be disproved by subsequent campaign developments.

This chapter reports on a reanalysis of media polls conducted early in the 1992 campaign, looking at whether there was a more interesting and telling news story than the obvious one presented through marginal frequencies for selected variables. The analysis is based upon a secondary analysis of a single poll and a subsequent story published by *The Washington Post* in February, just before the New Hampshire primary. However, we believe that the results could be replicated in any of the many polls conducted at the same time. The examination was performed in two stages. First, the original *Post* article, based on poll findings, was examined in the context of similar reporting during the campaign.[1] The next stage involved a secondary analysis of the poll data used in preparing the original story. This reanalysis suggests that public opinion on the central issues discussed was not as clear as the *Post* article might have led some readers to believe. The analysis reveals that a different, more interesting news story might have been written from the same data. We conclude that news organizations could have provided their audiences with more relevant and useful news coverage with only slightly more analytical effort, thus more closely approaching their professed goal of informing the public.

Politics and political campaigns have been a staple of news coverage for some time because the media have found it easy to report the conflict (campaigning) and its resolution (elections). The complexity of these processes can be neatly packaged by the news media for public consumption because they are familiar and recurring events. Polls have become a central measurement tool of "precision journalists" in this process of simplification across the last two decades, and as a result they too have become a standard feature of American political reporting.

George Gallup, Elmo Roper, and Archibald Crossley developed political polling during the 1930's with the support of media organizations (see Cantril, 1991, p.10). They were well aware of how powerful a research tool polling could be; they had witnessed its effectiveness in the advertising field. Public opinion polling originated in the retail business in order to determine the product preferences of consumers. Crossley, Roper, and Gallup envisioned public opinion polls contributing to more responsive leadership and resulting in better government. But the widespread dissemination of their early results was based upon standing relationships with leading newspapers and magazines of the day.

The founding fathers of political polling experienced success as long as the polls were reliable. When they failed, as happened in the 1948 "upset" victory of Truman over Dewey, public support for polls suffered a serious setback. Academic researchers were concerned that the actions of their commercial counterparts would reduce the credibility of all surveys; and public confidence in polls was not fully restored until the 1960 presidential election. In that year, every poll indicated either that John Kennedy would win in a close election or that if Richard Nixon did win, the margin would be quite small (Crespi 1989). One consequences of this "successful" prediction was news organizations' increased interest in polls, strengthened by the growing use of polls by political candidates and special interest groups in the 1960s. The print media's growing competition with television news operations, especially in election coverage, also stimulated this interest in polls (Mendelson & Crespi, 1970). The resulting proliferation of polls was a reflection of the ease with which a news story could be generated and the gain in respect for polls among those in government and business. By the mid–1970s, polls had become an integral and essential part of campaign coverage in the media.

Out of a concern about newsworthiness, including the timing and content of polls, news organizations considered the development of their own data collection activities. News organizations initially decided to collect data themselves in order to increase their editorial control. Newspapers were at a clear advantage because of one particular resource that was readily available: telephone banks in their circulation and classified advertising offices. As the network news became more involved in polling, they formed alliances with newspapers. The economics of polling encouraged large circulation morning newspapers and the networks to share their polling costs, producing the joint polling operations of CBS News and *The New York Times*, *The Washington Post* and ABC News, and other media pairings (Gollin, 1987). In these arrangements, the two news organizations share the same evening deadline. The network typically broadcasts a summary of the main poll findings because story lengths on the evening news are constrained by the fixed length of a broadcast. The next day's paper often contains an extended analysis of the data because its news hole is bigger.

The prominence of poll results presented in the news media has greatly affected American society, especially in the political arena. Persistently, some politicians, candidates and social critics accuse the news media of improperly influencing the political process (Paletz et al, 1980; Von Hoffman, 1980; Wheeler, 1976). Charges of wrongdoing are especially prevalent during pre-election periods, when candidates are soliciting campaign support by making claims about electability, only to have their assertions rudely blunted by release of a media poll (Gollin, 1987). The combined effects of polls and extended media coverage of them are also critical during the primary season for at least two other reasons. First, there are usually multiple candidates seeking the party's nomination. Unable to cover all candidates equally, the news media give more attention to the candidates they think are most viable and have the best chance of winning either the next event or the nomination (Marshall, 1983a and b; Bartels, 1988; See also Mutz, Chapter 12). Second, the primaries can be viewed as a sequence of elections in which media coverage of the outcome in one state can dramatically effect later polls and primaries (Orren & Polsby, 1987). If coverage is poll–driven, then there are indirect effects on subsequent events that are a consequence of the current quality and quantity of coverage.

News organizations employ polls to support their well–known tendency to report campaigns in terms of strategy and candidate standing (Broh, 1980). The media use sporting metaphors to emphasize the "horse race" aspects of coverage, as well as the popularity, character and electability of a candidate.[2] The news media sometimes depict public opinion in a way that is inaccurate because they do not reveal the relationship between the survey respondents' partisanship, ideology, current candidate preference or other relevant characteristics. Such misrepresentations can influence and change the audience members' opinions and behavior, just as correct interpretations can.

There is little consensus on the manner in which the media's use of polls influences people, but there is also little doubt that it does have an effect (Traugott, 1992a). Some experts argue that polls showing one candidate far ahead increase the incentives for supporters of the trailing candidate to change their preference and climb on board the winning candidate's bandwagon. Others emphasize underdog effects, where sympathetic voters rally around the candidate trailing in the polls. One problem for those assessing such effects may be that they are likely to occur simultaneously and thereby offset each other (Lavrakas, Holley, & Miller, 1991).

Those who have observed the increased use of polls in campaign coverage express a range of concerns. Some worry about the methodological competence of journalists who report on polls (Morin, 1992b; Mitofsky, Chapter 5), while others focus on the style of reporting. The predominant form of reporting is to employ the frequency distribution of the responses to individual questions, especially the "trial heat" question that measures candidate preference. This single item most fuels the appetite of journalists and news organizations for horse race coverage. Late in the 1992 campaign, tracking polls conducted continuously by or for some news organizations became an integral part of reporting, resulting in daily reports of who was ahead and by how much. Some of these surveys suffered from significant methodological problems, and their use may have distorted reporting of the dynamics of the "end game" of the campaign (Traugott, 1992b). They may also produce differing versions of the folklore about how the 1992 presidential campaign ended and interpretations of its broader political significance.

This chapter takes a closer look at a different example of poll–based reporting early in the 1992 campaign, using it to illustrate how the news media seldom report the complexity of poll results to their audiences. Through secondary analysis, it raises the question of whether the same data could have produced alternate stories. The potential ramifications of these two stories — the "original" oversimplified portrayal and a more "nuanced" version — are discussed in the conclusions.

The Case Study

Many reporters covering the 1992 presidential campaign believed that the candidates' policy positions were important but also knew their audience wanted to know the intimate details of the candidates' personal lives in order to judge their character. For the last several presidential election cycles, a candidate's character, and all that is associated with it, has been considered legitimate news. Reporters have considered the candidates' personal lives fair game and have been prepared to cover them. Before the first ballot of the New Hampshire primary was cast, the Gennifer Flowers story broke, immediately jeopardizing the nascent candidacy of Bill Clinton. News organizations used the flimsiest of journalistic pegs — a press conference staged by a tabloid — to engage in brief flurries of reporting about the "character issue" and "family values."[3]

Much of the subsequent coverage was driven by the results of quick turnaround opinion polls reported to show that many voters were concerned with a candidate's marital infidelity. For example, Robert Shogan (1992), writing in *The Los Angeles Times*, cited three polls to illustrate his point that some voters were unable to support an unfaithful candidate. He used such pessimistic phrases as "gravely damaged" and "wounded standard bearer" to describe Clinton's predicament. This "character issue" story took on a life of its own. Even two months later, Richard Benedetto (1992) used data from a *USA Today*/CNN Gallup poll to indicate that respondents rated Bush more favorably than Clinton on traits such as "upholding family values" and "honesty and trustworthiness."

When candidates get in trouble early in the campaign, the consequences can sometimes be fatal. Both organizational and financial support can wither, especially if opponents can take advantage of a candidate's vulnerable position. However, other candidates (both Democratic and Republican) could not exploit the flurry of coverage surrounding Clinton and the infidelity charges and deal a fatal blow to the front- runner. The other Democratic candidates found it difficult to get the news media to cover their positions on more substantive issues like the economy and taxes. George Bush was also ultimately unable to capitalize on the Clinton "feeding frenzy" because of questions later raised about his own alleged infidelity.

The level of such coverage ebbed and flowed during the campaign, often in conjunction with the timing of important events on the road to the nominating conventions and election day. Using data bases in Lexis/Nexis, the national news stream was scanned for coverage relating to "Bill Clinton," " George Bush," and "infidelity." The results, aggregated to biweekly totals across the entire campaign period, are presented in Figure 10.1.[4] The dramatic increase in Clinton infidelity coverage between early January and early February of 1992, peaking at ninety–five stories in mid–January, is evident. Throughout the early Democratic primaries, the Clinton staff was constantly bombarded with questions about their candidate's character as it related to the marital infidelity charges. Although this coverage subsided in April, interest grew again as the summer's Democratic and Republican conventions approached. The stories providing a general election perspective in late August and early September returned to this issue as well. During this period, the Bush allegations never received an equivalent amount of coverage. The greatest amount of coverage that the Bush infidelity charge received was eleven articles during mid–August, at the time that the Trento book was being promoted upon publication.[5]

The fact that Gennifer Flowers' disclosure became a story at all reflects a long term trend in changing standards of newsworthiness for political coverage, the point in the campaign at which the story arose, and the

199

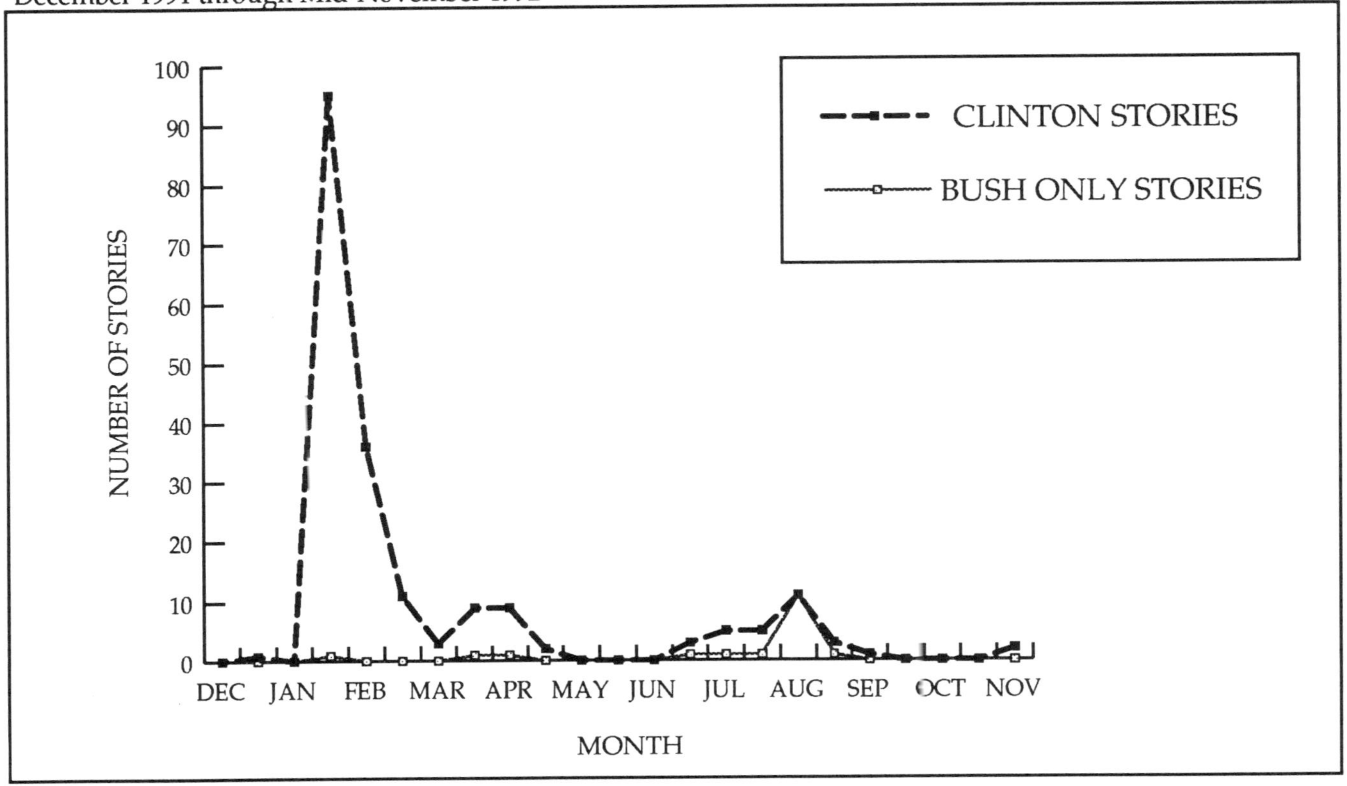

FIGURE 10.1 The Relative Coverage of Infidelity and Bill Clinton and George Bush in Major Newspapers from December 1991 through Mid-November 1992

marketing skills of the publishers of *The Star*.[6] In a sense, the increasing reliance of presidential candidates on campaigns that emphasize personal traits like trustworthiness and honesty also contributes to the press's sense of appropriateness. Therefore, it should come as no surprise that the polling operations of major news organizations turned to the topic as well. The incident had all of the classic ingredients of a good story — conflict, novelty, high impact and timeliness — and it involved the presidential campaign at a point when media interest was peaking just before the New Hampshire primary.

The attractions of polling for news organizations have been well documented. The methodology provides a direct measure of public reaction to events and individuals under conditions of editorial control over question wording and timing of the survey. A consensus about their newsworthiness explains why multiple polls are conducted around such events as debates, conventions, and incidents like the Gennifer Flowers press conference. However, a consensus about what is newsworthy in the findings of any particular poll is less likely to exist. While there may be general agreement on which topics or questions are most important to ask, there is no such agreement on how to report the results (Lewis, 1991). This lack of agreement leaves room for flexibility in reporting results, as well as the possibility of misreporting them.

This research is based upon the secondary analysis of a poll that supported an article originally appearing in *The Washington Post* National Weekly Edition . It was selected because it met several significant criteria. They included the presence of a major newspaper with a national readership as its source, a public opinion poll and its results as the focus of the article, issues and events in the 1992 presidential campaign, and the availability of the poll data for secondary analysis. We appreciate having early access to these data, but it is important to emphasize that virtually every major news organization conducted at least one poll about Flowers' allegations during this period. The analyses produced below suggest that alternative stories could have been produced from any of these other polls as well.

The *Washington Post* article was actually based upon two polls: data collected in an overnight survey by ABC News and The Post, and then a second survey the two organizations conducted just a few days later, using many of the same questions and a larger sample size. We used the data from the second survey, conducted from January 30 until February 2, 1992, for which the total sample size equalled 1,512 respondents.[7] The central question is whether a different story, equally newsworthy, could have been prepared from the same data. This is important because of the way in which initial reporting of the results framed subsequent coverage of the campaign. For example, *The Washington Post* was publishing articles about "character" two months later, after Super Tuesday when the nomination had virtually been assured, that continued to make references to the Flowers' allegations and their potential for disrupting the Clinton campaign (Maraniss, 1992).

The original *Washington Post* story portrayed the issue of marital infidelity as a serious concern for many survey respondents. The article suggested that many Americans could not tolerate adultery committed by a presidential candidate. This analysis was based upon the marginals for three central questions: Whether respondents could vote for a candidate who had an extramarital affair, whether Clinton's alleged affair should be an issue, and whether he should withdraw if the affair were confirmed. When asked if they could vote for a candidate for president who had an extramarital affair, 30% of the sample said they could not. On the question of whether Clinton's affair, if he had one, should be an issue, 21% said it should. Further, 54% were reported as saying Clinton should withdraw from the race if the affair were confirmed. These results suggested a sobering campaign ahead for Bill Clinton.

A single survey cannot explain whether attitudes precede candidate preferences or simply reflect a projection of prior predispositions. But partisanship and candidate preference are politically relevant factors for assessing the significance of public reactions to allegations about marital infidelity, and the exploration of these relationships formed the basis for the extended analysis. A somewhat different story emerges when public attitudes toward marital infidelity are evaluated by respondents' party identification and candidate preference.

The survey responses to the three basic questions (about the respondents' position on adultery committed by a presidential candidate, adultery as a campaign issue, and the prospect of a Clinton withdrawal if the allegations were true) were analyzed by these two politically relevant characteristics. Under these conditions, a more revealing picture of the impact of the incident emerges. As shown in Table 10.1, the data strongly suggest that projection was at work. Those who supported Bush over Clinton at the time — Democrats and Independents as well as Republicans — were equally likely to express concern about the general issue of marital infidelity and its particular relevance to Bill Clinton as were those who had already decided to support him. Although 24% of all the Democrats said they could not vote for an unfaithful candidate, those who supported Bush over Clinton were twice as likely to feel this way (40% compared to 19%). The views of self–described independents were essentially the same. Overall, 35% said they could not support an unfaithful candidate. But Republicans who favored Bush were three

TABLE 10.1 The Relationship Between Candidate Preference and Support for a Candidate Who Was Unfaithful in his Marriage, Controlling for Party ID[a]

	Could you vote for an unfaithful candidate?			Should Clinton's marital infidelity be an issue?			Should an untruthful Clinton Withdraw?[b]			N
	YES %	NO %	DK %	YES %	NO %	DK %	YES %	NO %	DK %	
TOTAL SAMPLE	69	28	3	19	80	1	50	46	4	1,512
Prefer BUSH[c]	60	37	3	29	70	1	62	36	2	777
Prefer CLINTON	79	18	3	8	91	1	37	58	4	627
Don't Know/ Won't Vote	68	24	8	19	78	3	53	33	14	108
DEMOCRATS[d]	72	24	4	16	83	1	44	52	4	498
Prefer BUSH	57	40	3	35	63	1	63	36	1	118
Prefer CLINTON	77	19	4	9	90	1	37	59	4	342
Don't Know/ Won't Vote	63	26	11	16	82	2	61	26	13	38
REPUBLICANS	62	35	3	25	74	1	60	38	3	433
Prefer BUSH	59	38	3	28	71	1	63	35	2	380
Prefer CLINTON	88	12	-	4	94	2	41	54	5	45
Don't Know/ Won't Vote	75	25	-	12	88	-	13	75	12	8
INDEPENDENTS	71	26	3	17	82	1	49	46	5	539
Prefer BUSH	63	35	2	27	73	-	60	39	1	253
Prefer CLINTON	80	18	2	7	92	1	37	58	5	230
Don't Know/ Won't Vote	68	23	9	23	73	4	55	29	16	56

[a] Data are from a Jan. 30 - Feb. 2, 1992, telephone survey conducted by the Washington Post / ABC News.
[b] Exact question wording: "On a different matter, could you vote for a candidate who had an extramarital affair, or not?," "Do you think the question of whether or not Clinton had an extramarital affair should be ar issue in the presidential election, or not?," and "A woman named Gennifer Flowers says that she had an affair with Clinton, and Clinton says this is not true. If it turned out that Clinton has not told the truth and did have an affair with this woman, do you think he should withdraw from the race or not?"
[c] Exact question wording: "If the 1992 presidential election were being held today, and the candidates were George Bush, the Republican, and Bill Clinton, the Democrat, for whom would you vote?"
[d] Exact question wording: "Generally speaking do you usually think of yourself as: a Democrat, a Republican, an Independent, or what?"

times as likely as those who favored Clinton, admittedly a small group, to feel this way (38% compared to 12%).

Similar relationships appear when the two questions about the appropriateness of marital infidelity as a campaign issue and Clinton's withdrawal from the race if the affair were later found to be true were analyzed. Supporters of George Bush were more likely to think this was an issue (by margins of between 20 to 26 percentage points) and that Clinton should withdraw if the allegations were true (by the same margins), independent of their partisanship. These results suggest that Clinton's political future was not as dim as the news coverage might have led readers to believe. Clinton was "suffering" disproportionately among groups where he had little support to begin with and probably stood little chance of gaining, even if the Gennifer Flowers' scandal had never broken — respondents who were already predisposed to support Bush.

Looking at the respondents' registration status and likelihood of voting in November would have been another politically relevant way to evaluate these poll results. In the early stage of the campaign, respondents who were unregistered and preferred Clinton were twice as likely to express concern about an unfaithful candidate (27% compared to 14%). And among the respondents who were registered to vote, 34% of those who were unlikely to vote and were Clinton supporters indicated that they were concerned about an unfaithful candidate, compared to 13% of those describing themselves as likely voters. There was no difference in the attitudes of the Bush supporters by their registration status and likelihood of voting. The data presented in Table 10.2 also demonstrate that there were no differences in these relationships for the question of whether Clinton's alleged infidelity should be an issue and whether an untruthful Clinton should withdraw, controlling on registration status and likelihood of voting. In the general election campaign, registration status and likelihood of voting obviously become more critical characteristics that should be a part of the presentation of any survey results. But even in the spring, they could have been used to define these basic relationships.

To summarize these findings, a re-examination of the ABC News/*Washington Post* poll shows that most of those concerned about the infidelity issue were individuals who were not predisposed to support Clinton (Republicans, Independents, and Bush supporters in general) and who, at the time of the poll, were not likely to vote for Clinton (unregistered respondents and unlikely voters). These "alternative" results produce an interesting but different conclusion about the impact of the Gennifer Flowers' allegations, one that bears some resemblance to subsequent campaign events. One conclusion of this analysis is that if

TABLE 10.2 The Relationship Between Candidate Preference and Support for a Candidate Who Was Unfaithful in his Marriage, Controlling for Voter Registration and Turnout[a]

	Could you vote for an unfaithful candidate?			Should Clinton's marital infidelity be an issue?			Should an untruthful Clinton Withdraw?[b]			
	YES %	NO %	DK %	YES %	NO %	DK %	YES %	NO %	DK %	N
REGISTERED[c]	70	25	5	19	79	2	50	44	6	1,110
Prefer BUSH[d]	59	38	3	31	68	1	62	37	1	575
Prefer CLINTON	83	14	2	7	92	1	36	60	4	462
No Preference/Won't Vote	69	22	9	18	78	4	51	34	15	73
NOT REGISTERED	66	30	4	20	80	0	52	41	7	396
Prefer BUSH	63	34	3	26	74	0	62	36	2	198
Prefer CLINTON	70	27	3	11	89	0	39	55	6	165
No Preference/Won't Vote	64	30	6	24	76	0	55	33	12	33
LIKELY VOTER[e]	73	23	4	19	81	0	52	43	6	1,308
Prefer BUSH	61	36	3	29	70	1	62	36	2	689
Prefer CLINTON	85	13	2	8	91	0	38	59	3	538
No Preference/Won't Vote	74	19	7	19	81	0	52	35	13	81
UNLIKELY VOTER	58	37	5	21	75	4	52	41	7	203
Prefer BUSH	63	36	1	32	68	0	61	36	3	88
Prefer CLINTON	63	34	3	10	90	0	38	59	3	88
No Preference/Won't Vote	48	41	11	22	67	11	56	29	15	27

[a] Data are from a Jan. 30 - Feb. 2, 1992, telephone survey conducted by the *Washington Post*/ABC News.
[b] Exact question wording: "On a different matter, could you vote for a candidate who had an extramarital affair, or not?" "Do you think the question of 'whether or not Clinton had an extramarital affair should be an issue in the presidential election, or not?" and "A woman named Gennifer Flowers says that she had an affair with Clinton, and Clinton says this is not true. If it turned out that Clinton has not told the truth and did have an affair with this woman, do you think he should withdraw from the race or not?"
[c] Exact question wording: "Can you tell me whether you are registered to vote at your present address?"
[d] Exact question wording: "If the 1992 presidential election were being held today, and the candidates were George Bush, the Republican, and Bill Clinton, the Democrat, for whom would you vote?"
[e] Exact question wording: "Some people have busier schedules than others. Because of this, some people who plan to vote can't always get around to it on election day. With your own personal schedule in mind, I'd like you to rate the chances that you will vote in the 1992 presidential election next November: are you absolutely certain to vote, will probably vote, are the chances about 50-50, less than 50-50, or don't you think you will vote in the 1992 presidential election next November?" The grouping of "likely voters" is the combination of the first two categories, and "unlikely voters" are formed by combining the last three responses.

Clinton could provide a credible response to the allegations and get back to discussing issues of interest and concern to his supporters, his candidacy could probably be sustained.

Conclusion

This analysis is not intended to reduce the political significance of the Gennifer Flowers incident or its potential impact in what turned out to be a close general election contest. But a news story suggesting that there was a partisan or candidate preference–based explanation for the voters' attitudes provides a different way of assessing the political consequences of the incident. The newsworthiness of the data is not diminished; rather it is altered by placing the results in a somewhat different context.

Traditional journalistic approaches to survey data and the limited analytical skills of many reporters explain the reporting of marginals rather than the relationships between variables. The oversimplification of survey findings does a disservice to readers and viewers in two ways. It does not fully represent the subtlety and complexity of the real world. And the cumulative nature of campaign coverage means that results presented at an early stage of the campaign can take on a durable life of their own, structuring the emphasis and tone of what follows. Candidates and their handlers understand this principle well, and they work continuously to affect the "spin" placed on events along the way.

Especially when quick turnaround polls support coverage, news organizations operate under serious time pressures to produce news stories based upon such polls. Nothing in the analysis presented above suggest the need to collect more data. Any of these analyses could have been specified in advance and the tables scanned before writing the copy. The main point is that politically relevant independent variables should be used to investigate alternative explanations for the marginal distributions of attitudes and opinions. Reporters must take care to analyze and report data in ways that add to citizen's understanding of the political process and the dynamics of the campaign rather than contribute to a misunderstanding of the significance of important events.

Notes

An earlier version of this chapter was prepared for delivery at the Annual Conference of the Midwest Association for Public Opinion Research in Chicago, in November, 1992. We gratefully acknowledge the receipt of computer-readable versions of surveys conducted by *The Washington Post* and ABC News from Richard Morin, director of polling for *The Washington Post*. The analyses and interpretations presented here are the sole responsibility of the authors.

1. The original article was written by Richard Morin (1992a) and entitled "Caring Less About Adultery, More About Mendacity: The Clinton Scandal Tests the Limits of Public Tolerance."

2. Albert H. Cantril, The Opinion Connection, p. 22. The four standard criteria of newsworthiness used by the new media include the presence of conflict, the public's familiarity with the actors or situations portrayed, the timeliness of the story, and the impact the story will have on an audience.

3. Later in the campaign, the media would seize upon a footnote in a book entitled *The Power House* (Trento, 1992) that raised a similar issue about George Bush's marital fidelity. For a variety of reasons, the Bush story did not receive as much coverage as the Clinton story. One reason is that no individual came forward to hold a press conference, and the president categorically denied the allegation when asked about it during a White House press conference (Harwood, 1992).

4. The search revealed that many articles that referred to Clinton's alleged infidelity also contained references to the consequences for his campaign against Bush. However, there were few articles that contained references only to Bush's alleged infidelity and its consequences for his campaign against Clinton.

5. There were in fact some surveys conducted to measure public reaction to the allegations about Bush, but they were not as numerous nor published as widely as those conducted about Clinton in the spring. Typical of the scant coverage they received was this reference in a story by Jonathan Alter in *Newsweek* (1992):

> This year's unmistakable consensus is for privacy — to let both candidates and women do largely what they want with their bodies. A *Newsweek* Poll shows 85 percent think the press should drop the entire infidelity question and that it's "not a serious issue" — for either candidate.

6. The first part of the story appeared under the headline "My 12–Year Affair with Bill Clinton" (February 4, 1992), and the second installment appeared under the headline "I Won't Go to Jail for Bill Clinton" (February 11, 1992).

7. We started by producing initial cross tabulations to see whether the findings of the original overnight survey could be replicated in the second survey with the larger sample. When the marginals for the key questions were found to be within sampling error in the two polls, we continued our analysis with the second survey with the larger sample.

PART FIVE

Public Reactions to Media Polls

11

The People, the Press and Campaign '92

Andrew Kohut
Larry Hugick

In 1985 the Times Mirror Company, the publisher of the *Los Angeles Times* and other leading newspapers and magazines began a program of survey research designed to elicit a better understanding of American attitudes toward the news media. An important component of this research has been to monitor public reaction to press coverage of national elections. For the 1988 presidential election Times Mirror commissioned the Gallup Organization to conduct seven nationwide public opinion surveys that elicited the public's views about the way the press was covering the campaign (cf. Traugott, 1991). In 1990 the Times Mirror Center, which had been established to carry on this program, conducted four nationwide surveys to gauge public opinion of coverage of the off-year elections.

Times Mirror Center and its principal polling agency, Princeton Survey Research Associates, conducted thirteen surveys during the 1992 campaign. As in previous elections, all of the Times Mirror Campaign '92 surveys were national in scope and included a mix of open-ended and closed-ended questions. Many of the questions asked in 1992 were identical to those posed in earlier campaigns so as to facilitate comparisons of public response.

Generally, Times Mirror's polling has been designed to examine how the public reacts to campaign coverage over the course of the election cycle. Times Mirror's work culminates in a survey that is conducted immediately after election day, to get a "bottom line response" from the public as to how well the press and other institutions and campaign processes performed or operated.

The research has attempted to determine the public's overall evaluation of the press's performance, as well as to find out how the public judged the press with regard to fairness, intrusiveness, and amount and tone of coverage. In addition, the program has monitored the level of public attentiveness to election news over the course of the campaign so as to provide a record of how interest in campaign news develops over the course of the campaign cycle and how these patterns differ between elections. Given the amount of self criticism of press performance in 1988, surveys of the press itself were added to the program in 1992.

In each election Times Mirror has also conducted special surveys to gauge in depth reaction to controversial aspects of media coverage in each campaign. In 1988 this included polling about coverage of Gary Hart's extramarital affairs, and the issue of Dan Quayle's National Guard service during the Vietnam era. In 1990 Times Mirror polled the public about the desirability of the news media evaluating campaign advertising. And in 1992 coverage of the Gennifer Flowers matter was a subject of Times Mirror surveys.

Taken as a whole these surveys provide a fairly comprehensive assessment of public attitudes toward not only media coverage of campaigns, but also toward the candidates and campaign processes. In reviewing the survey results from 1988, 1990, and 1992, it becomes apparent that these public attitudes have impacted on the evolution of presidential campaigns and how they are covered by the news media.

Overview of the 1992 Campaign

By almost all measures the 1992 presidential campaign was a better experience for the American public than the previous one. After falling to the 50% level in 1988, voter turnout in the 1992 presidential election increased by nearly five percentage points. People evaluated the campaign process more positively and many more voters believed they made an informed choice when they cast their ballots. The public felt less manipulated and significantly greater numbers thought that issues mattered in 1992 than felt that way in 1988.[1]

Yet the public was again disappointed with the news media's performance in covering the presidential campaign. In a nationwide Times Mirror survey completed on the weekend following the election the average grade afforded the press by the public was a "C+", a slight improvement on the average grade of "C" reflected in a 1988 survey.[2] In contrast, voter evaluations of themselves and the campaign process were considerably more positive than they had been in 1988. In the 1992 post-election survey, 61% of those surveyed gave "The Voters" a grade of either A or B, compared to only 49% in 1988.[3] Nearly 8 out of 10 respondents felt they had learned enough from the '92 campaign to make an informed choice, up from 59% who felt that way in 1988.[4] And, finally, some 70% of respondents in the '92 survey felt the presidential debates were helpful in deciding who to vote for. In 1988 just 48% of those surveyed rated the debates as helpful.[5]

How could voters be so much more satisfied with the 1992 election campaign but still rate the press so poorly? Times Mirror's program of People & The Press surveys suggests that people's general feelings about the media's role in society were as much responsible for these low ratings as their beliefs about actual press performance during the campaign. The public was unhappy with the same aspects of press coverage in 1992 as it was in 1988. These specific complaints about reporting on the presidential race are a reflection of more general areas of dissatisfaction with the way the media operates.

In recent years, growing numbers of people have come to believe that the press is often unfair in the way it covers national issues. Americans have also become extremely wary of the intrusiveness of the media, and are more likely to feel the press sensationalizes the private lives of public figures.

All three of these elements were at work in the public's response to the presidential campaign and are evident throughout the findings of 18 nationwide Times Mirror Center surveys conducted to gauge voter reaction to press performance. Times Mirror's survey program in 1992 built upon polling from the 1988 presidential campaign that revealed a significant amount of discontent with the way the press covered that election (Traugott, 1991).

The public voiced three major criticisms of press coverage during the 1988 campaign that set the backdrop for voter opinion of the media in 1992:

1. Most Americans thought that the press had over-covered that election. As the first "open" race in 30 years (the 22nd Amendment barred incumbent Ronald Reagan from seeking another term), it cost more and lasted longer than any U.S. presidential campaign in history.[6]
2. The public complained that the press had too much influence on the outcome of the '88 election. Too often, people believed that journalists crossed the line between reporting the news and creating news themselves.[7]
3. The public felt the media placed too much emphasis on covering the personal character of presidential candidates, as a result setting a negative tone that resonated throughout the political process.

Well before the first presidential primary took place, two
Democrats — Gary Hart and Joseph Biden — withdrew their candidacies after the media raised questions about their personal
integrity and judgment.[8]

Four years later, the public was still unhappy with the press on two of
these three counts. Public complaints about over-coverage of the race in
1992, however, were obviated by a shortened campaign — few
Democratic candidates came forward early to challenge a seemingly
invincible George Bush. The media, also not seeing much chance that
Bush would be defeated, put Campaign '92 on more of a back burner
than Campaign '88 (Rosensteil, 1993). In turn, many fewer Americans
complained about too much coverage in this election cycle than had done
so the last time around.

In October 1987, 59% of a nationwide sample thought news organizations were giving too much coverage to the presidential election campaign. Four years later, only 12% of the public held that opinion, while
most (58%) thought the news media was devoting about the right
amount of coverage to the campaign.[9]

Ironically, even though Americans observed less early media coverage
of the '92 presidential race than the '88 race, initially the public expressed
almost as much interest in following the campaign. Times Mirror surveys in the fall of 1987 and the fall of 1991 show roughly comparable levels of public attention to campaign news. Once the '92 primaries began,
the level of public attentiveness to campaign coverage rose sharply.
During the rest of the year, Americans were likely to express an equal or
higher level of interest in campaign coverage (following "very closely")
than they were at comparable points in 1988 (See Table 11.1).

TABLE 11.1 Attentiveness to 1988 and 1992 Campaign Coverage

	Percent Following News of Presidential Campaign "Very Closely"[a]	
	1988 Campaign	1992 Campaign
Month	%	%
Sept./Oct. ('87, '91)	14	12
May ('88, '92)	24	35
August ('88, '92)	39	36
Oct./Nov. ('88, '92)	43	55

[a]See Times Mirror Center for the People and The Press, News Interest Indexes
for months and years included. The monthly Times Mirror News Interest Index
measures how closely the public is following the major news stories of the month,
and how well they think the press is covering those stories.

The view that the press was not guilty of over-covering the race, however, was the only marked improvement in press performance evaluations reflected in Times Mirror surveys. In contrast, many of the criticisms about the way the press did its job remained as evident in 1992 as they had been in 1988.

The 1988 Backdrop to 1992 Opinions

Discontent with press performance in reporting on Campaign '88 revealed itself even before the field of candidates took shape. By mid-1987, there was a strong consensus that press scrutiny of adultery charges against Gary Hart had unfairly forced the Democratic front-runner out of the race. Joe Biden's exit under pressure from the media soon followed. Public unhappiness with the way the press was doing its job was reinforced in a number of subsequent incidents. Most notably, Dan Rather's verbal dual with George Bush over the Vice President's role in Iran-Contra on the CBS Evening News raised questions about the impartiality of the press, and the tendency of journalists to overstep their role.[10]

Press treatment of Dan Quayle, after the relatively unknown Indiana Senator was tapped for the second spot on the GOP ticket, also produced a backlash against the media. Although Quayle enjoyed little public support, relentless press probes of his enlistment in the National Guard during the Vietnam era and other personal matters raised questions about the fairness of the press and its tendency to "pile on" when a candidate comes under fire for some (seemingly minor) past indiscretion.

Between elections, Americans' exposure to media coverage of the trials and travails of a wide range of public figures who had fallen on hard times increased public antagonism toward the press. Coverage of the alleged wrong-doings of Jim Wright, Pete Rose, Leona Helmsley, the Keating Five, evangelical minister Jim Bakker and a score of state and local public figures spurred criticism about the increasing tabloid tendencies of the mainstream press.

Public discontent with the way the press reported on Gary Hart, Dan Quayle, and the personal problems of powerful people in trouble took its toll on the overall image of the press. At the end of 1989 Times Mirror concluded:

> Since Times Mirror began its People and The Press Research program five years ago, there has been a significant erosion of public confidence in the press as an impartial observer of the political and social scene. . . . Americans from all walks of life find fault with the way the press reports on the personal and ethical behavior of political leaders. These criticisms are now shaping opinions of the press and shadowing its credibility.[11]

Gennifer Flowers, a Bridge Between the Elections

As the '92 presidential campaign got under way, the experience of the last campaign was fresh in the minds of both the press and the candidates. In no uncertain terms, the 1988 experience made it clear that the old rules governing press coverage of candidates' personal lives no longer applied. A generation ago, John F. Kennedy could count on the journalistic community to keep their knowledge of his extramarital affairs out of their reporting. In the 1990s, Democratic hopeful Bill Clinton had no such assurances that the news media would refrain from reporting on his rumored romantic liaisons. As a result, Clinton tried to put the issue of marital infidelity behind him when he first announced his candidacy. The Arkansas governor acknowledged having had "difficulties" in his marriage and admitted he had not been a "perfect" husband, but said he and his wife, Hillary, had worked out their problems and were committed to each other (*The New Republic*, 1992).

The Clinton adultery rumors provided an early test of how the press would handle the "character" issue in 1992. After the Gary Hart/Donna Rice affair, news organizations took considerable heat from the public for going beyond reasonable limits in investigating the candidates' sex lives. More than two-thirds (68%) of Americans interviewed by Times Mirror months after Hart withdrew from the race said the press went too far in their reporting of that story.[12] Most Americans were not sympathetic to arguments that Hart's actions revealed a recklessness or lack of judgment unsuitable for a president, and thus justified a newspaper stakeout of his townhouse.

Even as they criticized the news media's handling of this specific case, however, the public did not identify marital infidelity as a topic that should *never* be part of campaign coverage. In late 1987, two-thirds of Americans (66%) said that stories about a candidate's extramarital affairs should be reported in some circumstances. Less than half of the public (41%), however, thought such stories should *always* be reported.[13]

The circumstances in Clinton's case were indeed different from those in Hart's case. First of all, while Hart was charged with having ongoing affairs, accusations against Clinton primarily dealt with past indiscretions. Secondly, while Hart had dismissed the marital infidelity charges against him as "ridiculous" and invited reporters to follow him around, Clinton did not flatly deny ever having an affair (Alter, 1992a).

Initially, the press appeared determined not to make an issue of marital infidelity in Campaign '92. After reporting on Clinton's statements about his marital problems, major national news organizations kept the rumors out of their campaign coverage. But when *The Star*, a supermarket tabloid, printed a story in late January 1992 detailing allegations by cabaret singer Gennifer Flowers of a 12-year-affair with the governor, the story moved up the media food chain. Big city tabloids like the New York Post and Boston Herald ran screaming headlines about Flowers's accusations. Tabloid television shows like Fox Television's *A Current Affair* gave the story significant air time. Soon, the story so dominated the campaign that even the major networks and national print media felt obliged to drop their voluntary boycott (Clift et al., 1992).

As a result of these developments, the fairness of the press was again called into question early in the campaign. Public response to the Flowers story paralleled voter reactions during the Hart/Rice affair. Surveys taken immediately before and after the Clintons appeared on CBS Television's top-rated *60 Minutes* (January 28, 1992) to respond to the charges generally revealed sympathy for the candidate and mixed reviews, at best, of the news media. In a CNN/*USA Today*/Gallup survey taken later that week, viewers of George Bush's State of the Union address — a more Republican group than the public at large — expressed a majority view (58%) that the media had been unfair in its handling of the marital infidelity charges against Clinton.[14] Five years earlier, 64% of the broader public had responded similarly to an identical question about Gary Hart in a *Newsweek* poll.[15]

In a Times Mirror survey started before and completed after the *60 Minutes* appearance, 40% of Americans agreed that marital infidelity is a legitimate issue for voters to consider when evaluating presidential candidates — but a larger proportion (52%) rejected this notion. Again, survey results closely matched those of similar questions reported after news of Hart's alleged affair broke in 1987.[16]

The Times Mirror survey showed, in broad terms, an almost even division in public opinion of the news media's handling of the Flowers charges: 44% believed the press had acted very or fairly responsibly; 41% thought the press had acted not too or not at all responsibly. But those with the strongest opinions on this matter tended to be press critics rather than supporters (see Traugott & Means, Chapter 10). Twice as many said the media had behaved not at all responsibly as said it had behaved very responsibly (17% vs. 8%).[17]

Press handling of the Clinton/Flowers controversy opened the media to charges of sensationalism. Public perceptions that news organizations are motivated by self-interest rather than by a commitment to serving the public interest were reinforced. Seventy-one percent in the Times Mirror survey thought the media's decision to cover the Flowers story was primarily motivated by a desire to attract large audiences; only 21% thought the chief motivation was to provide voters with important information about the character of a presidential candidate.[18]

By seeming to follow the tabloids' lead in making news judgments, the more respectable media lost their moral high ground on the "character" issue. Press handling of the Flowers story suggested to many that assessing character was merely an excuse for cheap sensationalism. In Times Mirror surveys, the public has consistently asked that coverage focus on things other than personal character. Three months before Flowers went public with her allegations, a survey found only 7% of the public saying they wanted to hear most about character in 1992 campaign coverage, while 46% wanted to hear most about issues and 42% wanted to hear most about the candidates' experience.[19]

As the 1992 campaign continued, Clinton was not the only candidate who attempted to capitalize on public resentment toward the news media. George Bush, who had skillfully used the Dan Rather interview to catapult his candidacy forward in 1988, frequently used the media as a foil in 1992. Dan Quayle, savaged by the press during the last campaign, included the Washington press corps in the "cultural elite" he said were hopelessly out of touch with the average citizen. Ross Perot, who ran his own anti-establishment campaign, chose to virtually ignore the traditional political media and take his message to the people directly and through the talk show circuit.

The Flowers controversy was also an early signal that the prestige of the political press — including network TV news departments, nationally influential newspapers and the weekly newsmagazines — had lost some of its power to set the tone for presidential campaign coverage. As the campaign progressed, debate about press performance focused not only on charges of sensationalism, bias and intrusiveness, but also on whether the public was better served by a more diverse, decentralized media environment.

How the Press Saw It

Many of the public's reservations about coverage of Gennifer Flowers were shared by the press itself. Times Mirror conducted two surveys of the national press corps over the course of the presidential campaign. In late spring of 1992, a poll of more than 400 members of the press community found them sharply divided on their collective performance. A majority in that survey believed that the barriers between mainstream and tabloid press had broken down.[20] The most common complaint was a belief that campaign coverage had focused on irrelevant or trivial issues.[21]

The relationship between press coverage and the success of Clinton's presidential effort to that point in the Democratic nomination contest best explains the press's ambivalent views of its performance. Bill Clinton was seen by all segments of the press community as having himself to blame for the difficulties he had encountered during his run (67%). Only 12% of the media — national, local, print and broadcast — believed the press was *principally* responsible for Clinton's difficulties with the "character issue,"[22] but almost half (46%) regarded this issue as the most significant element of campaign coverage at that juncture.[23] One in five (19%) believed that the character shadow over Clinton was the result of a combination of the candidate's own actions and the manner in which the press had responded to them.

The press as a whole believed it had covered the Clinton character issue fairly responsibly (55%). But very few journalists would go so far as to call the coverage "very responsible" (7%), and as many as 36% thought the press had not acted responsibly.[24] One respondent's view that "the issues getting most attention are not what is most important in making a choice for president" reflected a significant cross section of press response.

Despite these reservations about coverage of Clinton's character, at the midpoint of the campaign almost half the press corps (49%) believed that 1992 coverage was superior to that of the 1988 campaign.[25] As to improvements in coverage, 89% of the national press thought the frequent debates between the Democratic candidates during the primary season had a positive effect on campaign reporting. Press coverage of campaign commercials also received high marks from the press: 85% of respondents thought that describing and analyzing the campaign's TV spots had improved the quality of coverage.[26]

The advent of C-SPAN as a major source of campaign coverage, and the expanded role of Cable News Network (CNN), were almost universally applauded. Nine in ten press members (91%) thought that C-SPAN was having a positive effect on campaign coverage to that point, and CNN's efforts were approved by the same proportion (91%). CNN was even more popular among the local press than it was among its competitors and colleagues at the national level.[27]

Reduced coverage of the national political conventions and the decision by the four networks to rely on a single source for exit poll results were the only changes in the pattern of coverage that drew substantial criticism. While only 29% of the press as a whole believed that a single exit polling source would have a negative effect there were sharp divergences within the community. Forty percent of the top field people in national TV news, including news division executives and executive producers, disapproved of the change and 44% of print press reporters and editors were also unhappy that the networks did not commission separate exit polls (see Mitofsky & Edelman, Chapter 6).[28]

The Media Changes Its Report Card

A second Times Mirror survey of press opinion conducted in the final weeks of the campaign found that members of the press corps themselves had changed their minds about who was helped and who was hurt by news coverage of the campaign. A substantial majority (55%) of American journalists interviewed in the fall said that George Bush's candidacy was damaged by the way the press covered it. The earlier poll, taken as Bush turned back the challenge of an insurgent Pat Buchanan, found most journalists (50%) thinking that press coverage was having a neutral effect on Bush's candidacy.[29] In that earlier survey, a 64% majority also thought that Bill Clinton was being hurt by media coverage as he struggled with the "character" problems that plagued his primary campaign. In contrast, as the Arkansas governor seemed headed toward victory in the fall, only 11% felt that the Clinton campaign was harmed by the way the press covered his drive to the presidency.[30]

Both surveys found journalists lauding press coverage generally, despite their widespread belief that coverage was having a negative impact on one of the campaigns. In late October eight in ten journalists rated press coverage of Campaign '92 as excellent or good. Fewer than one in five (18%) rated press performance as only fair or poor. That survey also found the press thinking it did a good job on most of the major elements of campaign coverage (see Table 11.2).[31]

TABLE 11.2 Rating of 1992 Press Coverage[a]

	Press	Voters			
	Nov. '92	Sept. '92	May '92	Mar. '92	Feb. '92
Rating	%	%	%	%	%
Excellent	10	12	10	12	11
Good	70	45	44	51	45
Only Fair	16	27	33	28	32
Poor	2	11	10	6	7
Can't say	2	5	3	3	5
	100	100	100	100	100

[a]"The Press and Campaign '92: A Self Assesment," December 20, 1992. See Table 1, page 2 for November '92 numbers and trend. For results on the public alone see Times Mirror News Interest Index September 1992 (Survey September 10-13, 1992, N=1,508): Q.7.

The People and the Press Differ

The public rendered a more critical judgment of presidential campaign coverage than journalists did. While 80% of the news media sample rated the '92 coverage as either good or excellent, surveys of the public throughout the campaign found fewer than six in ten rating press coverage of the campaign positively and *more than one in three voters feeling that the press was doing an only a fair or poor job.*[32]

The public also became sensitive to differences in the way the press covered Bush and Clinton over the course of the campaign. The percentage of voters who thought that the press was unfair in the way it covered George Bush steadily increased throughout the year. In March, only 13% of voters believed the press was being unfair to the President.[33] By mid September that sentiment grew to 22%. In Times Mirror's post-election survey, 35% took the view that the press was unfair to Bush in its coverage while 61% saw the press as fair in its coverage.[34] (By comparison, 77% believed the press was fair to Clinton and 67% believed the press was fair to Ross Perot.)[35]

Both the public and press agreed, however, that the media had improved somewhat on its 1988 effort. Times Mirror's post-election follow-up survey of voters found that more than a third (36%) gave the press an "A" or "B" for its campaign coverage, compared with 30% who gave the press similar grades after the '88 campaign. However, the percentage giving the press a "D" or "F" for its campaign performance remained relatively high (31% in '92, 35% in '88).[36]

In 1992, the public's biggest complaint was that the press got too involved in the election process. A 54% majority believed the press had *too much* influence on the outcome of the election, while just 4% thought the press played too small a role, and 37% thought that it had the right amount of influence. These findings parallel those obtained by Times Mirror four years earlier. In the fall of 1988, 58% thought that the press had too great an influence on the outcome of that contest.[37]

Republicans, who are usually more critical of the press than other voters, found more fault with press coverage of Campaign '92 than Democrats or Independents did. More than two-thirds of GOP voters thought the press was shaping the outcome of the election (65%), compared with 29% of Democrats and 47% of political Independents.[38] As a result, the bottom-line assessment of press performance in Campaign '92 had a very pronounced partisan skew. Republican opinion divided pretty much evenly between those who thought the press had done an excellent or good job and those who gave the media bad marks overall for its

TABLE 11.3 Rating of 1992 Press Coverage by Party

	Party Affiliation		
Rating	Republican %	Democrat %	Independent %
Excellent	8	15	12
Good	44	49	42
Only Fair	30	25	28
Poor	14	8	12
Can't say	4	3	6
	100	100	100

election coverage. In contrast, a solid majority of Democrats (64%) thought the press had done an excellent or good job. Independents fell in between the two (See Table 11.3).

In 1992, there was significant sentiment that both major party presidential candidates had been subjected to excessive personal criticism from the media. Forty-one percent of Times Mirror's nationwide sampling believed that the press had been too tough on George Bush, and 42% believed that the press had been too hard on Bill Clinton.[39]

Four years earlier somewhat smaller percentages of voters believed the press had been too tough on the two major party candidates. In October 1988, Times Mirror found that a third (33%) of the voters thought the press was being too personally critical of George Bush and slightly more than a third (37%) felt that way about coverage of his opponent, Governor Michael Dukakis.[40] At that time, a solid majority (55%) of the public also thought that the press was being *unfair* in its coverage of GOP vice presidential candidate Dan Quayle.[41]

By the general election campaign in 1992, Republicans were more apt to think that the press was being too personally critical of George Bush (58%) than Democrats were to think the media had been too tough on Bill Clinton (45%). Ironically, Republicans were almost as likely to believe the press had been too hard on Clinton (39%), as members of his own party (45%).[42]

Not only was the press seen as less fair to George Bush, most voters also believed that reporters wanted to see Clinton, not Bush win the election. Fifty-two percent thought most media people wanted Clinton to win in November; 17% thought that the press wanted Bush to win and 31% could not say (See Table 11.4).[43]

In a follow-up question, about half (49%) of Times Mirror's sample said they thought that press people often let their own political prefer-

TABLE 11.4 Perception of Press Bias[a]

	Candidate Press Thought to Favor		
How Often Press Lets *Preferences Influence Reporting*	*Bush* %	*Clinton* %	*Neither/DK* %
Often	51	54	39
Sometimes	32	36	35
Seldom	14	9	17
Never	3	1	4
Don't Know	0	*	5
	100	100	100

[a]Times Mirror News Interest Index, September 1992.

ences influence the way they report the news. More than a third (35%) said this happened sometimes while only 14% thought it occurred seldom or never.[44]

Voters who thought the press wanted a Clinton victory and those who thought the press favored Bush were about equally likely to think the media lets its bias show. In fact, even voters who did not identify a media-favored candidate were inclined to believe that the press lets its preferences affect its reporting.

Since every election has a winner and a loser (or losers), such perceptions of media bias are to some degree inevitable. The press is often a scapegoat for supporters of a defeated candidate. This factor, plus the general belief that the press favors Democrats, would make people more apt to see a pro-Clinton bias in campaign coverage. This makes the finding that four in ten said the press was too hard on Clinton all the more remarkable.

The People, the Press and Perot

In 1992, the news media faced a unique challenge in dealing with the on again, off-again candidacy of Ross Perot. Both those who supported Perot and those who opposed his candidacy had reasons to be critical of the press. If journalists seemed too aggressive in their coverage of Perot, they were vulnerable to charges of elitism and of again taking the "character" issue too far. But if they were perceived as going too easy on Perot, they might be accused of shirking their "watchdog" responsibility to examine the background and qualifications of a man with no previous experience as a political candidate.

Pleasing both sides proved to be difficult. In June 1992, when Perot's popularity crested, a *Newsweek* Poll found that fewer than half (44%) the voters thought the news media was being generally fair in its coverage of Perot. The criticism came from both directions, but more thought the press was trying to make Perot look bad (24%) than believed it was letting him off too easy (18%).[45]

Many suspected that the harsh glare of the media spotlight was the major reason Perot suddenly withdrew from the race the following month, yet there was no major backlash against the media in the aftermath of Perot's exit. A CNN/*USA Today*/Gallup poll conducted the evening of Perot's announcement showed that voters were more angry with the candidate — who said he acted out of concern for the political process — than they were with the media. Only about one in five (21%) voters overall, and three in ten (31%) of those who had been supportive of Perot's candidacy, thought that the news media and the political establishment had unfairly forced the Texas entrepreneur out of the race (Newport & McAneny, 1992).

When asked to evaluate press coverage of Perot retrospectively the following October, before he re-entered the race, journalists themselves saw it neither as their finest nor their darkest hour. A majority said the press deserved a positive rating (63%), but only 15% said it did an excellent job of covering Perot's candidacy. And one-third (34%) of journalists interviewed gave the press a rating of only fair or poor.[46]

In the Times Mirror post-election survey, two-thirds of the voters (67%) said the press had been fair in covering Perot. Roughly one-fourth (27%) took the view that the coverage had been unfair. Those who reported having voted for Perot were sharply divided on this question: 49% thought the press was fair while 45% thought it was unfair.[47]

Alternative Media a Hit with Public, Press

The role of alternative media in the campaign was another aspect of the 1992 presidential race that set it apart from 1988. Media outlets other than traditional new shows — such as CNN's *Larry King Live*, NBC's *Today* show, talk radio and MTV — played a more visible role in the last campaign, in part because the candidates saw them as an effective way to get their message to voters without the usual filters.

While some criticized the effects of alternative media on 1992 campaign coverage, in the end, both the people and the press took a positive view. In the October 1992 Times Mirror press opinion survey, two-thirds (68%) of media people said the increased importance of talk shows such as Larry King and Rush Limbaugh were having a positive effect on the campaign process. Only one in five press members (19%) saw the overall effect as negative.[48] After the election, Times Mirror found that the public were as likely to give talk show hosts an "A" or "B" grade for their performance in the campaign as they were to give similar grades to the press as a whole (39% vs. 36%).[49]

Surveys by Princeton Survey Research Associates for the Markle Foundation found radio and television talk shows gaining prominence as the fall campaign progressed, thus challenging the notion that these "infotainment" outlets were undercutting the ability of the traditional media to keep the public properly informed about substantive issues. In the first of these surveys, taken in September, 40% of Americans said they sometimes got news about the campaign from these alternative sources. By the end of the campaign, that proportion increased to half (50%). Analysis suggested that these talk shows were a supplemental, rather than a primary source of information for their audiences. Seeing or hearing the candidates on talk shows was not associated with being uninformed or disinterested in substance. In fact, those who turned to talk and call-in shows actually had *above average* scores on a knowledge test of candidate issue positions.[50]

Concluding Observations

Campaign 1992 did mark some significant changes in the electorate, the media and the way the two interact.   One important trend that became particularly apparent during the '92 campaign was the changing role of the traditional news media. The expansion of cable television and advances in communications technology combined to offer the public new sources of direct access to the candidates, and the public responded favorably. While television remained the primary outlet for campaign news and information, the viewing public was offered a wider variety of options and allowed a more participatory role.

These new technologies gave rise to a slightly different dynamic between the public and the news media. While the public was by no means enamored with the press or the job it did in covering the '92 campaign, popular sentiment did reflect an improvement over assessments of 1988 coverage.

In addition, the public felt more equipped to make an informed choice in the election of 1992 than had been the case in 1988. This may have been due in part to the fact that the media did less "mediating" *per se* in Campaign '92. They seemed to serve more as purveyors of campaign news and information, while the candidates reached out to the voters directly. Nonetheless, a substantial percentage of the public continued to believe the media were unfair in their coverage of the candidates. Many complained, as they had in 1988, that the media put too much emphasis on candidates' private lives.

Perot's re-entry into the race and the fall debates deflected much attention away from the "horserace" polling that has become such a staple of modern campaign coverage, as well as a major target for media critics. While some news organizations made a concerted effort to downplay poll results in their coverage, there was certainly no lack of media-sponsored polling on the 1992 presidential race. But in contrast to 1988, surveys were more often put to uses other than keeping score (see Morin, Chapter 8 and Kagay, Chapter 9). They also provided a means for the public to state its priorities and opinions on issues and comment on the conduct of the various campaigns.

During the 1988 campaign, the onslaught of national media surveys showing George Bush with a comfortable lead over Michael Dukakis led to criticism that, by making the election outcome seem a foregone conclusion, the polls were discouraging people from voting. In 1992, there was little controversy about the polls driving the election or dampening voter interest. The polls made it clear that Ross Perot had little or no chance to win, but did not seem to keep his supporters from participating. In fact, Perot's share of the actual vote was higher, not lower, than his support in most major media polls.

In conclusion, if journalists want to improve on their overall C+ grade in their coverage of the next presidential campaign, they must address two key issues. First, they must confront the issue of how to cover questions about a candidate's character or allegations of personal misconduct without succumbing to sensationalism. The practice of ignoring the story initially, then seemingly following the lead of the tabloids, only undermined the credibility of the TV networks and the prestige press in 1992.

Second, public perception of media bias — historically liberal and pro-Democratic — persists despite the sometimes tough press treatment of Bill Clinton, Gary Hart, Ted Kennedy and other prominent Democrats. Changing public opinion on the issue of fairness is not likely to get easier for the news media. If Ross Perot is a harbinger of future major independent or third party presidential candidacies, the news media is likely to be charged with yet another kind of bias — this time for siding with the established parties against proponents of reform and change.

Notes

1. "Campaign '92: Voters Say 'Thumbs Up' to Campaign, Process Coverage." News Release from the Times Mirror Center for The People & The Press, November 15, 1992 (Survey Novemer 5-8, 1992, N=1,012).

2. Ibid. The average grade for 1992 was 3.0 on a scale from 1.0 (A) to 5.0 (F); the average grade for 1988 was 3.2. See page 3 and Q.11.

3. Ibid. Here the average grade for the voters in 1992 was 2.2; the average grade in 1988 was 2.6. See page 3 and Q.11.

4. Ibid., 77% in the 1992 survey said they had learned enough. See page 7 and Q.9.

5. Ibid., 70% characterized the debates as "very helpful" or "somewhat helpful." See page 1 and Q.10.

6. The People, The Press, & Politics Survey III, June 1988 (Survey May 13-22, 1988, N=3,021). See Q.503.

7. See for example, "The People, the Press & Politics October Pre-Election Typology Survey." Conducted for Times Mirror by The Gallup Organization, Inc., October 1988 (Survey October 23-26, 1988, N=2006). Fifty-eight percent of respondents said media organizations have too much influence. See page 38 and Q.603.

8. See for example, "The Press and the '88 Campaign," conducted for Times Mirror by The Gallup Organization, October/November 1987 (Survey October 25-November 4, 1987, N=1,501). Sixty-eight percent of respondents felt news organizations went too far in the way they reported charges that Gary Hart was having an affair with Donna Rice; 36% felt they went too far in reporting the charges of plagiarism against Joe Biden. See Q.22.

9. Times Mirror Center for The People & The Press, News Release, October 13, 1991 (Survey October 3-6, 1991, N=1,211). See page 5 and Q.12.

10. "The People, The Press and the 1988 Campaign," conducted for Times Mirror by The Gallup Organization, October/November 1987 (Survey October 25-November 4, 1987, N=1,501).

11. "The People & The Press Part 5: Attitudes Toward News Organizations — An Examination of the Opinions of the Press, The General Public and American Leadership," conducted for Times Mirror by The Gallup Organization, November 1989 (Survey August 9-28, 1989, N for the public=1,507). See pages 9-10. For example, in 1989, 62% of the public saw the press as influenced by powerful people and organizations, compared with only 53% in 1985 (Q.9). In 1989 44% of respondents said they thought press reports are often inaccurate, compared to 34% in 1985 (Q.7). And in 1992, 63% of respondents said that when news organizations cover stories about the personal and ethical behavior of politicians they are driving the controversy itself, not merely reporting the news (Q.26).

12. "The People, Press & The '88 Campaign," see Q.22.

13. Ibid., see Q.23.

14. Larry Hugick, "Public Assesses Clinton Controversy." *The Gallup Poll Monthly* (January 1992): pp. 33-35. Results are based on a telephone survey of 462 adults, 18 years and older, who watched all or most of President George Bush's State of the Union address on January 28, 1992. Respondents were recruited in advance and called back immediately after the speech ended at 10:30 PM EST. Respondents were asked, "Do you think the news media have been fair or unfair in their handling of charges of marital infidelity made against Democratic presidential candidate Bill Clinton?" (31% fair; 58% unfair; 11% no opinion).

15. *Newsweek* Poll of 812 adults, 18 years and older, conducted May 6-7, 1987

by the Gallup Organization. Respondents were asked, "Do you think the media has been fair or unfair in its treatment of marital infidelity charges against Gary Hart?" (22% fair; 64% unfair; 14% no opinion)

16. "The People, The Press & Politics Campaign '92: The Governor & The Press," January 30, 1992 (Survey January 24-28, 1992, N=1,008). See Q.2.

17. Ibid., see Q.3.

18. Ibid., see Q.5.

19. Times Mirror Center for the People & The Press, News Release, October 13, 1991 (Survey October 3-6, 1991, N=1,211). See Q.13.

20. Times Mirror Center for The People & The Press, News Release, June 4, 1992 (Survey April 20-May 8, 1992, N=413 total: 213 national, 200 local). Fifty-four percent of the total agreed that the barriers between the tabloid press and mainstream press have broken down, 40% disagreed. See Q.22B

21. Ibid., see Q.2.2. When asked to identify their biggest complaints about press coverage of the 1992 campaign, 36% of the respondents said "too much focus on irrelevant issues," 21% said "trivializing issues/focus on real issues."

22. Ibid., see Q.15. Respondents were asked, "In your opinion, which is a better explanation for the problems Bill Clinton has had in his campaign so far?" Twelve percent said the way the press has covered him; 67% said Clinton's personal actions and views themselves; 19% volunteered both or neither.

23. Ibid., see Q.1. Respondents were asked, "All in all, what campaign event has had the greatest impact on the presidential election campaign so far?" Forty-six percent said either coverage of Clinton character issues (23%) or the Gennifer Flowers press conference (20%).

24. Ibid., see Q.14.

25. Ibid., see Q.3. Eighteen percent characterized the coverage as worse; 29% said it was about the same.

26. Ibid., see Q.27B.

27. Ibid. Ninety-four percent of local press people viewed CNN positively, compared to 88% from the national sample.

28. Ibid., see page 11 and Q.27B.

29. "The Press And Campaign '92: A Self Assessment," December 20, 1992 (Survey October 7-29, 1992; Press/N=267, Powers That Be/N=48, Talk Show Hosts/N=23). See Q.3.

30. Ibid., see Q.5.

31. Ibid., see Q.2. Respondents were asked, "All in all, how would you rate the press coverage of the '92 Campaign? Would you say the coverage has been excellent, good, only fair, or poor?" Ten percent said excellent, 70% said good, 16% said only fair, and 2% said poor.

32. See for example, Times Mirror News Interest Index, February 1992 (Survey February 20-23, 1992, N=1,227). Fifty-six percent of respondents rated news coverage of the presidential campaign as excellent or good; 39% said it was only fair or poor. See Q.9.

33. "The People, The Press & Politics Campaign '92 — Electability: Bush, Clinton & Congress," Survey IV, April 3, 1992 (Survey March 26-29, 1992, N=1,668). See Q.34 F1,2.

34. "The People, The Press & Politics Campaign '92: Voters Say 'Thumbs Up'

To Campaign, Process & Coverage," Survey XIII, November 15, 1992. See Q.19 for November '92 numbers and trend.

35. Ibid., see Q.20 and Q.21.

36. Ibid., see Q.11 for November 1992 and trend.

37. Times Mirror Campaign '92 Survey XIII, November 15, 1992. See Q.18 for September '92 numbers and trend.

38. Ibid., see page 5 and Q.18. Numbers reflect the percentage of respondents who felt the press had too much influence on the outcome of the presidential election.

39. Ibid., see Q.39 for Bush and Q.40 for Clinton. Respondents were asked, "In the presidential campaign so far, have news organizations been too personally critical of George Bush/Bill Clinton or not?"

40. The People, The Press & Politics Survey VI, October 1988 (Survey October 23-26, 1988, N=2,006). See Q.605 for Bush, Q.606 for Dukakis.

41. The People, The Press & Politics Survey IV, August 1988 (Survey August 24-25, N=1,000). See Q.10.

42. Times Mirror News Interest Index, September 1992, see Q.39 and Q.40.

43. Ibid., see Q.37. Polling on this question was conducted in late September, before Ross Perot re-entered the race.

44. Ibid., see Q.38.

45. *Newsweek* Poll Release, "Perot Edging Ahead of Bush, Clinton Trailing" (June 6, 1992).

46. "The Press And Campaign '92: A Self Assessment," December 20, 1992, see Q.7. Fifteen percent rated press coverage of Perot as excellent, 48% said it was good, 27% said only fair, and 7% said poor.

47. Times Mirror Campaign '92 Survey XIII, November 15, 1992. See Q.21.

48. "The Press And Campaign '92: A Self Assessment," December 20, 1992. See Q.9.

49. Times Mirror Campaign '92 Survey XIII, November 15, 1992. See Q.11.

50. "Markle Foundation Political Awareness Survey Campaign '92," unpublished report prepared by Princeton Survey Research Associates, July 1993. (The survey was taken in two waves: Wave 1 September 8-21, 1992, N=1,882; Wave 2 October 20-November 2, 1992, N=1,882.) See pages 56-58 and Q.4.

12

Media, Momentum and Money: Horse Race Spin in the 1988 Republican Primaries

Diana C. Mutz

Polling is often implicated in the rising concern over horse race coverage of political candidates — that is, news emphasizing which candidate is ahead or behind, or who is gaining or losing ground based on which strategy or tactics. Although the horse race emphasis in election news predates the advent of scientific opinion polls (see Sigelman & Bullock, 1991; Herbst, 1993), polling is an integral part of today's horse race coverage. The extent of horse race emphasis is well-documented and widely decried (see, e.g., Broh, 1977; Patterson, 1980), but its consequences for political campaigns are less well understood.

This chapter examines the impact of horse race media coverage on candidates' abilities to obtain campaign donations. Popular wisdom suggests that the fate of campaign fund raising is closely tied to perceptions of campaign viability (cf. Hickman, 1991). Although considerable research has focused on the translation of money into winning campaigns, very little is known about the factors that influence fund-raising success. Moreover, much that is widely believed about the relationship between horse race coverage and campaign coffers is speculative or anecdotal in nature. The purpose of this chapter is to explore this relationship using systematically gathered information on both media coverage and campaign contributions.

For a number of reasons, presidential primary campaigns are an excellent place to begin understanding these processes. First and foremost, a race with three or more candidates provides a greater opportunity for strategic considerations to enter into decisions to contribute to one candidate over another, or whether to donate at all. While a variety of motivations may induce contributors to give money to candidates portrayed by media as "front runners," this motivation is peculiar to multi-candidate contests (see Bartels, 1988).

In multi-candidate contests, potential donors may consider the perceived viability or electability of candidates because they want to avoid "wasting" their money on a candidate without a chance. By the same token, contributors donating to candidates to whom they know many others are also donating may strategically enhance the return on their investment (see Jacobson & Kernell, 1983). Abramson and colleagues (1990) estimate that strategic considerations enter into voting decisions only around 10 percent of the time; however, strategic considerations might be expected in greater magnitude when potential contributors consider the possibility of throwing money — as opposed to votes — away on a candidate who has little chance of success. In one extreme example of this phenomenon, a group of contributors tried to hire Gallup to assess a candidate's chances of success before donating to him (Dionne, 1980).

Horse race emphasis is at its most extreme in coverage of the sequential primary contests, further contributing to the likelihood of influence in nomination races. Organizational and audience considerations dictate that both print and television journalists narrow the field to a manageable number of candidates as quickly as possible. For journalists, this places a premium on analyzing any available standards or benchmarks relevant to candidates' prospects (Arterton, 1984; Brady & Johnston, 1987). In addition to the polling and horse race fare common to coverage of all types of elections, the sequential nature of the presidential nomination system means that reporting on the results of previous primaries may affect the outcomes of subsequent contests, thus accentuating the horse race theme.

When it comes to fund raising, the stakes are also particularly high in primaries. While campaign finance regulations have reduced the importance of money in presidential general elections, they have heightened its role in primary races (Orren, 1983; Jacobson, 1975). The Federal Election Campaign Act of 1971 and its amendments all encourage fund-raising efforts aimed at attracting many small donations from large numbers of individuals rather than a few major donors.[1] These changes have inadvertently enhanced the importance of mass media in the process of winnowing presidential aspirants (Traugott, 1985).[2]

Finally, primaries are also an excellent place to begin exploring this relationship because candidates in primaries are competing for essentially the same pool of potential contributors, putting them on even footing with respect to the ease of generating funds from party supporters. If the influence of viability on fund raising is, in fact, as powerful and far-reaching as popularly supposed, it should be apparent during the primary season.

Before examining the relationship between campaign contributions and the media-portrayed viability of candidates in the 1988 primaries, I examine previous theories of the relationship between horse race coverage, polling, and primary success. Next I formulate a rationale for when and why horse race coverage should have these effects by examining research on the motivations underlying decisions to donate to political candidates. Finally, using data derived from Federal Election Commission reports and large samples of election coverage, I look at the relationships between horse race spin and contributions to the four leading candidates in the 1988 Republican primaries.

In 1988 the primary races attracted attention unusually early, leaving ample time for media-based public expectations of the candidates' chances to influence potential contributors. Findings from both Republican and Democratic candidates suggest that the extent to which media coverage implies that someone is a viable candidate is an important determinant of the frequency of campaign contributions. However, the way in which horse race coverage matters appears to differ according to candidates' initial status and characteristics of their constituencies. Just as poll results have been known to produce "boomerang" or "backlash" effects as well as bandwagon ones, so too knowledge that candidates are leading or gaining ground can both help and hurt fund raising.

Media's Role in the Primary Process

In the years following the reforms of the primary system, media's importance in the process of selecting presidential nominees has gone without question. Nonetheless, scholars have had markedly different conceptions of its role. One common conceptualization suggests that media are simply mirrors of the primary system itself; they cover primary outcomes because these contests have real consequences for candidates' chances of nomination. Media relay information as events unfold; the tone and amount of coverage candidates receive waxes and wanes according to their electoral fortunes in the sequential state primaries and caucuses. Patterson (1989: 98), for example, suggests that news coverage of candidates reflects their standing in national polls, arguing that "even brief spurts of news coverage often can be explained by indicators of electoral popularity" (see also, Adams, 1987). Potential contributors may learn of a candidate's latest polls or primary successes through the mass media, but media do little more than relay the outcomes of real world events (see also Aldrich, 1980).

An alternative conceptualization of media's role in primaries suggests that the interpretation of those outcomes is often more important than the results of the polls or primaries themselves. New Hampshire is not very important in terms of the number of delegates it has to offer, but media attention has made it an important early benchmark for candidates. In early primaries such as this, media play an important role in creating expectations and in deciding whether the candidate has lived up to them (Matthews, 1978). In some cases a close first place finish is a "loss," while in others, a narrow second place finish is a "win." According to this formulation, media may play an important, *leading* role in the interpretation of electoral preferences.

Unfortunately, in most studies candidates' successes in primaries and caucuses are typically lumped together with coverage of them as if they were a single entity.[3] While there is nothing inherently wrong with this practice, it does little to help disentangle the primary-driven and media-driven components of this process.

A third interpretation of media's importance suggests that it is the sheer amount of coverage concerning a candidate that matters rather than interpretations of winners and losers. Bartels (1988) suggests that people may "respond quite unthinkingly to changes in simple political stimuli such as the frequency with which candidates' names appear on television and in the newspaper" (Bartels, 1988: 111). Social psychological research on the effects of "mere exposure" on liking corroborate the potential for opinion change through processes of this kind (Zajonc, 1968; 1980). This process may seem unlikely for the highly politically involved type of person likely to vote in a primary, but it is possible that the sheer amount of coverage is interpreted by the public as connoting viability. After all, one might reason that only a truly competitive candidate would receive large amounts of coverage, thus one who is covered very little could not be a real contender. According to these formulations of the media's role, support for the candidate would be expected to respond to the sheer amount of coverage rather than the spin on horse race portrayals of candidate viability.

On first examination, the notion of momentum in presidential primary voting may seem closely related to the process proposed here; momentum suggests that media-generated expectations about a candidate's chances of winning influence vote choice, while in this case these same expectations influence the behavior of campaign contributors. But some caution should be exercised in assuming that the same mechanisms underlying momentum will be at work in influencing contributors. There is a tremendous amount of uncertainty surrounding presidential primary voting because of the general lack of public familiarity with candidates. Voter uncertainty and lack of information are said to fan the flames of momentum and increase the extent to which expectations influence vote choice (see Bartels, 1988).

It is difficult to extend these same generalizations to potential political contributors. Although the amount of information about candidates in a large pre-nomination field tends to be low, potential contributors — particularly at the primary stage — are likely to be among the most actively involved and well-informed (see, e.g., Brown, Hedges & Powell, 1980). In 1988, only around seven percent of the public gave money to either a Republican or Democratic candidate (see Alexander & Bauer, 1991). Primary activists are also more likely to be ideological in their preferences. These characteristics make it less likely that their attitudes toward candidates will be altered by horse race coverage.

At the same time, these same characteristics make it highly likely that these people will take strategic considerations into account. Although strategic voting has been found to account for only a tiny portion of momentum's influence, strategic contributing is likely to be a major factor in understanding the relationship between horse race coverage and contributor behavior.

Strategic Motivations Among Campaign Contributors

Changes brought about by the Federal Election Commission such as the growth of political action committees and the rise of candidate-centered campaigns have been widely studied, but less interest has been directed toward understanding how this affects the motivations underlying campaign contributing (Jones & Miller, 1985; Dunn, 1974). Instead contributing has been viewed as but one of many forms of political participation (e.g., Verba & Nie, 1972; Heard, 1960). What little we do know about the influence of horse race coverage on campaign coffers stems primarily from conventional wisdom as accumulated by pundits, politicians and their campaign consultants.

Meager research notwithstanding, the notion that popularity breeds even greater popularity is not something new to American politics, nor is it specific to the current primary system. This same principle has long been assumed to apply to the behavior of campaign contributors. As early as 1932, an analysis of incentives underlying campaign contributions claimed that people "give much as they put money on a winning horse . . . . Individuals grow to root for, and contribute to, one or the other of the political parties much as one roots for, and bets on, the Cubs or the White Sox, though with somewhat less enthusiasm perhaps"

(Overacker, 1932: 190-191). In more recent elections, candidates such as Carter in 1976, Anderson in 1980, and Hart in 1984 are all widely believed to have benefitted from early primary victories in the form of increased financial contributions (see Pomper, 1989; Marshall, 1983).

But even conventional wisdom is not all of one cloth when it comes to the anticipated effects of horse race coverage on fund raising. Among strategic motivations, the notion that nothing succeeds like success is probably the more common theory, but the contradictory assumption also has been incorporated into many direct mail appeals. As Kayden (1985: p. 95) notes, "The small donor derives satisfaction — a moral uplift — from contributing to a campaign. The issues that provide satisfaction are apt to be issues in which the donor is in the minority. After all, if one is in the majority, why worry?" Since there are limitations on the amount of money that may be given to a presidential primary candidate, people are more likely to be motivated by psychological than tangible rewards. By portraying a candidate's campaign as losing ground and in potential jeopardy, direct mail experts hope to provoke immediate action from loyal followers. This approach is, in essence, an attempt to invoke another form of strategic contributing; just as strategic contributors may want to contribute to a viable candidate in order to avoid wasting their money, loyal supporters may want to give to an embattled but strongly preferred candidate while their money still has a chance of helping his or her candidacy.

In short, despite widespread agreement as to the importance of horse race coverage in influencing fund raising, there is little empirical evidence bearing on its validity, and widespread confusion as to its role[4]. But assuming for the moment that horse race coverage does in fact influence fund-raising capabilities, one would not logically expect this pattern to apply equally well to all candidates and their constituencies. Candidates with clear front-runner status, for example, should be less susceptible to the short term ups and downs in horse race coverage than would be candidates of unknown status. Viability should matter most for the also-rans, that is, candidates who are not front runners and who have trouble differentiating themselves from the rest of the pack. If any candidate's supporters are going to respond positively to negative horse race spin, it should be constituencies who are intensely supportive of their chosen candidate; people who strongly support a given candidate are less likely to shift their support to another, and more likely to rally behind their candidate in the face of adversity.

Candidates in the 1988 primaries provided approximations of some of the types of candidacies described above. Among the four leading Democratic candidates, relationships between horse race coverage and contributions fit these general expectations (see Mutz, 1995). Since there was no clear front runner among the "seven dwarfs" running on the Democratic side, many of the candidates could potentially have benefitted from positive horse race spin. Dukakis and Gephardt supporters were, in fact, drawn toward greater giving when their respective candidacies were portrayed more positively in horse race spin. On the other hand, Jesse Jackson's strongly committed supporters were motivated to donate by news that his candidacy was threatened. Gore's supporters were strongly committed ideologically and also appeared to rally when his campaign fortunes were sliding.

If we assume that the same logic will apply to potential contributors to the Republican party, then one would anticipate several different relationships among the supporters of these four candidacies. As a standing vice-president, Bush was the clear front runner in the nomination race, making his supporters least likely to be influenced by horse race news. Dole and Kemp were less well-known also-rans, thus giving their supporters ample reason to be concerned about viability. Pat Robertson's candidacy was altogether different; he was a political outsider but with a ready-made constituency from his work as a well-known televangelist on the Christian Broadcasting Network. Moreover, the religious fervor of his supporters should make them more likely to stand by their man than supporters of other candidates. Eighty-four percent of Robertson supporters considered their support for him "strong," compared to 68, 71 and 77 percent for Kemp, Dole and Bush, respectively.[5] If any constituency was likely to have rallied behind its candidate in the face of adverse media spin, it would likely have been Robertson's.

Study Approach

To analyze the relationships between horse race spin and contributor behavior, several different kinds of data were gathered spanning a 43-week period running from July 1987 through the end of the 1988 primary season. Indicators of the number of donations received by each candidate each week were constructed from information available from the Federal Election Commission.[6]

Media portrayals of candidate viability were gauged through a content analysis of a random sample of AP wire service stories.[7] One thousand stories per candidate were randomly selected from the period July 1, 1987 through the date when only one candidate remained in the primary.[8] These stories were used to measure the sheer amount of coverage of each candidate over time, and the "spin" regarding whether the candidate was portrayed as winning or losing, or gaining or losing ground.[9] Care was taken not to code positive or negative general statements about the candidate or his campaign; strictly horse race statements dealing with the chances of victory or amount of public support for a candidate were included.[10]

To create a composite measure indicating the amount of positive spin relative to negative spin for each candidate, I constructed a weekly ratio of the number of positive to negative spin news stories. In addition to media spin measures, I also constructed indicators of changes in the sheer amount of coverage each candidate was receiving over time.

Looking at horse race spin and contributor behavior alone, it might be easy to mistake people's reactions to other events in the political environment for reactions to horse race coverage. For example, increases in the number of contributions might occur because the candidate is attracting more supporters as a result of newly espoused policy stands, or for any of a variety of reasons. Or perhaps it is not media coverage so much as the results of primaries themselves that are influencing contributors. Undoubtedly most people hear about these results through mass media, but the ambiguity of results from nomination contests means that journalists often have considerable discretion in how results are reported (Orren, 1985).

In order to sort out these possibilities, indicators were constructed to represent major ongoing primary events that might also influence public perceptions of the candidates' chances, and their share of contributions. These included an indicator of each candidate's objective probability of being nominated based on primary results to date,[11] the proportion of voters supporting each candidate according to the latest national poll of party members,[12] and the size of the campaign war chest to date.[13]

Measures of the size of a candidate's constituency make it possible to take into account the extent to which candidates are receiving money and votes for the same reasons unrelated to candidate viability.[14] For example, if changes in the amount of public support occurred, this might also enhance or detract from a candidate's fund-raising capacity by changing the size of his pool of potential contributors.

Taking into account the size of the campaign war chest allows for the fact that it generally takes money to raise more money. In order to receive donations, one generally has to ask, and this can become quite expensive when asking via mass mediated methods such as direct mail and advertising. Some question whether the amount spent on solicitation of funds should have much to do with the flow of contributions over time. As Jones (1990, p.40) noted in her study of recent patterns of campaign giving, "While it is true that more and more people are now asked, by phone and mail, to make political contributions, the response rate is generally very low . . . . There does not seem to be a large, undifferentiated electorate just waiting for an invitation to contribute to campaigns."

Others have suggested that it is personal associations rather than costly mass solicitations that are the driving force behind most individual decisions to donate (e.g., Brownstein, 1987). In either case, to the extent that contributing is driven by vast differences in the kinds of fund-raising efforts in which campaigns can afford to engage, taking into account the size of the war chest should incorporate this constraint.

Patterns of Contributor Behavior

It is tempting to assume that the number of donations to each of the four candidates should be related to one another in an interlocking series of relationships whereby an increase in donations to one candidate drives donations to the others down. As a quick glance at Figure 12.1 indicates, this was clearly not the case for the 1988 Republicans. Similar over time trends in patterns of giving seem to influence all four of the leading Republican candidates. The simultaneous peaks and valleys are most visible for Bush and Dole, but Kemp and Robertson donations also tend to rise and fall during roughly the same time periods. For the leading Democrats in 1988, there was a similar tendency to attract greater numbers of contributors during the same time periods. These patterns suggest that some external factors such as awareness or interest in the impending campaign are influencing all candidates' potential donors over time. Rather than taking donations away from other candidates, an increase in the number of donations to one candidate means that others are probably also experiencing upswings, though perhaps not of the same magnitude.

In looking at the effects of perceived viability on fund raising, it is important to take these influences into account so that seasonal increases that influence all candidates at once are not falsely attributed to changes in a particular candidate's viability. To do this, I calculated each candidate's competitive advantage in fund raising for each week by taking the number of donations a candidate received in any given week and subtracting the average number of donations received by all other leading Republican candidates that same week. These scores represent each candidate's competitive advantage in individual fund raising relative to the fund raising successes concurrently enjoyed by his opponents.

Ideally it would be possible to isolate the exact time that a contributor makes a decision. However, keeping in mind that available information on donations is dated according to when they are received at campaign headquarters, and that much fund raising occurs through the mail, it seems unlikely that a relationship between donations and horse race spin would be visible within a lag as short as one week. Even fund raising

238

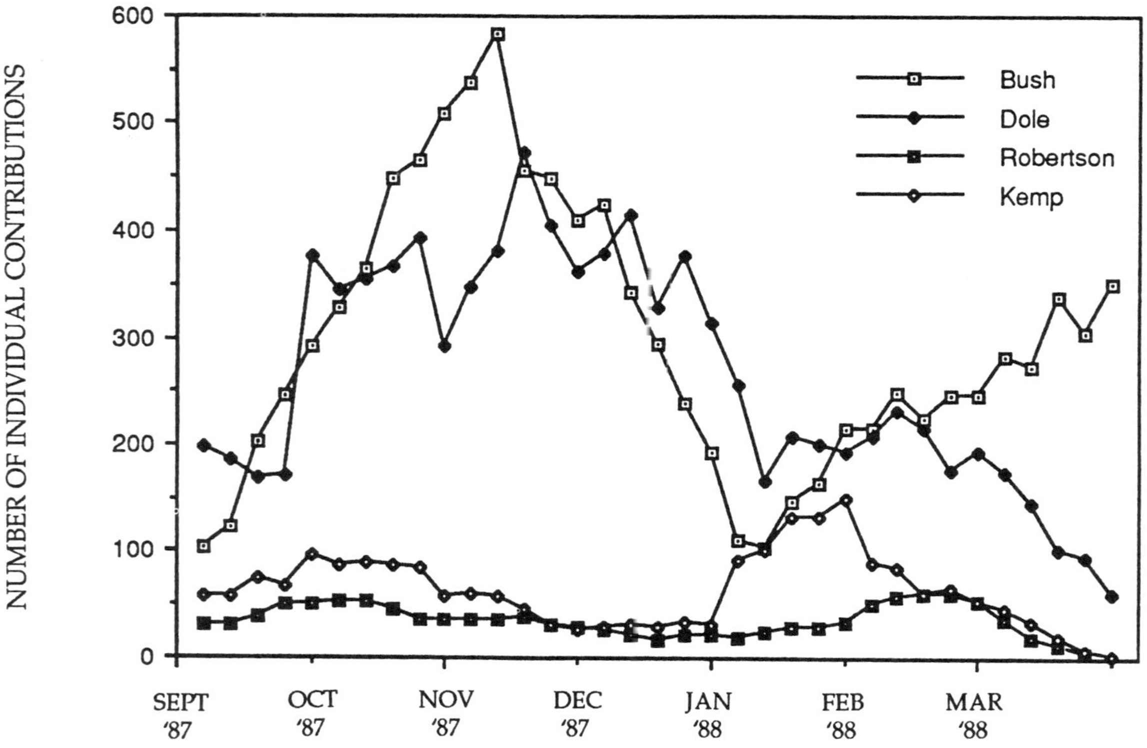

FIGURE 12.1 Number of Individual Donations to Four Leading Republican Primary Candidates

that occurs in face-to-face settings is generally planned in advance. This suggests a minimal lag of at least two weeks before one would expect changes in media spin to show up in larger numbers of checks at campaign headquarters.

As a rule of thumb, direct mail experts suggest that almost all of the responses to a request for money will be returned within three to four weeks of the original plea (approximately five weeks after the initial mailing), or not at all. Since direct mail is a slow, but common method of soliciting money, the time frame in which one could safely expect contributors to respond to changes in perceived viability and have their contributions noted at headquarters would be in the range of from two to five weeks. For these reasons, I used indicators of the average amount of media spin, voter support, etc., during the period two to five weeks prior to the week donations were recorded at campaign headquarters.

Based on these assumptions, these data were analyzed using multivariate regression techniques specially suited for analyzing trends over time.[15] Results are reported only for those factors that have a statistically significant influence on the flow of campaign contributions. Since potential contributors are likely to be influenced by their perceptions of the fortunes of opposing candidates as well, I also took into account the kind of horse race spin simultaneously being received by opposing candidates.[16]

I begin analyzing each candidate's donations by looking at the straightforward relationship between donations and media spin over time. Since it could be misleading to draw conclusions on this type of evidence alone, I then examine these same relationships while taking into account other factors that might simultaneously be influencing the flow of donations. I first describe results for each individual candidate, and then summarize the general pattern of findings for both Republican and Democratic candidates. Finally, I speculate about what these results suggest with respect to future elections.

Findings

Tracking Kemp Contributors

Figure 12.2 plots the ratio of positive to negative spin in Kemp's campaign coverage and the number of donations to the Kemp campaign each week. Here the effects of horse race coverage appear quite pronounced. The peak in spin in early September is followed a few weeks later by a peak in donations. Media spin dips in early October, followed four to five weeks later by a parallel dip in the number of donations received. In

240

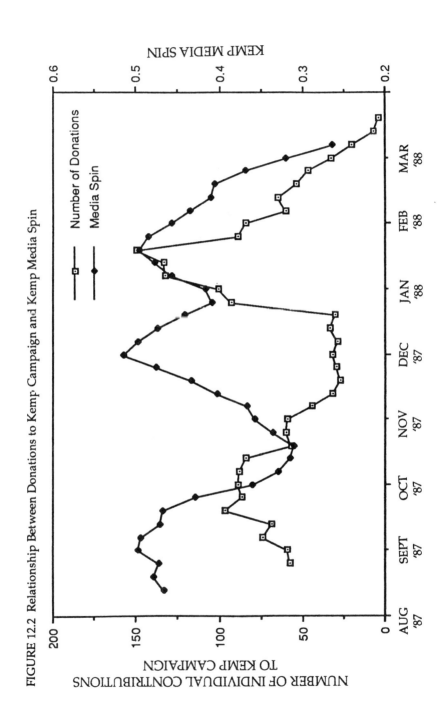

FIGURE 12.2 Relationship Between Donations to Kemp Campaign and Kemp Media Spin

a similar pattern, the peak in positive Kemp spin in early December is followed four to five weeks hence by a climb in the number of contributions. The third peak in Kemp's spin corresponds to a much smaller but still visible donation surge in mid February.

Kemp's early positive spin is likely to have resulted from a series of conservative endorsements in August and September including an Iowa Right-to-Life straw poll, The National Congressional Club, and U.S. Senator Gordon Humphrey of New Hampshire. By late October, this drops off considerably as a CBS News/*New York Times* poll showed Kemp running fourth with only six percent of Republican voters nationally, and also fourth among likely Iowa Republican voters. Reasons for the strong positive spin in December are less clear, although Kemp won a victory of sorts in Michigan by combining forces with Robertson to strike down redistricting and apportionment decisions. The January surge in positive spin coincides with several polls showing Kemp surging in New Hampshire. But Kemp's actual performance in Iowa and subsequent contests led to a quick falloff.

Simultaneously taking into account other influences on donations to Kemp gives a clearer picture of what was driving this trend. Even taking into account changes in the size of his constituency, the total amount of coverage he was receiving, ongoing primary events, the size of his war chest, and the kind of media spin other alternative candidates were receiving, the frequency of donations to Kemp was clearly a function of the media spin presented in coverage of his campaign. When coverage reflected a more positive outlook, donations began to roll in shortly thereafter. Results of the multivariate analysis suggest that for a week with a two to one ratio of positive to negative coverage, the Kemp campaign could expect roughly 650 more donations relative to what would be expected with coverage balancing positive and negative spin. Likewise, a week with twice as much negative as positive spin would cut the flow of donations in half. Given the very modest number of donations Kemp was receiving, this effect represents a substantial influence.

But in addition to media spin, Kemp's donations also were driven by the size of his primary constituency. As the number of Kemp supporters waxed and waned, so did the number of donations to his campaign. Interestingly, the number of donations that the Kemp campaign received also grew as a function of negative media spin on Dole's campaign. A favorable ratio of horse race stories concerning Dole's campaign drove donations to Kemp's campaign down. In fact, for a week in which coverage ran two-to-one negative toward Dole's campaign, Kemp received more than 300 more donations, thus suggesting that he was seen as a likely alternative by some Dole supporters. This effect is only about half the size of the positive effect that Kemp's media spin had on his donations, but it is still a major influence.

Tracking Dole Contributors

Figure 12.3 illustrates the relationship between Dole's media spin and donations to the Dole campaign over time. The early peak in media spin in late September is followed by a parallel peak in donations that begins in late September but reaches its apex in mid-October. A less dramatic upswing in Dole's portrayed viability in early November coincides with fund-raising successes that began at roughly the same point, but continued throughout late November and early December. The lag time seems to apply less well as the primary season progresses. Shortly after his victory in Iowa and the positive media spin it brought, Dole supporters rallied with a surge in donations, but this was short-lived and fell off quickly with shifting media coverage.

Positive spin on the Dole campaign peaked in mid-September of 1987. Most likely this surge of viability was due to a *Des Moines Register* poll showing Dole leading Bush 32 percent to 29 percent with Kemp at only 10 percent. In addition, an NBC News/*Wall Street Journal* poll released in late September showed Dole within one percentage point of Bush. This was the first and the last time Dole was shown to be within striking distance of Bush. Media spin indicators confirm that he never again regained such high viability coverage.

The unusually high peak in Dole donations occurring in early November resulted from a Hollywood fund-raiser on October 30 at where Dole raised nearly 1.1 million in a single evening. The two later peaks in December 1987 more closely conform to the earlier media spin pattern. The media spin peak in mid-November coincided with a November 15 *Des Moines Register* poll showing Dole in first place among Republicans likely to vote in the Iowa caucuses. A surge in positive media spin in early February resulted from Dole's clear victory in the Iowa caucuses and subsequent polls showing him surging in New Hampshire. By late February, coverage was turning less optimistic as Bush defeated Dole in New Hampshire. Again, donations increased shortly after these peaks and then fell off, but the overall level of donations never went back up to pre-primary season levels.

Even when taking into account primary results and the many other potential influences on contributing, Dole's donations still were strongly affected by horse race spin. In fact, results of the multivariate analysis suggest that Dole's contributors were influenced to virtually the same extent as Kemp's by horse race coverage of their favored candidate. Again similarly, Dole's donations were negatively influenced by the positive media spin received by one of his opponents. The more negative spin Robertson received, the better Dole fared financially. But unlike Kemp, Dole's donations were also driven by the size of his campaign war chest, although the translation of money into more money appeared to be

243

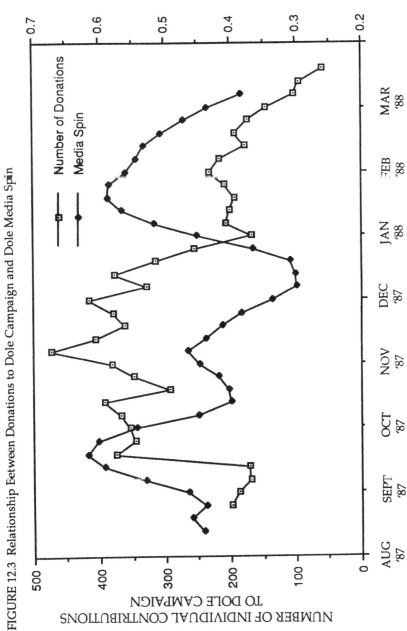

FIGURE 12.3 Relationship Between Donations to Dole Campaign and Dole Media Spin

far from an efficient one: the war chest had to increase by approximately $23,000 in order to produce a single new donation. This figure is misleading since the amount spent on fund raising was probably only a fraction of the total war chest. Nevertheless, it suggests that while money is important to fund-raising success, it is not easily converted into the numerous small donations on which primary candidates depend.

Tracking Bush Contributors

Bush's donations represent a departure from the pattern seen with Kemp and Dole. In this case, the analysis suggests that the spin on Bush's own campaign had no effect on his potential contributors, but coverage of Kemp's chances of victory had a very strong and significant negative effect. The less viable the media portrayed Kemp to be, the more contributions flowed into the Bush campaign. Although media spin surrounding the other two candidates was also negatively related to donations to Bush, these influences were not strong enough to reach conventional levels of statistical significance. Apparently early Kemp supporters — most likely those in the conservative wing of the Republican party — moved into Bush's camp when the media portrayed Kemp's chances as low, and away from the Bush camp when media coverage portrayed him as more viable.

Figure 12.4 illustrates the relationship between Kemp's media spin and donations to Bush over time. The pattern suggested by the multivariate analysis is clear. When Kemp's spin peaks briefly in early August, for example, it is followed a few weeks later by a downturn in Bush donations. When Kemp's spin falls in early October, it is followed a few weeks later by a tremendous surge in contributions to Bush. Again in early December, when media coverage portrayed Kemp as at the height of his viability in this campaign, this was followed shortly thereafter by the biggest dip in Bush donations of the entire primary and pre-primary season. Like Dole, most of his fund raising was accomplished in advance of the actual primary season. For a front runner then, the question in potential donors' minds is not whether the candidate is viable, but rather how viable the likely alternatives are.

Tracking Robertson Contributors

The beginning of the upswing in positive spin surrounding Robertson's campaign occurred on September 12, 1987 when Robertson placed first in an Iowa straw poll sponsored by the Iowa State GOP Committee. This was the first real face-off among Republican candidates, and the surprising results were interpreted as indicative of Robertson's organizational strength as well as his popularity. Interestingly, this pat-

245

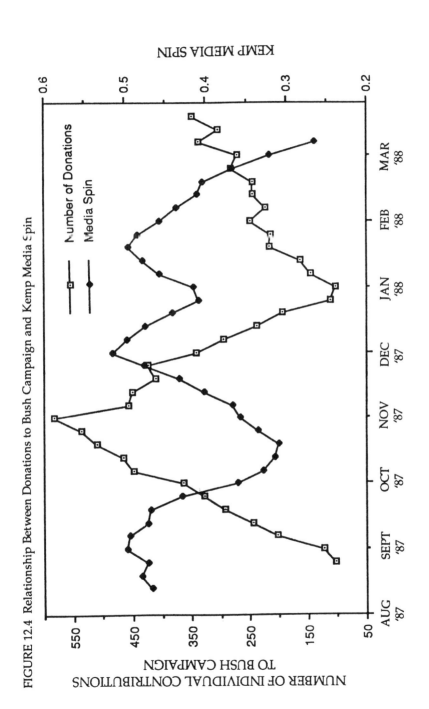

FIGURE 12.4 Relationship Between Donations to Bush Campaign and Kemp Media Spin

tern of coverage continued right up to the beginning of the primary season. His all-time high in positive spin occurred in February 1987, the month in which he came in second in Iowa, shocking many pundits by finishing ahead of George Bush. In this same month, Robertson also won the Hawaiian caucuses and placed second behind Dole in the Minnesota caucuses and in the South Dakota primary.

Multivariate examination of donations from Robertson supporters showed a very different pattern from that of the other candidates. Media spin on Robertson's campaign was related to the flow of donations, but unlike any of the other candidates, this influence was a negative one, indicating that an increasing number of donations flowed into the Robertson coffers when he was portrayed as losing ground, and these numbers generally fell off shortly after he was portrayed as gaining ground.

In examining Figure 12.5, it is tempting to interpret the negative relationship between Robertson's media spin and the flow of donations as simply a matter of using the wrong time lag. Perhaps altering the assumed time between the change in media spin and the time the contribution is received would reverse the relationship to a more familiar, positive one. However, as Figure 12.5 indicates, there is no time lag that could account for this pattern short of an unreasonably long one lasting four or five months.

Another alternative is that fund-raising ability is driving media spin rather than vice-versa. Figure 12.5 could support this idea in the first four months or so, but the trends are more or less simultaneous toward the end of the time series. A third alternative is that because of their intensity of commitment, Robertson's supporters were truly more motivated by loyalty and the threat of loss than by viability and the fear of throwing money away on a candidate without a chance. Since the pattern changes somewhat from the exhibition season to the actual primaries, no one explanation fits extremely well in this case. However, among the Democratic candidates, donations to Jesse Jackson demonstrated a similar relationship, thus suggesting that this pattern is not unique to Robertson, and that it may indeed be tied to candidates with intensely supportive constituencies.

Summary and Implications

Recent history belies the conventional wisdom that unfavorable early perceptions of candidate viability will "cripple" and "destroy" a candidate's chances of winning the nomination (see, e.g., Sigelman, 1989; Bartels, 1988; c.f. Marshall, 1983). In 1988, for example, Dukakis and Bush both finished third in Iowa, thus prompting many candidates to rethink

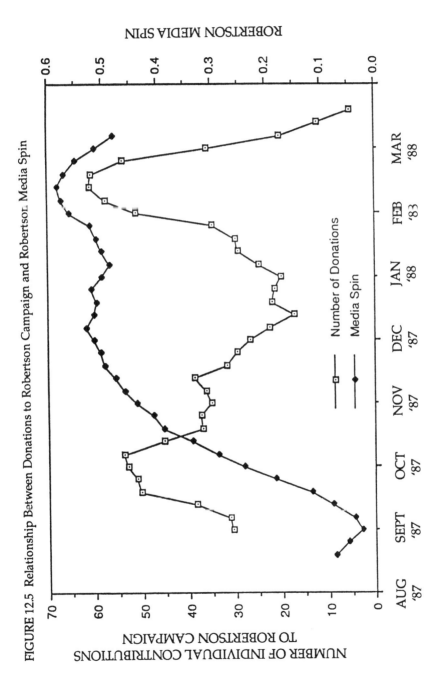

FIGURE 12.5 Relationship Between Donations to Robertson Campaign and Robertson Media Spin

the importance of a strong early showing (see Oreskes, 1990). In 1988, "The candidates who ultimately walked away with the prize began very slowly" (Sigelman, 1989: 38). Likewise, in 1992, Clinton lost New Hampshire to Tsongas, and Bush fared far worse than anticipated against Buchanan.

Winning the nomination clearly takes more than a strong showing in Iowa or New Hampshire. But perceived viability more generally may, nonetheless, be of substantial value in attracting campaign resources. Media coverage of the campaign horse race appears to play an important role in determining which candidates enter the primary season well funded, and which candidates continue to find supporters with checkbooks in hand.

The importance of media spin in the dynamics of fund raising for the candidates in 1988 is all the more impressive when one considers that this impact was above and beyond the influence of primary campaign victories, delegate counts, levels of voter support, and the size of the campaign war chest. These factors were typically overshadowed by media spin as predictors of the flow of campaign donations.

Although it can be dangerous to generalize from a single election year, the pattern of findings makes some intuitive sense. Portrayals of candidate viability mattered most for the Republican also-rans, Kemp and Dole. Front-runner George Bush's financial fortunes hinged more on coverage of his opponents than on coverage of his own viability. And Pat Robertson's highly committed supporters responded out of loyalty to a cause they were unlikely to abandon even in the face of adversity. Since their candidate could not easily be replaced by another similar one, they were motivated by the threat of a lost cause.

These results do not support the idea that viability and front-runner status benefit a candidate financially simply because of the increased free media coverage received (cf. Robinson, Conover & Sheehan, 1980). The total amount of coverage received bore no relation to patterns of contributor behavior. At least for these four candidates, the effects of media coverage were not due to the sheer amount of media attention directed toward them. Although media coverage may help to legitimize a candidacy, heavy press attention can just as easily be a liability as an asset since it may bring with it extra critical coverage of the candidate (see also Robinson & Sheehan, 1983).

Moreover, these findings suggest that the origins of horse race influence do not lie in the structure of primary events alone: they result from the discretion of reporters in interpreting the meaning of ongoing events. With respect to the impact of primary outcomes, this finding should come as no surprise since most fund raising occurred before the primary season itself was under way. There were few actual "events" to serve as guideposts during the most important fund-raising period except for the ones journalists constructed for these purposes. As a result, things such as polls and endorsements probably took on additional significance. I do not mean to suggest that polls and endorsements and the like are not newsworthy events, but interpretations of their significance to winning the nomination are often highly ambiguous, unlike primary results which have an easily interpretable, objective connection to delegate counts and ultimately winning the nomination.

As states continue to jockey for earlier and supposedly more powerful positions, some political observers have argued that we should seek to eliminate the potential for momentum-like processes by changing the structure of the primary system. The outcomes of sequential primaries influence expectations of candidate success or failure, and this inevitably alters the dynamics of the campaign, with fund raising being no exception. Moving to a system such as a national primary could eliminate these influences if it were the structure of the primary process itself driving it. But in general, the effects of horse race coverage on fund raising are more pronounced during the exhibition season when journalists have the most discretion in interpreting candidate standing. Condensing the primary season into a shorter period seems unlikely to eliminate the over time emphasis since other standards and benchmarks will simply be adopted to fill this vacuum.

Not surprisingly, many of the peaks and valleys in horse race spin can be traced to the release of polls indicating that a candidate is doing better or worse than anticipated. Poll results are an integral part of horse race reporting, particularly during the early campaign. However, these peaks and valleys in horse race spin are still evident even if one eliminates all news stories based on polls or even those making any reference to them. So while polls may influence the current spin placed on coverage of a candidate, the effects of polls on campaign news apparently transcend the publication of poll-based news stories themselves. Once a horse race tone is established by poll results, it is picked up and carried over into campaign news stories on topics other than polls. This finding suggests that the impact of polls on the dynamics of campaigns is probably under-estimated by focusing on poll-based news alone.

Many political observers blame the journalistic norm emphasizing professional objectivity for the glut of horse race coverage; the desire to remain objective steers journalists away from issue-oriented news toward coverage of the strategic aspects of elections. Paradoxically, coverage designed to keep journalists outside the realm of political influence also has concrete political consequences. Putatively "neutral" coverage of who is ahead or behind has important consequences for attaining the resources necessary to run a competitive race. Although the candidates who did well in the early state primaries and caucuses did not ultimately walk away with the nominations, the two candidates who entered the primary season best funded did walk away with their respective parties' nominations.

These results also highlight the broader question of whether and to what extent horse race coverage is harmful to the political process. History suggests that eliminating poll results from political campaigns would do little to stem the tide of horse race coverage (see, e.g., Sigelman & Bullock, 1991, cf. Davis, 1985). This issue notwithstanding, a major criticism of horse race emphasis is that it encourages irrational decision making. But the strategic campaign contributor is anything but irrational; people quite sensibly want to put their money on a person who has a solid chance of being nominated, and to avoid wasting money on a favored candidate who is doing well without their financial assistance. In both cases, the potential donor is making a highly calculated decision.

More generally, these findings suggest that horse race coverage may play more than a superfluous, potentially anti-democratic role in campaigns. Broh (1987) makes this point in his assessment of television coverage of Jesse Jackson's bid for the 1984 nomination. He argues that while Jackson received more than his fair share of positive media spin, and plenty of media coverage in general, he was hurt by the fact that he did not receive as much horse race coverage as the other candidates: "It's not that TV news was unfair in describing Jackson's chances; rather, television news simply did not describe his chances" (Broh, 1987: 14).

Horse race coverage may be more than simply the most memorable and entertaining part of campaign coverage in the eyes of potential voters. It may also serve a valuable purpose by engaging voters in the campaign process to the extent that they are willing to place a "bet" on a candidate. The ups and downs of the campaign draw people into the process and involve them in a way that is important to facilitating political interest as well as donations. Thus horse race coverage may serve as an important trigger, motivating potential donors to take action. The motive may be to rush to the aid of an intensely favored underdog, or to attach one's self to a rising star. In either case, news about changes in candidate status draws potential donors' attention to the campaign and acts as an important motivating force fueling a campaign's progress.

There is, however, one critical difference between the campaign and a true horse race. While news of a particularly strong horse may encourage people to put their money on it, placing the bet does not change the horse's chances of running a good race. In politics, by contrast, decisions to bet on one candidate over another can make or break a candidacy. This fact makes it all the more important to understand how polling and the larger campaign horse race interact with the strategic nature of contributor behavior.

Notes

An earlier version of this chapter was presented to the American Association for Public Opinion Research in Phoenix, Arizona in May, 1991. I would like to thank David Fan, Murray Edelman and Cate Steele for their contributions to this study. This research was supported by a grant from the Graduate School of the University of Wisconsin-Madison.

1. Under these rules candidates for the presidential nominations may accept no more than $1000 from any individual contributor and no more than $5000 from any multi-candidate committee (see Alexander & Haggerty (1987)) for details). For candidates who are able to raise $5000 in each of 20 states from individual contributions of $250 or less, public matching funds are available from the federal government. Upon qualification, only individual contributions are matchable, and only up to $250 per contribution.

2. In an interesting departure from the conventional wisdom on effects of campaign reform, Reiter (1985) argues that changes in the character of nomination politics are more directly related to broader social changes than to specific procedural reforms.

3. For example, Bartels (1988) weights his measure of each candidate's cumulative primary vote share by the amount of media coverage the subsequent week. Aldrich (1980) examines actual and expected performances specifically in publicized primaries.

4. Nor is there conclusive evidence bearing on closely related claims such as the influence of publicized poll results on public opinion in non-sequential electoral processes (for a review, see e.g., Traugott, 1990).

5. The source of these figures is the 1988 NES Super Tuesday study.

6. Only private individual contributions received by the candidate's principal campaign committee or another authorized campaign committee were counted toward this total. Many candidates fund their pre-announcement activities through candidate PACs rather than campaign organizations in order to circumvent FECA limits. These organizations were particularly important in funding the wide open field of candidates in 1988. Contributions to these technically "independent" organizations such as Bush's Fund For America's Future, Kemp's Campaign For Prosperity, Robertson's Committee for Freedom, or Dole's Campaign America were not included in the data presented here. This money is typically spent in ways that indirectly benefit the candidate — most often on things such as travel expenses so that the candidate may travel to speaking engagements around the country — ostensibly on behalf of other candidates. Although these organizations play a major role in the pre-announcement stage when individual donations to candidates cannot yet be matched, they are less of a factor during the time period of interest in this study. By mid 1987, the candidates all had a vested interest in accumulating many small individual donations that would help them qualify for matching funds. Separate analyses including donations to pre-candidacy PACs did not change the general pattern of findings.

I used the number, rather than the monetary total of donations received each week in these analyses. Although amounts are obviously important as well, in modeling the decision making process prompting people to donate money, amount is more likely to be affected by idiosyncratic factors such as personal affluence, while the number of donations should be more evenly influenced by outside factors such as media coverage. Moreover, the campaign finance system puts a premium on the number of individual donations, so it makes even more sense to concentrate on the number of individual contributors. Since the FEC only requires records for individual donations of more than $200, these analyses must exclude small donations.

7. The major television networks and national newspapers generally agree in their assessments of candidates' performances and prospects (Marshall, 1983), thus suggesting that American newspaper readers and television viewers receive essentially the same representation of the primary race. Great similarities in the nature of horse race coverage make it unnecessary to assess multiple media sources in order to gauge media portrayals of the campaign environment. Since the AP wire service crosses over all of these channels — both print and broadcast — it serves as an appropriate source from which to measure the amount and nature of horse race coverage surrounding individual candidacies over time.

8. The precise specification for the universe of stories sampled was simply any story including the candidate's first and last name. For a detailed description of all coding rules, please contact the author.

9. This was done using a computer program designed to identify and score word and phrase combinations by paragraph. The rules used to code the content were quite complex; they took into account the distance between words, the order in which words appeared, and the presence of negatives or other concepts in the paragraph. For example, in an analysis of Bush stories, "Bush . . . outscored . . . Dole" was recognized as positive spin for Bush, while "Dole . . . outscored . . . Bush" was scored as negative spin for Bush. Similarly "Bush . . . outscored . . . by . . . Dole" would be recognized as negative spin for Bush.. To estimate the reliability of coding, a random subsample of 250 paragraphs from the 1000 stories for each candidate was coded by an independent coder whose scores were then compared to those generated by the computer program. This process resulted in 89 percent of paragraphs classified correctly. Most errors were Type II errors, that is, they resulted from not scoring paragraphs that did involve candidate viability rather than inappropriately coding coverage that did not involve horse race considerations. For details on this procedure and examples of its use in other contexts, see Fan (1988).

10. Attempts to reliably differentiate references to whether candidates are ahead versus gaining ground or behind versus losing ground proved impossible since most horse race coverage blended the two, even within single sentences. Attempts to differentiate speculation ("If Dole wins this one, . . . ") from descriptions of past or likely future events were also abandoned on the grounds that speculation formed an integral part of the type of coverage expected to bring about changes in fund-raising capabilities.

11. Measures of the candidates' probabilities of nomination were constructed from a comparison of each candidate's share of all of the delegates selected at a given point in the campaign relative to the total number needed to secure the

nomination. A second indicator of ongoing events was comprised of the share of the primary vote the candidate won in the most recent primary. As Bartels (1988) argues, public perceptions of the candidates' chances "respond with special force, at any given point in the campaign, to the most recent primary results." The candidate's cumulative percentage of the primary vote to date served as yet another indicator of accumulating support. These three items turned out to be highly intercorrelated (r= .81). To avoid multicollinearity problems, they were combined into a single index representing primary outcomes.

12. These data were drawn from a variety of sources using the Roper archive's Public Opinion Location Library. When more than one poll was available for a given week, the percentages were averaged. Since minor differences in question wording might make for erroneous comparisons of the absolute percentage support from week to week, each candidate's competitive standing was calculated with respect to the amount of support for all candidates using that particular question. For an analysis of problems peculiar to primary polling, see Bartels and Broh (1989).

13. Ideally it would be possible to assess the amount of money a campaign is spending on advertising, direct mail or other types of direct appeals for money, but detailed information on the amount of money spent on fund-raising efforts is not available, particularly on an over time basis (see McBurnett, 1991). Nonetheless, if one assumes that the percentage of the campaign budget spent on such activities is fairly consistent across candidates, then the size of the war chest itself can serve as a reasonable surrogate. Cook (1989) reports that in 1988 candidates all adopted basically the same strategy, starting early and focusing their energies on fund raising during the exhibition season.

14. Including a measure of voter intentions in the analysis eliminates the indirect effects that horse race coverage might have on contributors. If horse race coverage makes potential contributors more likely to vote for a particular candidate, which in turn leads to more contributions, then this impact will be registered in the impact of voter support measures since they are the more immediate precursors to increased contributions. The goal of these analyses is to identify media impact resulting in increased contributions due to strategic motivations — that is, without any concurrent change in the candidate's base of voter support.

15. Autocorrelation of the error terms was detected when using OLS regression estimates. Durbin-Watson statistics were 2.11, 2.36, 2.06, and 1.82 for Kemp, Dole, Bush and Robertson, respectively. For this reason, a two-step full transform (EGLS) method was used to take into account first order autoregressive processes (see Judge et al., 1980 or Harvey, 1981 for details). This resulted in Durbin-Watson statistics within acceptable ranges (see Johnston, 1972).

16. The hypothesized relationships are as follows:

$$y_t = a + b_1 x_{1(t-q)} + b_2 x_{2(t-q)} + b_3 x_{3(t-q)} + b_4 x_{4(t-q)} + b_5 x_{5(t-q)} + b_6 x_{6(t-q)} + b_7 x_{7(t-q)} + b_8 x_{8(t-q)} + e.$$

where:

y_t = the number of donations received by a candidate at week t, measured as a deviation from the average number of donations received by the other candidates during week t

q =   the proposed time lag of two to five weeks prior
a =   a constant
x_1 =   the ratio of positive to negative media spin
       surrounding the candidate two to five weeks prior
x_2 =   the index of primary events two to five weeks prior
x_3 =   the total amount of media coverage the candidate received two
       to five weeks prior
x_4 =   the size of the candidate's campaign war chest
       two to five weeks prior
x_5 =   the candidate's competitive advantage in voter
       support two to five weeks prior
x_6, x_7, x_8 = the ratio of positive to negative media spin surrounding
       other leading candidates two to five weeks prior

PART SIX

Conclusion

13

The Media's Use of Election Polls: A Synthesis and Recommendations for 1996 and Beyond

Paul J. Lavrakas
Michael W. Traugott

The previous chapters have discussed recent developments in the news media's use of information gathered by election polls and other social science techniques, such as focus groups, to frame their election coverage and compose their news stories. Various technical or methodological aspects of election polling were discussed in relation to the collection of the data and to its interpretation. Examples of exactly how polling information was used in coverage of the Bush/Clinton/Perot election campaign were presented and critiqued. Finally, some of the likely direct and indirect effects of this type of news on journalists and the news media and, thereby, on the public and the campaigns, were addressed.

In closing this volume, we see four themes that integrate the individual chapters and strongly suggest the need to change — that is, enhance — the manner in which most journalists and news organizations utilize polling in election coverage. First, we believe there is no longer any need to question the "power of the polls" and the news they generate. Second, the news media are almost without exception "data-rich but analysis poor." Third, traditional approaches to formulating and "packaging" election news coverage should be modified to accommodate modern enhancements to information gathering and interpretation. And finally, media executives and journalists should accept more responsibility for the effects of their work on the values and processes they profess to serve and recommit themselves and their organizations to doing a better job.

The Power of the Polls

We believe that this volume and other scholarly works in the past two decades (e.g., Bartels, 1988; Broh, 1980; Cantril, 1991; Jamieson, 1992; Lavrakas and Holley, 1991; Mann and Orren, 1991; Meyer, 1990; Patterson, 1980, 1989; Traugott, 1992; and Yankelovich, 1991) have presented compelling arguments about the power of election polls, and the information and news they generate, to influence election campaign outcomes. There are important direct effects and important indirect effects associated with election polls.

The impact of poll-based media coverage is significant throughout the campaign, although the effects vary at different stages of the campaign. Most of the impact has to do with candidate viability and electability, because most of the poll-based coverage, heretofore, has been used to support horse-race coverage. Poll findings are likely to have their greatest direct effects during the primaries, especially when emerging candidates are most reliant upon financial contributions and volunteer efforts. During this period, however, the resources the media commit to polling and to campaign coverage are relatively modest, and measuring the public's attitudes and preferences is relatively difficult because information levels are low. During the general election phase of the campaign, most potential voters have developed their candidate preferences. At this phase, extensive amounts of poll-based horse-race coverage may affect the size of voter turnout as well as the preferences of late deciders, thereby impacting the election outcome. At the very end of the campaign and in the immediate post mortem, the media's use of exit polls of voters leaving the voting booth can frame the meaning and contribute to the political spin that is used by journalists and political elites to attach meaning and significance to the election.

Logic suggests, and research findings reinforce, the belief that the increase in the use of election polls has had a considerable and growing impact on reporters, editors, and producers, and the manner in which they cover election campaigns; it directly affects *what* they choose to report and *how* they report it. These effects of the poll findings on journalists *indirectly*, but no less powerfully, influence the campaigns, as candidates and their supporters are forever attending to poll-driven media coverage to make decisions about their candidate's viability. Too much of this coverage focuses on the horse-race aspects of the campaign. However, the power of the polls likely would remain strong even if the typical election coverage focused more on issues than is currently thought to happen. As candidate viability is impacted by poll results, the electorate's choices are constrained or, at a minimum, narrowed. To the extent that potential voters decide that their vote will not matter because they believe that the election's major ballot outcomes are foregone conclusions predicted by the polls, other down-ballot races may be affected.

Towards the end of the campaign, when many in the potential electorate are deciding *how to vote* and, especially at the very end, when many are deciding *whether or not to vote*, journalists and their news organizations need to attend more closely to what the possible election outcomes will mean for various segments of their readers, viewers, and the public at large. This suggests the need for added attention to issue coverage, including public attitudes on the issues as measured by pre-election surveys. The media should not allow candidates solely to dictate the issues and rhetoric of the campaign. Here, polling should be used more creatively to illuminate congruencies and incongruities between a candidate's position on specific issues and the public's. For example, if there are "litmus-test" issues that determine the vote of certain groups of citizens, shouldn't it be the responsibility of the media to identify these issues and pin down the candidates as to their policy positions on these issues? Isn't this just good reporting, and doesn't this make good business sense for a newspaper, magazine, television or radio station?

Although we believe that any reasonable review of current research documents beyond any substantial doubt that reporting about polls has an impact on elections and the nation's political processes, additional, detailed research is needed on the nature and magnitude of the effects. Regardless of our conclusions about the direct and indirect power of the polls, we believe the public policy debate must continue over what, if anything, to do about election polls and the media's use of them. This debate — one that involves important constitutional as well as policy issues — must be informed by the best available empirical knowledge base.

We hope it is obvious to readers what our own position is on this matter. Holding a deep regard for the potential benefits that can accrue to a society with a free press, we object to legislation or regulation that would impinge upon news decisions about the use and dissemination of information gathered via election polls. However, as strongly as we support the media's right to exercise their own news judgment, we submit that more news media must exercise *better* news judgment in planning and executing their election coverage, especially as it incorporates election polls and other information derived from social science techniques to gauge public preferences and opinions.

Data-Rich but Analysis Poor

Given the millions of dollars that the news media now spend on election polling and other social science techniques like focus groups to gather information to supplement traditional "shoe-leather" journalism, it is somewhat of a wonder that they do so little in making use of the information they gather. Most news organizations barely scratch the surface of their data; in many instances, they only report simple (univariate) frequencies in the form of the percentage of the likely electorate supporting each candidate.

Perhaps it is not surprising that news organizations have embraced "new" news-gathering techniques, such as election polling methods, long before they learned what could *and should* be done with the information they generated. However, As has been shown countless times before, giving someone a new tool well before that person understands how it is best used can have serious unintended and undesired consequences.

We believe that news media decision-makers — in particular, editors, producers, publishers, and station managers — must recognize the power of the information gathered through election polls and insist that adequate time and resources be allocated to in-depth analyses and framing of election coverage. Their goal should be not only to assure that their reporters write accurate stories, but more importantly, that they write the *right* stories. Currently, this does not happen frequently enough at news organizations, and it appears unlikely that this kind of coverage will improve given the present *modus operandi* of most news media. Somehow the vicious cycle of focusing on the short-term demands of deadline pressures and ignoring potential long-term implications must be broken for significant change to occur. Given the public's well-documented disenchantment with the news media, news executives are living on borrowed time if they fail to take corrective action. Is it surprising that we have witnessed an increase in the public's attention to "infotainment" media such as radio call-in shows and television "news magazines" at the same time there has been a decline in the public's respect for traditional news outlets?

In the short-run, it may appear impossible to many news executives that they could increase resources to allow for more thorough internal analysis of election polls. Warren Mitofsky has suggested one way this might be accomplished — by retaining the services of a polling "expert" who would take the first pass at writing about the *meaning* of the numbers that polls generate. Other ways may be developed as well and additional effort must be devoted to this task. To us, the current state of affairs wherein considerable resources are utilized to gather election poll data but inadequate planning and resources are given to making the best use of them is not only bad journalism, it is bad business.

New Packaging of Election Coverage

We propose that a new way is needed for news organizations to plan and package their election news coverage, especially as it relates to the use of election polls. We hold that few who observe or participate in our nation's political processes, including many journalists and news executives, are satisfied with the present form of election coverage and the small number of news organizations that are getting it done right. We are not advocating a rejection of longstanding approaches to covering public opinion, elections, and the political process. Rather, we believe that most news organizations must supplement the old and more properly use the new.

First, knowledgeable coverage by expert political reporters should be central to comprehensive election news coverage. So-called "shoe-leather" journalism techniques that involve extensive background research, interviews with candidates and campaign officials, and even off-the-record contact with key players in political campaigns, must continue in order to keep reporters in touch with breaking news and alerted to future events. However, the information gathered by the standard journalistic interview with knowledgeable sources should be used in an iterative process. What reporters seek from these sources should be guided, at least in part, by what a news organization is learning from "precision journalism" sources, e.g., election surveys. Likewise, the information learned from the traditional reporting methods must be woven into the development of survey questionnaires and the analyses that are conducted with these data.

Second, quality election surveys should be used throughout the campaign, from before the primaries through the weeks following the election. By quality surveys we mean those that are planned and conducted by people who are methodologically and statistically competent, and therefore well aware of the pitfalls and other challenges of surveying an electorate at different stages in the campaign. Potential problems include biased questionnaire items, low response rates, and unreliable identification of likely voters, as well as superficial and otherwise inappropriate analytical strategies. An example of an enhancement to survey techniques would be to routinely include specific items in pre-primary questionnaires to allow analysts to disentangle candidate name recognition from candidate preferences (cf. Lavrakas and Merkle, 1991).

Election surveys should be used to both plan campaign news coverage and as part of what is reported as news. A proactive approach for guiding coverage by using election survey findings would make it more likely that reporters, editors, and producers have a major say in setting the agenda for the issues that the candidates address. Of course, we believe this should occur in a nonpartisan manner with the news media looking to serve the public by raising the level of political dialogue beyond campaign strategy and personalities issues.

For this to happen, a team approach to covering the campaign should be developed and implemented by the individual news organization — one suited to their resources and needs. The key players on this election coverage team would be the organization's news editors, political reporters, and election survey experts. Other players on this team would likely include columnists, editorial writers, feature writers, sound and video technicians, photographers, and graphic designers. Although some news organizations, especially the "prestige" national daily newspapers, have been developing their own versions of this team approach during the past twenty years, many have not.

The difference between what we are describing and the "team" approach traditionally taken by most news organizations is the *central* role we propose for the election survey expert(s). Through an interactive series of meetings that would continue for the entire campaign, it would be the survey expert's responsibility to advise editors and reporters of the meaning of election poll results — similar to Mitofsky's suggestions in Chapter 5 — and work together with them to decide *what is newsworthy and what is not*, from a public opinion perspective. We can envision the survey expert routinely holding "internal seminars" for the journalists to brief them on the import of the latest poll results. For many news organizations this model presupposes that they are sponsoring or conducting their own election polls. Given that approximately half of all daily newspapers do so at present, with more newspapers and other news organizations making this commitment each year, the model could be applied by hundreds of news organizations, which in turn would affect the election news coverage received by millions of readers, viewers, and listeners. Even if a news organization did not have its own polls, these briefings could still be useful for its news staff if they were conducted by an expert who could explain the findings of other available election surveys.

Another major responsibility of the survey expert would be to listen closely to what the editors' and reporters' own news savvy portended for future surveying. Similar to the process Mike Kagay described in Chapter 9 that occurs at *The New York Times*, journalists will have expert opinions and even hunches about what should be learned to better cover an evolving campaign. However, the journalists on the news team will not be expert in turning these ideas into valid survey research. That is the survey expert's job.

The third part of our action package includes the use of other techniques to gather information about the public's attitudes towards issues and the candidates, in particular focus groups. We are not sanguine about the value of using focus groups in the absence of quality election surveying. There simply is too great a chance for journalists to draw unreliable conclusions that do not generalize beyond the small number of participants in the focus groups. However, when used in tandem with surveys, both to help plan future survey questionnaires and to "humanize" the sterile numbers that polls generate, focus groups are a solid partner in our proposed package.

Finally, news organizations must get beyond merely increasing the types of sources they use to gather information about an election campaign. It is arguably more important that they allow adequate time and resources to make good sense of the information they gather, so, for example, they don't end up reporting accurately on the *wrong* story. Although traditional journalistic interviewing and qualitative techniques, such as focus groups, are not likely to require extensive technical skills to determine the *meaning* of what has been learned, extracting meaning from election surveys requires sophistication that heretofore has not been present in most newsrooms.

As noted above, we believe that a much needed source of expertise is the inclusion of a local survey expert, even for medium and small sized news organizations. These experts could be either private-sector pollsters or academic ones. At a minimum, the involvement of social science specialists would begin a few months before the primaries and continue through to a few weeks after the election. While it may seem straightforward to some news executives to utilize the indigenous quantitative research resources available in many news organization's marketing departments, these researchers often will not be adequately trained in valid survey methods or political science. However, by bringing in an outside expert for the first few years to serve this purpose, a news organization could also provide training to an internal researcher who would be assigned to work with the survey expert.

The chapters in this book and other recent writing about the media's use of election polls provide a wealth of ideas for news executives to think about and accommodate to their organization's needs and resources. We hope many executives will make a commitment to think critically about how the resources that have been allocated for election campaign coverage might be redeployed and possibly increased. We believe strongly that this can produce better journalism *and* enhance the bottom-line.

Developing Wisdom in a Free Society's Electorate

Even as the sample survey was becoming an integral part of American journalism earlier in this century, its proponents were debating its role in a democracy and its appropriate relationship to the press that reports its results. George Gallup was fond of quoting James Bryce, the 19th century commentator on American political culture, about the place of public opinion in American democracy and using him to substantiate the new venture Gallup had embarked upon. Bryce believed that the highest form of democracy, the "fourth stage," would be reached when "the will of the majority of citizens were to become ascertainable at all times" (Gallup & Rae, 1940, p. 125). Gallup felt that his own operationalization of the concept in the form of a "sampling referendum" was key to measuring public opinion on a timely basis.

Beyond measurement, however, Gallup understood that the dissemination of poll results by the news media was an important part of the democratic process. Again borrowing from Bryce, he acknowledged that, "the press occupy a key position in the democratic structure . . . not a single but a threefold role . . . [as] 'narrators,' 'advocates,' and 'weatherworks.'" (Gallup & Rae, 1940, p. 125). The media's role was — and is — important because of the need to keep citizens informed of what others like them are thinking and the degree to which their views converge with or diverge from those of organized interests, elected officials, and other politicians.

George Gallup's view of democracy was clearly from the bottom up. He felt that "unless the ordinary citizen can find channels of self-expression, the common man may become the *forgotten* man" (Gallup & Rae, 1940, p.14; italics added). Gallup's view of elected officials was:

> In a democracy, most legislators give some attention to public opinion. And to the extent to which they heed public opinion, to that extent they should have an impartial and accurate appraisal of their constituents' views. If the legislator does not agree with the majority opinion, he has an opportunity and a responsibility to correct the views of the public. (Gallup, 1944, p.90).

And Gallup was optimistic that news media could play a key beneficial role in the process.

However, half a century later, social critic and pollster, Daniel Yankelovich, presents a bleak assessment of the effects the news media are currently having on America's search for viable public policy solutions to the nation's and the world's problems (Yankelovich, 1991). In explaining the potential of the news media to help political solutions, rather than hinder them, he observes:

> There is a missing concept in American democracy, with a mystery attached to it. The mystery is not what the concept is — that is easy to state — but rather, why it is missing . . .
>
> The missing concept is a set of terms to describe the *quality* of public opinion and to distinguish "good" public opinion from "bad." (p.15)

Although not focusing on election polls per se, Yankelovich provides a complicated, yet nonetheless compelling, treatise on how the news media and others should learn to distinguish between good quality public opinion and bad. He chastises "the villains," whom he sees as the mass media, for:

> [devoting] unlimited amounts of space to trumpeting how poorly informed the public is. But [letting] their eyes glaze over when it comes to efforts to grasp and report the subtlety and complexity of the public mind. (p.36)

He also explains *why* it is important for democratic society that the media change.

Yankelovich details the barriers that are formed by devising public policies that rely too heavily on the "judgment of experts." He believes the media rely far too much on experts as informed sources and vastly under-utilize the "wisdom" of the public. However, he makes it clear that this wisdom — he calls it "public judgment" to distinguish it from "mass opinion" — does not exist on all policy issues. Yankelovich challenges the news media to help develop this wisdom in the citizenry.

As defined by Yankelovich, *public judgment* exists on an issue when the citizenry's measured views are stable, consistent, "and most important of all, . . . those who hold the opinions recognize the implications and take responsibility for them" (p. 234). "'Public judgment' is the state of highly developed public opinion that exists once people have engaged an issue, considered it from all sides, understood the choices it leads to, and accepted the full consequences of the choices they make" (p.6).

Yankelovich cites policy areas about which he believes Americans reached collective wisdom (e.g., U.S.-Soviet relations) and others for which they have not (e.g., AIDS). He presents a detailed game-plan that operationalizes the steps a news organization would take to raise the wisdom of its public on a given policy issue. In short, this involves the news media using sample surveys first to determine the "stage" at which the public's opinions on an issue exist. That is, where on the continuum from "low quality" mass opinion to "high quality" public judgment does the public fall? Is the public in the first stage of *Consciousness Raising* in which people are beginning to learn about an issue and starting to consider its socio-political meaning? Or, has the public advanced to a stage of *Working Through*, wherein people are grappling with the nature and magnitude of the societal changes that may need to be made regarding the issue? Or, has the final stage of *Resolution* been reached wherein the citizenry has "resolved where it stands cognitively, emotionally, and morally" (p. 65)?

Assuming that a state of public wisdom (i.e., the Resolution Stage) does not exist on an issue, the news media would use surveys to supplement traditional news gathering methods to help the public "work through" the volatility and inconsistencies of their opinions, and their lack of recognition of the implications of their opinions. This process could take decades to accomplish or it might take only a few months depending on the issue. What is explicit and implicit in Yankelovich's thinking is the significant positive role he envisions that the news media should be having in the process, as opposed to his severe disheartenment with the current state of affairs.

In closing, we believe that our concept of "packaging" election campaign coverage shares the spirit of Gallup's vision and is consistent with many of the important elements that Yankelovich has included in his framework. We share Yankelovich's view that to improve the current situation vis-a-vis the news media, election polls, and campaign coverage, "it will be necessary to support those in the media who see the standard for measuring journalism to be *its effect on the quality of public deliberations*" (1991, p.250; italics added). Not until improved models emerge will the balance shift from a state of growing disappointment and/or distress with much of how election campaigns are covered to a state of increasing appreciation for the contributions the coverage makes to our public discourse.

We hope that the great unactualized potential for the news media to contribute positively to democratic political processes starts being realized as this century ends and the next begins. We believe that a key part of this progress is the changes news organizations must make in the way they utilize election surveys.

References

Abramson, P.R., J.H. Aldrich, P. Paolino, and D.W. Rohde. 1990. "Sophisticated Voting in the 1988 Presidential Primaries." Paper presented to the annual meeting of the American Political Science Association, San Francisco, CA.

Achen, C.H. 1989. "Democracy, Media, and Presidential Primaries," in P. Squire, ed., *The Iowa Caucuses and the Presidential Nominating Process.* Boulder: Westview Press.

Adams, W.C. 1987. "As New Hampshire goes . . .," in G.R Orren and N.W. Polsby, eds., *Media and Momentum: The New Hampshire Primary and Nomination Politics.* Chatham, NJ: Chatham House.

Aldrich, J.H. 1980. *Before the Convention: Strategies and Choices in Presidential Nomination Campaigns.* Chicago: University of Chicago Press.

Alexander, H.E. and B.A. Haggerty. 1987. *Financing the 1984 Election.* Lexington: D.C Heath.

Alter, J. 1992a. "The Cycle of Sensationalism." *Newsweek* (February 3), p. 25.

_____. 1992b. "Sex, Abortion and Hypocrisy." *Newsweek* (August 24), p. 28.

Altschuler, B.E. 1982. *Keeping a Finger on the Public Pulse: Private Polling and Presidential Elections.* Westport, Conn.: Greenwood Press.

Arterton, F.C. 1984. *Media Politics: The News Strategies of Presidential Campaigns.* Lexington, MA: Lexington Books.

Asher, H. 1992. *Polling and the Public: What Every Citizen Should Know* (2nd edition), Washington, D.C.: Congressional Quarterly Press.

Baker, J. 1985. "The Ceremonies of Politics: Nineteenth-Century Rituals of National Affirmation," in W. Cooper, M. Holt, and J. McCardell, eds., *A Master's Due: Essays in Honor of David Herbert Donald.* Pp. 161-178. Baton Rouge: Louisiana State University Press.

Baldasty, G. 1992. *The Commercialization of News in the Nineteenth Century.* Madison: University of Wisconsin Press.

Bartels, L.M. 1988. *Presidential Primaries and the Dynamics of Public Choice.* Princeton: Princeton University Press.

Bartels, L.M. and C.A. Broh. 1989. "The polls - A Review : The 1988 Presidential Primaries." *Public Opinion Quarterly* 53(4): 563-89.

Bauman, S., and S. Herbst. 1994. "On Managing Perceptions of Public Opinion: Candidates' and Journalists' Reactions to the 1992 Polls." *Political Communication* 11:133-143.

Benedetto, R. 1992. "It's Hard to Decide Who to Vote For." *USA Today* (March 24), p. 6A.

Bogart, L. 1985. *Polls and the Awareness of Public Opinion.* New Brunswick: Transaction, Inc.

_____. 1991. *Preserving the Press: How Daily Newspapers Mobilized to Keep Their Readers.* New York: Columbia University Press.

Brady, H.E., and R. Johnston. 1987. "What's the Primary Message: Horse Race or Issue Journalism?" in G.R. Orren and N.W. Polsby, eds., *Media and Momentum.* Chatham, NJ: Chatham House.

Broh, C.A. 1980. "Horse-Race Journalism: Reporting the Polls in the 1976 Presidential Election." *Public Opinion Quarterly* 44:514-29.

_____. 1983. "Presidential Preference Polls and Network News," in W.C. Adams, ed., *Television Coverage of the 1980 Presidential Campaign.* Norwood, NJ: Ablex.

_____. 1987. *A Horse of a Different Color: Television's Treatment of Jesse Jackson's 1984 Presidential Campaign.* Washington, D.C.: Joint Center for Political Studies.

Brown, C.W., R.B. Hedges, and L.W. Powell. 1980. "Modes of Elite Political Participation: Contributors to the 1972 Presidential Candidates." *American Journal of Political Science.* 24: 259-290.

Brown, P. 1991. *Minority Party: Why Democrats Face Defeat in 1992 and Beyond.* Washington, D.C.: Regnery Gateway.

Brownstein, R. 1987. "Raising Bucks for Bush." *New York Times* (May 17), section 6, p. 42.

Cantril, A.H., ed. 1900. *Polling On The Issues.* Cabin John, Md.: Seven Locks Press.

_____. 1991. *The Opinion Connection: Polling, Politics, and the Press.* Washington, D.C.: Congressional Quarterly Press.

Chaffee, S.H. 1987. "Media Election Research Without Party Identification." Unpublished manuscript, Institute for Communication Research. Stanford, CA: Stanford University.

Clift, Eleanor, et al. 1992. "Character Questions." *Newsweek* (February 10), Pp. 26-27.

Cohen, P. 1982. *A Calculating People: The Spread of Numeracy in Early America.* Chicago: University of Chicago Press.

Converse, J.M. 1976. "Predicting No Opinion in the Polls." *Public Opinion Quarterly* 40: 515-530.

_____. 1987. *Survey Research in the United States: Roots and Emergence, 1890-1960.* Berkeley: University of California Press.

Converse, J.M. and S. Presser. 1986. *Survey Questions: Handcrafting the Standardized Questionnaire.* Newbury Park, CA: Sage Publications.

Cook, R. 1989. "The Nominating Process," in M. Nelson, ed., *The Elections of 1988.* Washington, D.C.:Congressional Quarterly Press.

Crespi, I. 1988. *Pre-election Polling: Sources of Accuracy and Error.* New York: Russell Sage Foundation.

_____. 1989. *Public Opinion, Polls, and Democracy.* Boulder: Westview Press.

Crotty, W., ed. 1992. *Political Participation and American Democracy.* New York: Greenwood Press.

Crouse, T. 1974. *The Boys on the Bus: Riding with the Campaign Press Corps.* New York: Ballantine.

Davis, R.J. 1985. "A National Circus: Trends in Newspaper Coverage of Eight Presidential Elections." Department of Politics, Princeton University.

de Tocqueville, A. 1969. *Democracy in America.* J. P. Mayer, ed. New York: Anchor.

Delli Carpini, M.X. and B. Williams. 1990. "The Method Is the Message: Focus Groups As a Means of Examining the Uses of Television in Political Discourse." Paper presented at the Annual Meeting of the International Society for Political Psychology, Washington, D.C.

Demers, D.P. 1987. "Use of Polls Changes Slightly Since 1978." *Jounrnalism Quarterly* 64: 839-842.

————. 1988. "Opinion Polling Practices of Chain and Independent Papers." *Journalism Quarterly* 65: 500-503.

Dinkin, R. 1989. *Campaigning in America: A History of Election Practices.* Westport, Conn.: Greenwood Press.

Dionne, E.J. 1980. "Experts Find Polls Influence Activists." *The New York Times* (May 4), p. 26.

————. 1991. *Why Americans Hate Politics.* New York: Simon & Schuster.

————. 1992. "The Illusion of Technique: The Impact of Polls on Reporters and Democracy," in T.E. Mann and G.R. Orren, eds., *Media Polls in American Politics..* Pp. 150-167. Washington, D.C.: The Brookings Institution.

Dunn, D.D. 1974. "Contributors in the American Electoral Process." *American Politics Quarterly* 2: 221-230.

Dykers, C.R. 1993. "Improving the Media's Role in the Public Sphere: The Case of the Wichita Eagle." Paper presented at the annual conference of the American Association for Public Opinion Research, St. Charles, IL.

Faulkenberry, D.G., and R. Mason. 1978. "Characteristics of Nonopinion and No Opinion Response Groups. *Public Opinion Quarterly* 42: 533-546.

Fenwick, I., F. Wiseman, J.F. Becker, and J.R. Heiman. 1982. "Classifying Undecided Voters in Pre-Election Polls." *Public Opinion Quarterly* 46: 383-391.

Fitzpatrick, C. 1992. "Some Liked What They Heard, but Others Weren't Impressed." *The Detroit News* (January 29), p. 1A.

Francis, J.D., and L. Busch. 1975. "What We Now Know About 'I don't knows'." *Public Opinion Quarterly* 39: 207-218.

Frankovic, K. 1994. "News Media Polling in a Changing Technological Environment." *12th Annual Van Zelst Lecture in Communication.* Evanston: Northwestern University.

Gallup, G. 1944. *A Guide to Public Opinion Polls.* Princeton: Princeton University Press.

Gallup, G. and S.F. Rae. 1940. *The Pulse of Democracy: The Public Opinion Poll and How It Works.* New York: Simon and Schuster.

Gamson, William A. 1992. *Talking Politics.* Cambridge: Cambridge University Press.

Gannon, J.P. 1991a. "Middle Class Boils About U.S. 'Decline'." *The Detroit News* (November 3), p. 1A.

————. 1991b. "Ordinary Voters Demand Candidates, Media Confront Real Issues in '92." *The Detroit News* (November 3), p. 1A.

————. 1991c. "Voters Overwhelmingly Believe Nation Is on the Wrong Course." *The Detroit News* (November 3), p. 1A.

————. 1992a. "Angry Voters Are in No Mood for Perot to Re-enter Race." *The Detroit News* (September 27), p. 3A.

_____. 1992b. "Clinton May Be Picked Clean by the Time He's Nominated." *The Detroit News* (February 9), p. 11A.

_____. 1992c. "Candidates Have a Long Way to Go." *The Detroit News* (February 9), p. 11A.

_____. 1992d. "Name of the Game: Style, 'Electability'." *The Detroit News* (March 7), p. 1A.

_____. 1992e. "Reagan Dems Fall out of Love with Bush." *The Detroit News* (July 5), p. 1A.

_____. 1992f. "Undecideds' Post-debate Verdict: Bush is Big Loser." *The Detroit News* (October 25), p. 1B.

Germond, J.W. and J. Witcover. 1989. *Whose Broad Stripes and Bright Stars?* New York: Warner Books.

Gitlin, T. 1990. "Blips, Bites and Savvy Talk: Television's Impact on American Politics." *Dissent* 37: 18-26.

Gollin, A.E. 1980. "Exploring the Liason Between Polling and the Press." *Public Opinion Quarterly* 44: 455-461.

_____. 1987. "Polling the News Media." *Public Opinion Quarterly* (supplement), 51(2):86–94.

Greenberg, D.S. 1992. "Political Polling: Just Say No. *Chicago Tribune* (September, 9).

Greer, S. 1993. "Evaluating an Alternative Model for Coverage of a Presidential Election: The Case of the Charlotte Observer." Paper presented at the annual conference of the American Association for Public Opinion Research, St. Charles, IL.

Greiter, W. 1992. *Who Will Tell the Pepole: The Betrayal of American Democracy.* New York: Simon & Schuster.

Harvey, A.C. 1981. *The Econometric Analyses of Time Series.* New York: John Wiley and Sons.

Harwood, J. 1992. "Allegations of Bush Affair May Blunt Possible GOP Tactic Against Clinton." *Wall Street Journal* (August 12), p. 12.

Heard, A. 1960. *The Costs of Democracy.* Chapel Hill: University of North Carolina Press.

Herbst, S. 1993. *Numbered Voices: How Opinion Polling Has Shaped American Politics.* Chicago: University of Chicago Press.

_____. *Politics at the Margin: Historical Studies of Public Expression Outside the Mainstream.* Cambridge: Cambridge University Press.

Hickman, H. 1991. "Public Polls and Election Participants," in P.J. Lavrakas and J.K. Holley, eds., *Polling and Presidential Election Coverage.* Pp. 100-133. Newbury Park, CA: Sage.

Holley, J. K. 1991. "The Press and Political Polling," in P.J. Lavrakas and J.K. Holley, eds., *Polling and Presidential Election Coverage.* Pp. 215-237. Newbury Park, CA: Sage.

Hoyt, M. 1992. The Wichita Experiment: What Happens When a Newspaper Tries to Connect Readership and Citizenship?" *Columbia Journalism Review* (July/August): 42-47.

Ismach, A. H. 1984. "Polling as a News-Gathering Tool," in L.J. Martin, ed., *Polling and the Democratic Consensus.* Pp. 106-118. Philadelphia: The Annals of the American Academy of Political and Social Science.

Jacobson, G.C. 1975. "The Impact of Broadcast Campaigning in Electoral Outcomes." *Journal of Politics* (August): 769-793.

_____. 1980. *Money in Congressional Elections.* New Haven: Yale University Press.

Jacobson, G.C. and S. Kernell. 1983. *Strategy and Choice in Congressional Elections* (2nd edition). New Haven: Yale University Press.

Jamieson, K.H. 1992. *Dirty Politics: Deception, Distraction and Democracy.* New York: Oxford University Press.

Johnston, J. 1972. *Econometric Methods* (2nd edition). New York: McGraw-Hill.

Jones, R.S., and W.E. Miller. 1985. "Financing Campaigns: Macro-level Innovations and Micro-level Response." *Western Political Quarterly* 38: 187-210.

Judge, G.G., W.E. Griffiths, R. C. Hill, and T. C. Lee. 1980. *The Theory and Practice of Econometrics.* New York: John Wiley and Sons.

Kagay, M.R. 1991. "The Use of Public Opinion Polls by *The New York Times:* Some Examples from the 1988 Presidential Election," in P.J. Lavrakas and J.K. Holley, eds., *Polling and Presidential Election Coverage.* Pp. 19-56. Newbury Park, CA: Sage.

Kayden, X. 1985. "Effects of the Present System of Campaign Financing on Special Interest Groups." in G. Grassmuck, ed., *Before Nomination: Our Primary Problems.* Washington, D.C.: American Enterprise Institute.

Kern, M. and M. Just. 1992a. "Constructing Candidate Images: Focus Group Discourse about Campaign News and Advertising." Paper presented at the New England Political Science Association, Providence, R.I.

_____. 1992b. "The Focus Group Method, Ads, News, and the Construction of Candidate Messages." Paper presented at the annual meeting of the American Political Science Association, Chicago.

Klecka, W.R. 1980. *Discriminant Analysis.* Pp. 1-86: Newbury Park, CA: Sage.

Kolbert, E. 1992. "Test-Marketing a President." *The New York Times Magazine* (August 30), Pp. 18-21, 60, 68, 72.

Krueger, R.A. 1988. *Focus Groups: A Practical Guide for Applied Research.* Newbury Park, CA: Sage.

Ladd, E.C. & J. Benson. 1992. "The Growth of News Polls in American Politics," in T. E. Mann & G. R. Orren, eds., *Media Polls in American Politics.* Pp. 19-31. Washington, D.C.: The Brookings Institution.

Lavrakas, P.J. 1991. "Introduction," in P.J. Lavrakas and J.K. Holley, eds., *Polling and Presidential Election Coverage.* Pp. 9-18. Newbury Park, CA: Sage.

Lavrakas, P.J. and D.M. Merkle. 1990. "Name Recognition and Pre-Primary Poll Measurement Error." Paper presented at the International Conference of Survey Measurement Error, Tucson, AZ.

Lavrakas, P.J. and Holley, J.K., eds. 1991. *Polling and Presidential Election Coverage.* Newbury Park, CA: Sage.

Lavrakas, P.J., J. K. Holley, and P.V. Miller. 1991. "Public Reactions to Polling News During the 1988 Presidential Election Campaign," in P.J. Lavrakas and J.K. Holley, eds., *Polling and Presidential Election Coverage.* Pp. 151-183. Newbury Park, CA: Sage.

Lewis, I.A. 1991. "Media Polls, the *Los Angeles Times* Poll, and the 1988 Presidential Election," in P.J. Lavrakas and J. K. Holley, eds., *Polling and*

Presidential Election Coverage. Pp. 57-82. Newbury Park, CA: Sage.

Looney, R. 1991. "Pollsters Fret as Americans Learn to Say No." *Chicago Tribune* (February 5).

Mann, T.E. & G.R. Orren. 1992. "To Poll or Not to Poll . . . And Other Questions," in T.E. Mann and G.R. Orren, eds., *Media Polls in American Politics*. Washington, D.C.: The Brookings Institution.

Maraniss, D. 1992. "A Question of Character: Despite His Success, Clinton Remains Defined by Doubts." *The Washington Post National Weekly Edition* (April 20–26), Pp. 6–7.

Marshall, T.R. 1983a. "Evaluating Presidential Nominees: Opinion Polls, Issues, and Personalities," *Western Political Quarterly* 36: 650–659.

_____. 1983b. "The News Verdict and Public Opinion During the Primaries," in William C. Adams, ed., *Television Coverage of the 1980 Presidential Campaign*. Pp. 127-186. Norwood, NJ: Ablex.

Matthews, D. 1978. "The news media and the 1976 presidential nominations," in J. D. Barber, ed., *Race for the Presidency: The Media and the Nominating Process*. Englewood Cliffs, NJ: Prentice-Hall.

McBride, F. 1991. "Media Use of Pre-election Polls," in P. J. Lavrakas and J.K. Holley, eds., *Polling and Presidential Election Coverage*. Pp. 184-199. Newbury Park, CA: Sage.

McBurnett, M. 1991. "The Dynamics of Voter Preference in Primary Campaigns." Paper presented to the Midwest Political Science Association, Chicago.

McCracken, G. 1988. *The Long Interview*. Newbury Park, CA: Sage.

McGerr, M. 1986. *The Decline of Popular Politics: The American North, 1865-1928*. New York: Oxford University Press.

Merton, R.K. and P.K. Hatt. 1949. "Election Polling Forecasts and Public Images of Social Science: A Case Study in the Shaping of Opinion among a Strategic Public." *Public Opinion Quarterly* 13: 185-222.

Meyer, P. 1973. *Precision Journalism: A Reporter's Introduction to Social Science Methods*. Bloomington: Indiana University Press.

_____. 1990. "Polling as Political Science and Polling as Journalism. *Public Opinion Quarterly* 54 (3): 451-459.

_____. 1991. "How to do an election." *The New Precision Journalism*. Pp. 214-235. Bloomington: Indiana University Press.

_____. 1992. "Numbers Turn On Undecided Voters." *USA Today* (November 2), p. 7A.

Meyrowitz, J. 1992. "The Press Rejects a Candidate." *Columbia Journalsim Review* (March/April), Pp. 46-47.

Miller, P.V. 1993. "The 1992 Horse Race in the Polls," in W. Crotty, ed., *America's Choice: The Election of 1992*. Pp. 139-148. Guilford, CT: Dushkin.

Miller, P.V., D.M. Merkle, and P. Wang. 1991. "Journalism with Footnotes: Reporting the "Technical Details" of Polls," in P. J. Lavrakas and J. K. Holley, eds., *Polling and Presidential Election Coverage*. Pp. 200-214. Newbury Park, CA: Sage.

Moore, D.W. 1992. *The Superpollsters: How They Measure and Manipulate Public Opinion in America*. New York: Four Walls Eight Windows.

Morgan, D. L. 1988. *Focus Groups as Qualitative Research*. Newbury Park, CA: Sage.

Morin, R. 1992a. "Caring Less About Adultery, More about Mendacity: The Clinton Scandal Tests the Limits of Public Tolerance." *The Washington Post National Weekly Edition* (February 2–3), p. 37.

_____.1992b. "Surveying the Surveyors." *The Washington Post National Weekly Edition* (March 2–8), p. 37.

Mutz, D.C. 1995 "Effects of Horse Race Coverage on Campaign Coffers: Strategic Contributing in Presidential Primaries." *Journal of Politics* (forthcoming).

The New Republic. 1992. "Sex and the Candidate" (editorial). 206(5): p. 7.

Newport, F. and L. McAneny. 1992. "Reaction to Perot's Withdrawl." *The Gallup Poll Monthly* (July), Pp. 31-32.

Norusis, M.N. 1990. *SPSS/PC+ Advanced Statistics 4.0 for the IBM PC/XT/AT and PS/2*. Pp. B1-B37. Chicago: SPSS, Inc.

Oreskes, M. 1990. "Few Approach Starting Gates for 1992 Presidential Stakes." *New York Times* (August, 13), p. 1.

Orren, G.R. 1980. "Presidential Campaign Finance: It's Impact and Future." *Commonsense* 2: 50-66.

_____. 1985. "The Nomination Process: Vicissitudes of Candidate Selection," in M. Nelson, ed., *The Elections of 1984*. Washington, D.C.: Congressional Quarterly Press.

Orren, G.R. and N.W. Polsby. 1987. *Media and Momentum: The New Hampshire Primary and Nomination Politics*. Chatham, N.J.: Chatham House Publishers.

Overacker, L. 1932. *Money in Elections*. New York: Macmillan.

Paletz, D.L., et al. 1980. "Polls in the Media: Content, Credibility, and Consequences." *Public Opinion Quarterly* 44 (4):495–512.

Panagakis, N. 1989. "Incumbent Races: Closer Than They Appear." *The Polling Report* 5: 1-3.

Patterson, T.E. 1980. *The Mass Media Election*. New York: Praeger.

_____. 1989. "The Press and Its Missed Assignment," in M. Nelson, ed., *The Elections of 1988*. Washington, D.C.: Congressional Quarterly Press.

Pomper, G.M. 1989. "The Presidential Nominations," in G. Pomper, et al., *The Election of 1988: Reports and Interpretations*. Chatham, NJ: Chatham House.

Pomper, G.M. et al. 1989. *The Election of 1988: Reports and Interpretations*. Chatham, NJ: Chatham House.

Porter, T. 1986. *The Rise of Statistical Thinking: 1820-1900*. Princeton: Princeton University Press.

Price, W. 1953. "What Daily News Executives Think of Public Opinion Polls." *Journalism Quarterly* 30:287-99.

Reiter, H.L. 1985. *Selecting the President: The Nominating Process in Transition*. Philadelphia: University of Pennsylvania Press.

Rippey, J.N. 1980. "Use of Polls as a Reporting Tool." *Journalism Quarterly* 57: 642-646, 721.

Robinson, M., N. Conover, and M. Sheehan, 1980. "The Media at Mid-year: A Bad Year for McLuhanites." *Public Opinion* 3: 41-45.

Rosenstiel, T. 1993. *Strange Bedfellows*. New York: Hyperion.

Royko, M. 1992. "Annoy Pollsters — Resort to Lying." *Chicago Tribune* (October 28).

SAS Institute, Inc. 1990. *SAS/STAT User's Guide* (version 6, fourth edition), Pp. 45-51.

Shafer, B.E. 1988. "Scholarship on Presidential Selection in the United States." *American Political Science Review* 82: 955-963.

Shogan, R. 1992. "Clinton Keeps Bid Afloat, but Polls Show Voters Wary." *Los Angeles Times* (January 31), p. A1.

Sigelman, L. 1989. "The 1988 Presidential Nomination: Whatever Happened to Momentum?" *PS: Political Science and Politics*, (March). Washington, D.C.: American Political Science Association.

Sigelman, L. and D. Bullock. 1991. "Candidates, Issues, Horse Races and Hoopla: Presidential Campaign Coverage 1888-1988." *American Politics Quarterly* 19: 5-32.

Smith, T. 1990. "The First Straw? A Study of the Origins of Election Polls." *Public Opinion Quarterly* 54:21-36.

Squire, P., ed. 1989. *The Iowa Caucuses and the Presidential Nominating Process.* Boulder: Westview Press.

Steeper, F.T. 1980. "Public Response to Gerald Ford's Statements on Eastern Europe in the Second Debate," in G. F. Bishop, R. G. Meadow, and M. Jackson-Beeck, eds., *The Presidential Debates: Media, Electoral, and Policy Perspectives.* New York: Praeger.

Stewart, D.W. and P.N. Shamdasani. 1990. *Focus Groups: Theory and Practice.* Newbury Park, CA: Sage.

Tankard, J.W. 1972. "Public Opinion Polling by Newspapers in the Presidential Election of 1024." *Journalism Quarterly* 49:361-365.

Taylor, P. and D.S. Broder. 1988. "Evolution of the TV Era's Nastiest Presidential Race: Bush Team Test-Marketed Negative Themes." *The Washington Post* (October 28), p. 1A.

Traugott, M.W. 1985. "The Media and the Nominating Process," in George Grassmuck, ed., *Before Nomination: Our Primary Problems.* Washington, D.C.: American Enterprise Institute.

_____. 1990. "The Proliferation of Media Polls in Campaign Coverage: Questions for Comparative Study." Paper presented to the convention of the International Communication Association, Dublin, Ireland.

_____. 1991. "Public Attitudes About News Organizations, Campaign Coverage and Polls," in P.J. Lavrakas and J.K. Holley, eds., *Polling and Presidential Election Coverage.* Pp. 134-150. Newbury Park, CA: Sage.

_____. 1992a. "The Impact of Media Polls on the Public," in T.E. Mann and G.R. Orren, eds., *Media Polls in American Politics.* Washington, D.C.: The Brookings Institution.

_____. 1992b. "The Polls in 1992: A Generally Good Show, But Much Work Needs to Be Done." *The Public Perspective* (November/December), Pp. 14–16.

Traugott, M.W. and R. Rusch. 1989. "Understanding the Proliferation of Media Polls in Presidential Campaign Coverage." Paper presented at the annual meeting of the Midwest Association for Public Opinion Research, Chicago.

Trento, S. 1992. *The Power House: Robert Keith Gray and the Selling of Access and Influence in Washington.* New York: St. Martin's Press.

Verba, S., and N.H. Nie. 1972. *Participation in America.* Chicago: University of Chicago Press.

Von Hoffman, N. 1980. "Public Opinion Polls: Newspapers Making Their Own

News?" *Public Opinion Quarterly,* 44 (4): 572-573.

Wheeler, M. 1976. *Lies, Damn Lies, and Statistics.* New York: Liveright.

Zajonc, R.B. 1968. "Attitudinal Effects of Mere Exposure." *Journal of Personality and Social Psychology Monograph Supplement* 9: 1-27.

_____. 1980. "Feeling and Thinking: Preferences Need No Inferences." *American Psychologist* 35: 151-175.

Index

About the Book

Most news media are "data rich but analysis poor" when it comes to election polling. Since election polls clearly have the power to influence campaigns and election postmortems, it is important that "spin" not take precedence over significance in the reporting of poll results. In this volume, experts in the media and in academe challenge the conventional approaches that most news media take in their poll-based campaign coverage. The book reports new research findings on news coverage of recent presidential elections and provides a myriad of examples of how journalists and news media executives can improve their analysis of poll data, thereby better serving our political processes.